Professionalism
Skills for Workplace Success

Business 12/15/17

Professionalism
Skills for Workplace Success

Third Edition

Lydia E. Anderson

Sandra B. Bolt

PEARSON

Boston   Columbus   Indianapolis   New York   San Francisco   Upper Saddle River
Amsterdam   Cape Town   Dubai   London   Madrid   Milan   Munich   Paris   Montreal   Toronto
Delhi   Mexico City   Sao Paulo   Sydney   Hong Kong   Seoul   Singapore   Taipei   Tokyo

Editorial Director: Vernon Anthony
Executive Acquisitions Editor: Gary Bauer
Editorial Assistant: Tanika Henderson
Director of Marketing: David Gesell
Marketing Manager: Stacey Martinez
Marketing Assistant: Les Roberts
Senior Managing Editor: JoEllen Gohr
Project Manager: Christina Taylor
Senior Operations Supervisor: Pat Tonneman
Senior Art Director: Diane Ernsberger

Text and Cover Designer: Rokusek Design
Manager, Visual Research: Mike Lackey
Photo Researcher: Lynsey Jacob
Cover Art: iStock
Full-Service Project Management: Abinaya Rajendran, Integra
Composition: Integra
Printer/Binder: R. R. Donnelly/Willard
Cover Printer: Lehigh Phoenix Color/Hagerstown
Text Font: 11/13 ITC Legacy Serif Std Book

Credits and acknowledgments borrowed from other sources and reproduced, with permission, in this textbook appear on appropriate page within text.

Microsoft® and Windows® are registered trademarks of the Microsoft Corporation in the U.S.A. and other countries. Screen shots and icons reprinted with permission from the Microsoft Corporation. This book is not sponsored or endorsed by or affiliated with the Microsoft Corporation.

Many of the designations by manufacturers and seller to distinguish their products are claimed as trademarks. Where those designations appear in this book, and the publisher was aware of a trademark claim, the designations have been printed in initial caps or all caps.

Library of Congress Cataloging-in-Publication Data

Anderson, Lydia E. (Lydia Elaine)
    Professionalism : skills for workplace success / Lydia E. Anderson, Sandra B. Bolt.—3rd ed.
        p. cm.
    ISBN-13: 978-0-13-262466-4 (alk. paper)
    ISBN-10: 0-13-262466-4 (alk. paper)
    1. Vocational qualifications. 2. Employability. 3. Performance. 4. Life skills. I. Bolt, Sandra B. II. Title.
HF5381.6.A53 2013
650.1—dc23
                                                                        2011039498

10 9 8 7 6 5 4 3

ISBN 10: 0-13-262466-4
ISBN 13: 978-0-13-262466-4

Brief Contents

Contents

Workplace Basics

Module 3   Relationships

Career Planning Tools

Module 4

Video Case Study Index

Professionalism: Skills for Workplace Success, Third Edition, remains committed to its original purpose of addressing employer concerns by providing those new to the workplace with basic skills for success on the job and providing job seekers the tools they need to secure the job of their dreams. This unique text prepares students for their first professional workplace experience by linking self-management issues to career planning tools and workplace basics, including expected behaviors. Text content is applicable to any individual who works within a traditional work environment. The book is designed not as a textbook, but as a workbook that can be kept and referred to throughout one's career.

Economics and technology were the primary factors that influenced revisions for this third edition. As our world continues to struggle with challenging economics and historic unemployment rates, it is imperative that job seekers and those new to the workplace not only demonstrate but exceed expectations regarding business etiquette, appropriate use of technology, and proper workplace attire, and understand how these expectations are different from those in social situations. In today's increasingly competitive work environment, it is essential that students communicate in a professional manner, maturely deal with conflict, and be accountable team members, consistently behaving in a fair and ethical manner. This third edition addresses these issues and provides readers with the current and practical skills necessary to maintain success on the job.

Unique Approach

Professionalism: Skills for Workplace Success extends beyond a typical résumé/job-search text to seamlessly emphasize the relationship between résumé development, job search skills, and human relations in the workplace. Developed with input from industry leaders, the text addresses topics students need to know when transitioning from campus to the workplace. Presented in a simple, highly interactive format, this text assists individuals in understanding the foundation of effective workplace relationships and how to appropriately manage these relationships toward career success. Beginning with the basic management principle that individual workplace performance affects organizational success and profitability, readers are able to integrate soft skills within the framework of a formal business structure. The topics and principles presented benefit all individuals, no matter their career goals. Using a gender-neutral character named Cory, mini-case studies give individuals valuable insight into Cory's real workplace dilemmas. Additionally, throughout the text are introductory assessments, exercises, web quizzes, student discussion topics, and activities designed to improve the reader's understanding and application of the material as well as their written and oral communication skills.

This book is written for individuals wanting to excel in their career. Attitude, communication, and human relations are the keys to surviving in today's challenging, competitive, and uncertain workplace. The text teaches realistic survival skills and motivates individuals to improve both personal and professional performance.

Organization

The text is divided into four modules and sixteen chapters that are arranged to accommodate quarter-, half-, or full-semester courses. Modules include:

Module 1: Self-Management
Module 2: Workplace Basics
Module 3: Relationships
Module 4: Career Planning Tools

New to This Edition

Integrating feedback from instructors, business leaders, and students, the third edition provides readers with current and necessary tools for both job search and career success. The third edition has been heavily revised to incorporate the economic and technological changes that have significantly affected today's work environment. New chapter features include the following:

- **How Do You Rate?** These assessments provide students an introduction to the chapter topic through brief, fun, and realistic applications.
- **Introductory paragraphs** for each chapter summarize key concepts and assist in understanding and application of content to a modern work environment.
- **Updated and expanded technology** references and treatment of technology's influence in both the job search process and the work environment are included.
- **Updated Cory Stories** better reflect current ethical and workplace dilemmas.

To appropriately reflect the current technological, economic, and employment challenges, the following chapter-specific changes have been incorporated into the third edition:

Changes to the **Self-Management** module include the following:

- Attitude and Personality (formerly chapter 1) merged with Goal Setting and Life Management (formerly chapter 2) to enable students to better link personal issues to long-term career success.
- an enhanced description of professionalism, explaining its necessity and contributions to workplace success in today's economy.
- an enhanced discussion on self-efficacy and its influences on self-esteem, self-image, and projection.
- the introduction of SMART goals.
- an updated personal finance discussion, including rearranged topics for increased student understanding and the integration of current money management technologies available through smart phones.
- an expanded discussion on stress and time management, including job burnout.
- a new discussion on procrastination and perfectionism.

- an expanded discussion on organization, including how to organize, behaviors of organized individuals, and organizing electronic files.
- Etiquette and Dress (formerly chapter 6) moved to Self-Management module.
- an enhanced discussion on dress codes and professional attire, including safety issues and geographical differences.
- addition of dental hygiene tips.
- a revised discussion on body art and body piercings.
- a new section on scheduling appointments.
- a new section on introductions and business networking.
- an enhanced discussion on dining etiquette.
- technology, phone, and e-mail etiquette content moved to a new chapter in another module (Chapter 10) dedicated to digital communication.

Changes to the **Workplace Basics** module include:

- an enhanced discussion on diversity and ethnocentrism.
- Accountability and Workplace Relationships (formerly chapter 10) moved to Workplace Basics module.
- an enhanced discussion on types of bosses.
- a more concise description of key organizational functions.
- a new discussion on how technology and social media increase the importance of providing exemplary customer service.
- a revised chapter title, Human Resources and Policies, to better reflect chapter content.
- a formal mentoring discussion moved from Goal Setting chapter and presented as an organizational resource in the Human Resources and Policies chapter.
- an updated benefits section to reflect the current economic climate and uncertainty of the federal Patient Protection and Government Care Act.

Changes to the **Relationships** module include:

- expansion of the Communication chapter (formerly chapter 9) to two chapters: the first chapter (chapter 9) focuses on communication fundamentals and traditional workplace communication; the second chapter (chapter 10) focuses on current communication technologies.
- a new discussion on proxemics.
- expanded discussions on presentations, handwritten notes, electronic thank-you notes, and greetings.
- digital content updates (formerly from chapter 9), such as the business e-mail, mobile communication devices, and phone etiquette.
- updated discussion on mobile communication devices, business texting, and instant messaging, and appropriate use for each tool.
- updated discussion on appropriate etiquette regarding the use of texting, phone, social media, laptops/tablets, and other electronic technologies in a work environment.
- a new discussion on how to protect your e-dentity.
- a new discussion on new media tools such as blogs and wikis.
- new content regarding the proper etiquette relating to video and teleconferencing.

- a retitled Motivation, Leadership, and Teams chapter to reflect appropriate order of topics for improved student understanding.
- a streamlined discussion on Maslow's theory and the addition of McClelland's Needs Theory and Vroom's Expectancy Theory.
- enhanced discussions on leadership, the use of teams in the workplace, team projects, and presentations.
- a dedicated section on meetings, including the meeting process and appropriate behaviors.
- an expanded discussion on conflict resolution and common types of conflict.
- a new discussion on technology's impact on workplace conflict.
- a new section on assumptions, misinterpreting information, and jumping to conclusions.
- an expanded discussion on workplace bullying, filing legitimate complaints, and zero-tolerance policies.

The **Career Planning Tools** module continues to include:

- individual chapters dedicated to job search planning, creating a résumé package, and the mastery of interview techniques.
- assessments, samples and examples, and hands-on, in-chapter activities that walk students through the process of creating and using the appropriate career planning tools.

Changes to the **Job Search** chapter include:

- an enhanced discussion on a realistic job preview that links skills and personal history to selecting the right career.
- a new discussion on cost-of-living considerations.
- a new discussion on DMV records and their influence on the job search process.
- a new section on electronic job search portfolios.
- new sections on collecting job applications, completing computer applications, utilizing workplace kiosks, and pre-employment tests.
- an enhanced discussion on references and technology.
- a new discussion on utilizing social networks in a job search.
- a new discussion on the increased use of on-the-spot interviews for entry-level positions.
- an expanded discussion on volunteering and the use of college career centers.

Changes to the **Résumé Package** chapter include:

- an enhanced discussion regarding sharing a résumé both traditionally and online.
- an enhanced discussion on when not to list dates on a résumé.

Changes to the **Interview Techniques** chapter include:

- a new discussion that guides students through the pre-interview process and preparation, beginning with the invitation to interview.
- an enhanced discussion on how to create and utilize a concise personal commercial.
- an expanded discussion on phone and online interviews.

- a new section on technology-based interviews, including online and video chat interviews.
- a new discussion on reading body language during an interview.
- a new discussion on post-interview follow-up.
- a discussion on the need to consistently "sell yourself" throughout the job search/interview process.
- an enhanced discussion on pre-employment tests.

Changes to the final chapter, **Career Changes**, include the following:

- a new title to better reflect common career changes.
- a new discussion on work furloughs.
- an expanded discussion of entrepreneurship.

Professionalism Video Case Studies

Video case studies are integrated into the textbook to focus on key challenges students face in getting a job, maintaining that job, and prospering in it. Topics include making ethical choices, workplace etiquette, proper dress and deportment, customer service orientation, conflict management, sexual harassment, meeting management, preparing for the job search, writing effective résumés and cover letters, interviewing techniques, and how to behave in a performance evaluation. For a complete listing of the videos, consult the video index on page ix, following the table of contents.

These videos are available on DVD for use in the classroom to facilitate discussion and are accessible by students online in MyStudentSuccessLab.

Supplemental Resources

INSTRUCTOR SUPPORT—Resources to simplify your life and support your students.

"Easy access to online, book-specific teaching support is now just a click away!"

Instructor Resource Center—Register. Redeem. Login. Three easy steps that open the door to a variety of print and media resources in downloadable, digital format, available to instructors exclusively through the Pearson IRC at www.pearsonhighered.com/irc

Online Instructor's Manual—This manual is intended to give professors a framework or blueprint of ideas and suggestions that may assist them in providing their students with activities, journal writing, thought-provoking situations, and group activities. The test bank, organized by chapter, includes multiple choice, true/false, and short-answer questions that support the key features in the book. This supplement is available for download from the Instructor's Resource Center at www.pearsonhighered.com/irc

Online PowerPoint Presentation—A comprehensive set of PowerPoint slides that can be used by instructors for class presentations or by students for lecture preview or review. The presentation includes all the graphs and tables in the textbook. The presentation contains bullet point PowerPoint slides for each chapter. These slides highlight the important points of each chapter to help students understand the concepts within each chapter. Instructors may download these PowerPoint presentations from the Instructor's Resource Center at www.pearsonhighered.com/irc

Online MyTest Test Bank—Pearson MyTest offers instructors a secure online environment and quality assessments to easily create print exams, study-guide questions, and quizzes from any computer with an Internet connection.

<u>Premium Assessment Content</u>
- Draw from a rich library of question test banks that complement the textbook and course learning objectives.
- Edit questions or tests to fit specific teaching needs.

<u>Instructor-Friendly Features</u>
- Easily create and store questions, including images, diagrams, and charts, using simple drag-and-drop and Word-like controls.
- Use additional information provided by Pearson, such as the question's difficulty level or learning objective, to help quickly build a test.

<u>Time-Saving Enhancements</u>
- Add headers or footers and easily scramble questions and answer choices all from one simple toolbar.
- Quickly create multiple versions of a test or answer key and, when ready, simply save to Word or PDF format and print!
- Export exams for import to Blackboard 6.0, CE (WebCT), or Vista (WebCT)! Additional information available at www.pearsonmytest.com

Instructor DVD for Professionalism—This DVD contains the videos featured in Professionalism in high-resolution format for instructors to use in class. They are available to qualified adopters upon request.

MyStudentSuccessLab—Are you teaching online, or in a hybrid setting, or looking to infuse technology into your classroom for the first time? MyStudentSuccessLab is an online solution designed to help students build the skills they need to succeed for ongoing personal and professional development at www.mystudentsuccesslab.com

Additional Resources

Robbins Self Assessment Library—This compilation teaches students to create a portfolio of skills. S.A.L. is a self-contained, interactive library of forty-nine behavioral questionnaires that help students discover new ideas about themselves, their attitudes, and their personal strengths and weaknesses. Available in paper, CD-rom, and online (Access Card) formats.

The Golden Personality Type Profiler™—This popular personality assessment provides students with information about five fundamental personality dimensions: where you direct your energy (introverted or extraverted), the way you gather and interpret information, how you make decisions, how you approach life (e.g., organizing versus adapting), and how you respond to stress. The Golden Personality Type Profiler is similar to the Myers-Briggs Step I assessment program. It takes about fifteen–twenty minutes to complete, and students receive an easy-to-use and practical feedback report based on their results. This tool helps students improve their self-knowledge and ability to work effectively with others by providing them with feedback on their leadership and organizational strengths, communication and teamwork preferences, motivation and learning style, and opportunities for personal growth. The Golden Personality Type Profiler is typically used in a classroom setting to help prepare students for entry into the workforce or for career development. Instructional support materials are available so that instructors can guide students through their feedback report and help them apply their results to build personal and interpersonal skills.

MyStudentSuccessLab

Start Strong. Finish Stronger.
www.MyStudentSuccessLab.com

MyStudentSuccessLab is an online solution designed to help students acquire the skills they need to succeed for ongoing personal and professional development. They will have access to peer-led video interviews and develop core skills through interactive practice exercises and activities that provide academic, life, and professionalism skills that will transfer to ANY course.

It can accompany any Student Success text or be used as a stand-alone course offering.

How will MyStudentSuccessLab make a difference?

Is motivation a challenge, and if so, how do you deal with it?

Video Interviews—Experience peer led video by students, for students of all ages and stages.

How would better class preparation improve the learning experience?

Practice Exercises—Practice skills for each topic, leveled by Bloom's taxonomy.

What could you gain by building critical thinking and problem-solving skills?

Activities—Apply what is being learned to create personally relevant resources through enhanced communication and self-reflection.

PEARSON

MyStudentSuccessLab

Start Strong. Finish Stronger.

www.MyStudentSuccessLab.com

As an instructor, how much easier would it be to assign and assess on MyStudentSuccessLab if you had a Learning Path Diagnostic that reported to the grade book?

Learning Path Diagnostic

- For the **course**, 65 Pre-Course questions (Levels I & II Bloom's) and 65 Post-Course questions (Levels III & IV Bloom's) that link to key learning objectives in each topic.

- For each **topic**, 20 Pre-Test questions (Levels I & II Bloom's) and 20 Post-Test questions (Levels III & IV Bloom's) that link to all learning objectives in the topic.

As a student, how much more engaged would you be if you had access to relevant YouTube videos within MyStudentSuccessLab?

Student Resources

A wealth of resources like our FinishStrong247 YouTube channel with "just in time" videos selected "by students, for students."

MyStudentSuccessLab Topic List:

1. A First Step: Goal Setting
2. Communication
3. Critical Thinking
4. Financial Literacy
5. Information Literacy

6. Learning Preferences
7. Listening and Taking Notes in Class
8. Majors and Careers
9. Memory and Studying
10. Problem Solving

11. Professionalism
12. Reading and Annotating
13. Stress Management
14. Test Taking Skills
15. Time Management

MyStudentSuccessLab Feature Set:

Learning Path Diagnostic: 65 Pre-Course (Levels I & II Bloom's) and 65 Post-Course (Levels III & IV Bloom's) / Pre-Test (Levels I & II Bloom's) and Post-Test (Levels III & IV Bloom's).

Topic Overview: Module objectives.

Video Interviews: Real video interviews "by students, for students" on key issues.

Practice Exercises: Skill-building exercises per topic provide interactive experience and practice.

Activities: Apply what is being learned to create 'personally relevant' resources through enhanced communication and self-reflection.

Student Resources: Pearson Students Facebook page, FinishStrong247 YouTube channel, MySearchLab, Online Dictionary, Plagiarism Guide, Student Planner, and Student Reflection Journal.

Implementation Guide: Grading rubric to support instruction with Overview, Time on Task, Suggested grading, etc.

Introducing CourseSmart, The world's largest online marketplace for digital texts and course materials.

▶ **CourseSmart saves time.** Instructors can review and compare textbooks and course materials from multiple publishers at one easy-to-navigate, secure website.

▶ **CourseSmart is environmentally sound.** When instructors use CourseSmart, they help reduce the time, cost, and environmental impact of mailing print exam copies.

▶ **CourseSmart reduces student costs.** Instructors can offer students a lower-cost alternative to traditional print textbooks.

▶ **"Add this overview to your syllabus today!"**
REQUIRED COURSE MATERIALS—ALTERNATE VERSION AVAILABLE:

CourseSmart is an exciting new choice for students looking to save money. As an alternative to purchasing the printed textbook, students can purchase an electronic version of the same content. With a CourseSmart eTextbook, students can search the text, make notes online, print out reading assignments that incorporate lecture notes, and bookmark important passages for later review.

To learn for yourself, visit www.coursesmart.com

This is an access-protected site, and you will need a password provided to you by a representative from a publishing partner.

Acknowledgments

The success of our first and second editions exceeded our wildest dreams, and we are tremendously thankful to those who have included our materials in their educational toolboxes. This third edition continues to integrate feedback from many business leaders and educators who continue to openly share their expertise and concerns regarding necessary workplace skills specific to today's tumultuous economic environment. Our hope is that this third edition continues to prepare students for real-world success and contributes to employer and economic success, as well. Updates in this third edition reflect the ever-changing and challenging business environment, specifically techno-logical and economic changes. We remain committed to providing readers a competitive advantage in successfully realizing and achieving their career goals and believe this updated edition does just that.

We continue to be thankful for Pearson and its talented staff, who provide both authors and text users incredible support. They are the definition of quality. We are specifically grateful to our executive editor, Gary Bauer, whose innovative leadership grew this text and its authors to where we are today.

Our grateful appreciation goes to the reviewers of this text for their honest and valued insight:

Dennis Nasco, Jr., Southern Illinois University
Susan Moak Nealy, Baton Rouge Community College
Heidi Lee Arrington, University of Hawai'i - Kapi'olai Community College
Brian Penberty, ECPI College of Technology
Laura Portolese Dias, Shoreline Community College
Dr. Raven Davenport, Houston Community College
Denver L. Riffe, National College
Thomas R. Smith, Prism Career Institute
Zachary Stahmer, Anthem Education Group
Anita Wofford, The Art Institute of Charlotte
Michael Bailey, Texas A&M University
Kevin Michael Bratton, West Georgia Technical College
Laure S. Burke, Kapiolani Community College
Kelley Ashby, The University of Iowa
Martha Hunt, NHTI-Concord's Community College
Denise Doyle, Institute of Technology
Regina D. Hartley, Ph.D., Caldwell Community College & Technical Institute
Tammy Mohler-Avery, Brandford Hall Career Institute
Gina P. Robinson, Brunswick Community College

Lydia E. Anderson has a master's in business administration with an emphasis in marketing. In addition to years of corporate marketing and strategic planning experience, she has been teaching for over fifteen years in both community college and university settings. She is currently a tenured faculty member and chair of the Business Administration and Marketing Department at Fresno City College in Fresno, California, and also an adjunct professor at California State University, Fresno. Her teaching areas of expertise include human relations in business, management, supervision, human resource management, and marketing. Ms. Anderson is also active in (California) statewide business curriculum development, and in Academic Senate, and she regularly consults with corporations on business topics relating to management and marketing.

Sandra B. Bolt has a master's in business administration with an emphasis in human resource management. She has been teaching in the college setting for over twenty years. She is currently a tenured faculty member and past chair of the Business and Technology Department at Fresno City College in Fresno, California. Her teaching areas of expertise include workplace relationships, office occupations, office technology, résumé/interview, and document formatting. She is currently the secretary/treasurer of the college district union. She has extensive secretarial and leadership experience and has served as a computer applications trainer. She is a certified Crown Financial leader and trainer and has led many personal financial management sessions for community groups. She has been a volunteer guest speaker at professional conferences and high school career fairs, in addition to her involvement with committees and student functions at Fresno City College.

Both authors have used their professional, educational, and personal experiences to provide readers with realistic stories and challenges experienced in a typical workplace.

Dedication

I dedicate this third edition to all the instructors who work diligently in preparing their students to become self-reliant and successful. Thank you for your often unacknowledged efforts. To my husband, Randy, and my son, Tim, thank you for being you and making us. And finally, to my God be the glory for the great things He has done.

—Lydia E. Anderson

To my husband, Bret, who has always been supportive, loving, and my best friend. To my son, Brandon, who makes my life wonderful and complete. To the memory of my parents, who taught me how to be self-sufficient and helped set me on the right path to my successful career and happy family life. And, of course, to God, for giving me the blessings and strength I have in my life.

—Sandra B. Bolt

Professionalism
Skills for Workplace Success

Attitude, Goal Setting, and Life Management

chapter 1

The future belongs to those who believe in the beauty of their dreams.

Eleanor Roosevelt (1884–1962)

MyStudentSuccessLab Visit www.mystudentsuccesslab.com for added practice, activities, assessment, and videos.

Objectives

- Define *professionalism*
- Define and describe *personality* and *attitude* and their influence in the workplace
- Identify individual personality traits and *values*
- Identify the influences of *self-efficacy*
- Identify and develop a strategy to deal with past negative experiences
- Define *locus of control*
- Identify primary and secondary *learning styles*
- Describe the importance of *goal setting*
- Identify the impact setting goals and objectives have on a life plan
- Set realistic goals
- Define goal-setting techniques
- Create *short-term* and *long-term goals*
- Describe the importance of setting *priorities*

How-Do-You-Rate

	Are you self-centered?	Yes	No
1.	Do you rarely use the word "I" in conversations?	❑	❑
2.	When in line with coworkers, do you let coworkers go ahead of you?	❑	❑
3.	Do you keep personal work accomplishments private?	❑	❑
4.	Do you rarely interrupt conversations?	❑	❑
5.	Do you celebrate special events (e.g., birthdays, holidays) with your coworkers by sending them a card, a note, or small gift?	❑	❑

If you answered "yes" to two or more of these questions, well done. Your actions are more focused on the needs of others and you are most likely not self-centered.

All About You

Congratulations! You are about to embark on a self-discovery to identify how to become and remain productive and successful in the workplace. The first step in this self-discovery is to perform a simple exercise. Look in a mirror and write the first three words that immediately come to mind.

1. _____.

2. _____.

3. _____.

These three words are your mirror words. **Mirror words** describe the foundation of how you view yourself, how you view others, and how you will most likely perform in the workplace.

This text is all about professionalism in the workplace. The goal of both your instructor and the authors is to not only help you secure the job of your dreams, but more importantly to keep that great job and advance your career based upon healthy, quality, and productive work habits that benefit you, your coworkers, and your organization. **Professionalism** is defined as workplace behaviors that result in positive business relationships. This text provides you tools to help you experience a more fulfilling and productive career. The secret to healthy relationships at work is to first understand you. Once you understand your personal needs, motivators, and irritants, it becomes easier to understand and successfully work with others. This is why the first part of this chapter focuses on your personality, your values, and your self-concept.

An individual's personality and attitude dictate how he or she responds to conflict, crisis, and other typical workplace situations. Each of these typical workplace situations involves working with and through people. Understanding your own personality and attitude makes it much easier to understand your reactions to others' personalities and attitudes.

The workplace is comprised of people. **Human relations** are the interactions that occur with and through people. These interactions create relationships. Therefore, you theoretically have relationships with everyone you come into contact with at work. For an organization to be profitable, its employees must be productive. It is difficult to be productive if you cannot work with your colleagues, bosses, vendors, and/or customers. Workplace productivity is a result of positive workplace interactions and relationships.

Personality is a result of influences, and there are many outside influences that affect workplace relationships. These influences may include immediate family, friends, extended family, religious affiliation, and even society as a whole. This means that your experiences and influences outside of work affect your workplace behavior. It also means that experiences and influences at work affect your personal life. Therefore, to understand workplace relationships, you must first understand yourself.

Personality and Values

Behavior is a reflection of personality. **Personality** is a stable set of traits that assist in explaining and predicting an individual's behavior. Personality traits can be positive, such as being caring, considerate, organized, enthusiastic, or reliable. However, personality traits can also be negative, such as being rude, unfocused, lazy, or immature. For example, if your personality typically reflects being organized at work and suddenly you become disorganized, others may believe something is wrong because your disorganized behavior is not in sync with your typical stable set of organized traits. An individual's personality is shaped by many variables, including past experience, family, friends, religion, and societal influences. Perhaps a family member was incredibly organized and passed this trait on to you. Maybe someone in your sphere of influence was incredibly unorganized, which influenced you to be very organized. These experiences (positive or not) shape your values. **Values** are things that are important to you as an individual based upon your personal experiences and influences. These influences include religion, family, and societal issues such as sexual preference, political affiliation, and materialism. Note that you may have good or bad values. You may value achievement, family, money, security, or freedom. For example, one individual may not value money because he or she has been told that "money is the root of all evil." Contrast this with an individual who values money because he or she has been taught that money is a valuable resource used to ensure a safe, secure future. Since values are things that are important to you, they will directly affect your personality. If you have been taught that money is a valuable resource, you may be very careful in your spending. Your personality trait will be that of a diligent, hardworking person who spends cautiously. A more in-depth discussion of values and how they relate to business ethics is presented in chapter 4.

Here is an example of how one's past experience shapes one's values. Cory's parents were both college graduates with successful careers. Cory worked hard to secure a new job. Cory continues to go to college and achieve success at work because the influences from the past impact Cory's values and beliefs in the ability to perform successfully at work. However, many of Cory's friends are

Talk It Out

What cartoon character best reflects you?

not attending college, and many have a hard time securing and/or maintaining employment. For this reason, Cory gets no support from these friends regarding earning a degree and securing employment.

As explained in the example of Cory's values, those values are affecting both career and life choices. These are positive choices for Cory, but negative choices for some of Cory's friends.

Attitude

An **attitude** is a strong belief toward people, things, and situations. For example, you either care or do not care how your classmates feel about you. Your past success and failures affect your attitude. Your attitude is related to your values and personality. Using the previous money example, if you value money, then your attitude will be positive toward work, because you value what you get in return for your work effort—a paycheck. Attitude affects performance. An individual's performance significantly influences a group's performance. A group's performance, in turn, impacts an organization's performance. Think about a barrel of juicy red apples. Place one bad apple in the barrel of good apples, and, over time, the entire barrel will be spoiled. That is why it is so important to evaluate your personal influences. The barrel reflects your personal goals and your workplace behavior. Your attitude affects not only your performance, but also the performance of those with whom you come in contact.

Does this mean you avoid anyone you believe is a bad influence? Not necessarily. You cannot avoid certain individuals, such as relatives and coworkers. However, you should be aware of the impact individuals have on your life. If certain individuals have a negative influence, avoid or limit your exposure to the negative influence (bad apple). If you continue to expose yourself to negative influences, you can lose sight of your goals, which may result in a poor attitude and poor performance.

Self-Efficacy and Its Influences

Let us review your "mirror words" from the beginning of this chapter. What did you see? Are your words positive, or negative? Whatever you are feeling is a result of your **self-concept.** Self-concept is how you view yourself. Thinking you are intelligent or believing you are attractive are examples of self-concept. **Self-image** is your belief of how others view you. If your self-concept is positive and strong, you will reflect confidence and not worry about how others view you and your actions. If you are insecure, you will rely heavily on what others think of you. While it is important to show concern for what others think of you, it is more important to have a positive self-concept. Note that there is a difference between being conceited and self-confident. Behaving in a conceited manner means you have too high an opinion of yourself as compared to others. People are drawn to individuals who are humble, display a good attitude, are confident, and are consistently positive. If you believe in yourself, a positive self-image will follow without effort. It is easy to see the tremendous impact both personality and attitude have in the development of your self-concept and self-image. One final factor that influences self-concept and performance is that of self-efficacy. **Self-efficacy** is your belief in your ability to perform a task. For example, if you are confident in your math abilities, you will most likely score high on a math exam because you believe you are strong in that subject. However, if you are required to take a math placement exam for a job and you are not confident in your math abilities, you will most likely not perform well. The way you feel about yourself and your environment is reflected in how you treat others. This is called **projection.** If you have a positive self-concept, this will be projected in a positive manner toward others.

Envision a hand mirror. The handle of the mirror (the foundation) is your personality. The frame of the mirror is your personal values. The mirror itself is your attitude, which is reflected for you and the world to see. The way you view yourself is your self-concept; the way you believe others see you is your self-image.

Exercise 1-1   All About You

Describe yourself. Include your personality traits, personal values and attitude toward achieving career success.

_____

_____

_____

Dealing with Negative "Baggage"

Many of us have experienced a person who appears to have a "chip on his or her shoulder" that negatively influences his or her behavior. This is reflected in the individual's personality. More often than not, this "chip" is a reflection of a painful past experience. What many do not realize is that our negative past experiences sometimes turn into personal baggage that creates barriers to career success. Examples of negative past experiences may include traumatic issues such as an unplanned pregnancy or a criminal offense. Other times, the negative experience involved a poor choice or a failure at something that had great meaning. These experiences are the ones that most heavily impact one's personality, values, and self-esteem. In turn, this will affect your attitude at the workplace, which will eventually affect your performance. Consider the following example concerning Cory. In high school, Cory made a poor choice and got in minor trouble with the law. Cory paid the dues, yet is still embarrassed and sometimes still feels unworthy of a successful future. Cory is trying to climb the mountain of success carrying a hundred-pound suitcase. The suitcase is filled with the thoughts of previous poor choices and embarrassment. From others' perspective, Cory does not need to carry this unnecessary baggage. In fact, because of Cory's motivation to complete college, most friends and acquaintances are unaware of Cory's past mistake. Cory's current self-efficacy leads Cory to believe success cannot be attained. Cory needs to learn from and forgive the past mistake and move forward. As self-image improves, Cory's belief in the ability to succeed will increase.

If you are one of these individuals who have had a negative experience that is hindering your ability to succeed, recognize the impact your past has on your future. Although you cannot change yesterday, you can most certainly improve your today and your future. Begin taking these steps toward a more productive future:

1. *Confront your past.* Whatever skeleton is in your past, admit that the event occurred. Do not try to hide or deny that it happened. There is no need to share the episode with everyone, but it may help to confidentially share the experience with one individual (close friend, family member, religious leader, or trained professional) who had no involvement with the negative experience. Self-talk is the first step toward healing. Verbally talk through your feelings, reminding yourself of your positive assets.

2. *Practice forgiveness.* Past negative experiences create hurt. A process in healing is to forgive whoever hurt you. This does not justify what was done as acceptable. The act of forgiveness does, however, reconcile in your heart that you are dealing with the experience and are beginning to heal. Identify who needs forgiveness. Maybe it is a family member, perhaps it is a friend or neighbor, or maybe it is you. Your act of forgiveness may involve a conversation with someone, or it may just involve a conversation with yourself. Practice forgiveness. In doing so, you will begin to feel a huge burden being lifted.

3. *Move forward.* Let go of guilt and/or embarrassment. Once you have begun dealing with your past, move forward. Do not keep dwelling on the past and using it as an excuse or barrier toward achieving your goals. If you are caught in this step, physically write the experience down on a piece of paper and the words "I forgive Joe" (replace the name with the individual who harmed you). Then take the paper and destroy it. This physical act puts you in control and allows you to visualize the negative experience being diminished. As you become more confident in yourself, your negative experience becomes enveloped with the rest of your past and frees you to create a positive future.

This sometimes painful process is necessary if your goal is to become the best individual you can be. It is not something that happens overnight. As mentioned previously, some individuals may need professional assistance to help them through the process. There is no shame in seeking help. In fact, there is great freedom when you have finally let go of the "baggage" and are able to climb to the top of the mountain unencumbered.

Exercise 1-2 Letting Go

How should Cory deal with the negative baggage?

_____

_____

_____

Locus of Control

The reality is that you will not always be surrounded by positive influences and you cannot control everything that happens in your life. Your attitude is affected by who you believe has control over situations that occur in your life, both personally and professionally. The **locus of control** identifies who you believe controls your future. An individual with an *internal* locus of control believes that he or she controls his or her own future. An individual with an *external* locus of control believes that others control his or her future.

Extremes on either end of the locus of control are not healthy. Realize that individual effort and a belief in the ability to perform well translate to individual success. However, external factors also influence your ability to achieve personal goals. Take responsibility for your actions and try your best. You cannot totally control the environment and future. Power, politics, and other factors discussed later in the text play an important part in the attainment of goals.

Learning Styles

Another element of personality is one's **learning style.** Learning styles define the method of how you best take in information and/or learn new ideas. There are three primary learning styles: visual, auditory, and tactile/kinesthetic.

To determine what your dominant learning style is, perform this simple exercise. Imagine you are lost and need directions. Do you:

   a.   want to see a map,
   b.   want someone to tell you the directions, or
   c.   need to draw or write down the directions yourself?

If you prefer answer *a*, you are a visual learner. You prefer learning by seeing. If you selected *b*, you are an auditory learner. You learn best by hearing. If you selected *c*, you are a tactile/kinesthetic learner, which means you learn best by feeling, touching, or holding. No one learning style is better than the other. However, it is important to recognize your primary and secondary learning styles so that you can get the most out of your world (in and out of the classroom or on the job). As a visual learner, you may digest material best by reading and researching. Auditory learners pay close attention to course lectures and class discussions. Tactile/kinesthetic learners will learn best by performing application exercises and physically writing course notes. Recognize what works best for you and implement that method to maximize your learning experience. Also recognize that not everyone learns the same way you do and not all information is presented in your preferred method. With that recognition, you can become a better classmate, team member, coworker, and boss.

Your Personal Handbook

The main idea of this discussion is that personality and attitude affect performance both personally and professionally. If you can honestly say that you have no concerns regarding personal confidence, attitude, and external influences (friends and family), congratulations. You have just crossed the first big hurdle toward workplace success. If you are like the majority of the population and can identify opportunities for improvement with either internal or external influences, a bigger congratulation is extended to you. Identifying areas for improvement is by far one of the most difficult hurdles to jump but certainly the most rewarding.

This book is designed as a personal handbook that leads you on an exciting journey toward creating both personal and career plans. On this journey you will also develop a respect and understanding of basic personal financial management and the influence finances have on many areas of your life. Self-management skills including time, stress, and organization will be addressed, as well as professional etiquette and dress. Workplace politics, their implications on performance, and how to successfully use these politics in your favor will be discussed, as will your rights as an employee. These newfound workplace skills will improve your ability to lead, motivate, and successfully work with others in a team setting. Finally, you will learn how to handle conflict and work with difficult coworkers.

As we move through key concepts in this text, begin developing a positive attitude and believe in yourself and your abilities. Equally important is that you learn from your past. Little by little, you will make lifestyle changes that will make you a better individual, which will make you an even better employee. It all translates to success at work and success in life.

The Importance of Personal Goal Setting

Everyone has dreams. These dreams may be for a college degree, a better life for loved ones, financial security, or the acquisition of material items such as a new car or home. Goal setting is the first step toward turning a dream into a reality. This important process provides focus and identifies specific steps that need to be accomplished. It is also a common practice used by successful individuals and organizations. A **goal** is a target. Think of a goal as a reward at the top of a ladder. Goals typically come in two forms: short-term goals and long-term goals. To reach a long-term goal, you need to progress up each step of the ladder. Each step contributes to the achievement of a goal and supports your personal values. More difficult goals typically take longer to achieve. Goals provide focus; increase self-concept; and help overcome procrastination, fear, and failure.

Influences of Goals

When you set and focus on goals, career plans become more clear and meaningful. They motivate you to continue working to improve yourself and help you achieve, not just hope for, what you want in life.

Consider Cory's goals. At twenty-two years of age, Cory had only a high-school education. After working as a service clerk since graduating from high school, Cory decided to go to college to become a Certified Public Accountant (CPA). Cory's long-term goal is to finish college in five years. Self-supporting and having to work, Cory set a realistic goal to obtain an associate degree in accounting within three years. After achieving that goal, Cory found a good job, has a good income, and has more self-confidence. Still committed to becoming a CPA, Cory needs to earn a bachelor's degree and has set a goal to do that within two years. This is motivating Cory to perform well.

In Cory's example, as one goal was reached, Cory became more motivated and self-confident enough to set a higher goal. Achieving goals results in continually striving for improvement.

Goals can and should be set in all major areas of your life, including personal, career, financial, educational, and physical. Goals help maintain a positive outlook. They also contribute to creating a more positive perception of you and will result in improved human relations with others.

Talk It Out

Discuss one goal that can be set for this class.

How to Set Goals

As explained earlier, achieving short- and long-term goals is like climbing a ladder. Imagine that there is a major prize (what you value most) at the top of the ladder. The prize can be considered your long-term goal, and each step on the ladder is a progressive short-term goal that helps you reach the major prize.

Set short-term and long-term goals and put them in writing. **Long-term goals** are goals that will take longer than a year to accomplish, with a realistic window of up to ten years.

To set a goal, first identify what you want to accomplish in your life. Write down everything you can think of, including personal, career, and educational dreams. Next, review the list and choose which items you most value. In reviewing your list, ask yourself where you want to be in one year, five years, and ten years. The items you identified are your long-term goals. Keep each goal realistic and something you truly want. Each goal should be challenging enough that you will work toward it but it should also be attainable. There should be a reason to reach each goal. Identify why each goal is important to you. This is a key step toward setting yourself up for success. Identify both opportunities and potential barriers toward reaching these goals. Remember Cory's goal to be a CPA? Cory believes becoming a CPA represents success. It is important to Cory, and it is a realistic goal that can be reached.

Exercise 1-3   Long-Term Career Goal

Write your long-term career goal.

_____

_____

_____

Short-term goals are goals that can be reached within a year's time. Short-term goals are commonly set to help reach long-term goals. Businesses often refer to short-term goals as **objectives,** because they are short-term, measurable, and have specific time lines. Short-term goals can be achieved in one day, a week, a month, or even several months. As short-term goals are met, long-term goals should be updated.

Just like long-term goals, short-term goals (objectives) must be realistic, achievable, and important to you. They need to be measurable so you know when you have actually reached them.

An additional long-term goal for Cory is to buy a car one year after graduation. Cory has set several short-term goals, one being to save a specific amount of money each month. To do this, Cory needs to work a certain number of hours each week. Cory also needs to be specific about the type of car, whether to buy used or new, and whether he needs to take out a loan. The answers to these questions will determine if the time frame is realistic and how much Cory needs to save every month.

Exercise 1-4   Short-Term Goals

Using your long-term career goal from Exercise 1-3, identify at least three short term goals.

_____

_____

_____

A popular and easy goal-setting method is the SMART method. SMART is an acronym for "specific, measurable, achievable, relevant, and time-based." Clearly identify what exactly you want to accomplish and, if possible, make your goal quantifiable. This makes your goal specific. Also, make your goal measurable. Identify how you know when you have achieved your goal. Keep your goal achievable but not too easily attainable nor too far out of reach. A good achievable goal is challenging, yet attainable and realistic. Relevant personal goals have meaning to its owner. The goal should belong to you, and you should have (or have access to) the appropriate resources to accomplish the goal. Finally, **SMART goals** are time-based. Attaching a specific date or time period provides a time frame for achieving the goal. For example, instead of writing, "I will become a manager in the future," write, "I will become a manager with a top accounting firm by the beginning of the year 2018." After you have written a goal, give it the SMART test to increase its probability for success.

Exercise 1-5   SMART Goals

Rewrite the goals from Exercise 1-4 into SMART goals.

_____

_____

_____

After you have written your goals in a positive and detailed manner, there are a few additional aspects of goal setting to consider. These include owning and being in control of your goals.

Owning the goal ensures that the goal belongs to you. You should decide your goals, not your parents, spouse, significant other, friends, relatives, or anyone else who may have influence over you. For example, if Cory goes to college because it is a personal dream to be a CPA, that goal will be accomplished. However, if Cory becomes a CPA because it was Cory's parents' idea to be a CPA, this would not be Cory's goal and it would make it harder to accomplish this goal.

Control your goal by securing the right information necessary to accomplish it. Know what resources and constraints are involved, including how you will be able to use resources and/or get around constraints. If your goal is related to a specific career, identify what attaining it will require in regard to finances, education, and other matters. Clarify the time needed to reach these goals by writing them as short-term or long-term goals. Referring back to the concept of locus of control, remember that not every factor is within your control. Therefore, be flexible and maintain realistic control over your goal.

Creating a Life Plan

Identifying goals contribute to the creation of a **life plan.** A life plan is a written document that identifies goals in all areas of your life, including your career and personal life (social, spiritual, financial, and activities).

Consider the following life issues:

- *Education and career:* Degree attainment, advanced degrees, job titles, specific employers.
- *Social and spiritual:* Marriage, family, friends, religion.
- *Financial:* Home ownership, car ownership, investments.
- *Activities:* Travel, hobbies, life experiences.

Create goals for each of these major life areas and note that some of your goals may blend into two or more areas. Some younger students are uncertain of their career goals. Others may feel overwhelmed that they have a life goal but perhaps lack the necessary resources to accomplish a goal. Goals can change over time. Stay focused but flexible. What is important is that you establish goals that reflect your values.

Just as your personal life goals and career goals are important, education is an important key to achieving your life plan. Consider the degrees/certificates required, the time frame, the financial resources, and the support network you will require for educational success.

No one can ever take your knowledge away from you. Make college course choices based upon your desired educational goals. Choose courses that will benefit you, help you explore new concepts, and challenge you. To be successful in your career, it is important to enjoy what you do. Select a career that supports your short-term and long-term goals.

When planning your career consider:

- Why your selected career is important to you.
- What resources are needed to achieve your career goals.
- How you will know you have achieved career success.

People choose careers for different reasons, including earning power, status, intellect, values, and self-satisfaction. If there is a career center available at your college, take time to visit and explore the various resources it offers. There are also several personality and career interest tests you can take that will help you determine your potential career. One popular and useful career assessment is the Golden Personality Type Profiler. The Golden Profiler is a well-respected personality assessment that assists users in identifying behaviors that support specific careers. Additional career assessments are offered at many college career centers and online. These useful assessments help identify interests, abilities, and

Web Quiz

Discover your personality

Take the Golden Personality Type Profiler or search for another online personality test to take.

www.mystudentsuccesslab.com.

personality traits to determine which career will suit you best. Use all resources available and gather information to assist you in making the best career decision. Conduct Internet searches, interview people who are already working in your field of interest, perform an internship, volunteer, or job shadow in a field that interests you. Doing so will help clarify your goals and life plan. An additional discussion on career exploration is presented in a later chapter.

Consider the type of personal relationships you want in the future. Goals should reflect your choice of marriage, family, friends, and religion. Identify where you want to be financially. Many people dream of becoming a millionaire, but you need to be realistic. Think about what kind of house you want to live in and what type of car you want to drive. If a spouse and children are in your future, account for their financial needs, as well. Also identify what outside activities you enjoy, including hobbies and travel. The personal financial plan you create will be a part of achieving these goals. This will be discussed in more detail in the next chapter. Think about what results and rewards will come from achieving your goals.

Intrinsic rewards include such things as self-satisfaction and pride of accomplishment. These come from within you and are what you value in life. **Extrinsic rewards** include such things as money and praise. These rewards come from external sources. Intrinsic and extrinsic rewards are needed to achieve satisfaction in your future. Both are equally important and should be recognized. They motivate you and help you maintain a positive outlook when working toward goals.

Talk It Out

Share common rewards that are important to you. Identify these rewards as intrinsic or extrinsic.

Priorities

Priorities determine what needs to be done and in what order. Properly managing priorities is the key to reaching goals. Not only is it important in your personal life, but it will be necessary at work.

You may need to adjust priorities to reach your goals. Before priorities can be placed in order, determine what they are. Sometimes your first priority is not necessarily what is most important in life; it is just that a particular activity demands the most attention at a specific point in time. For example, if Cory has a young child, that child is one of the most important things in Cory's life. However, if Cory is attending college to become a CPA and needs an evening to study for a big exam, the priority will be to study for the exam. That does not mean the exam is more important than the child. However, passing the exam is a step toward a better future for Cory and the child.

Cory's decision is called a **trade-off.** A trade-off is giving up one thing to do something else. Another example involving Cory is the decision to purchase a car in one year; Cory needs to save a certain amount of money each month. In order to do this, Cory may have to give up going to the coffee shop each morning and instead make coffee at home in order to set aside enough money to meet the savings goal to purchase the car.

Life plans require flexibility. When working toward goals, be flexible. Times change, technology changes, and priorities may change, which influence your goals. Reevaluate goals at least once a year. You may need to update or revise your goals and/or time lines more frequently than once a year because a situation changed. If that is the case, be flexible and update the goals. Do not abandon your goals because the situation changed.

Talk It Out

Identify priorities and trade-offs for successfully completing this course.

Workplace Dos and Don'ts

Do realize the impact your personality has on overall workplace performance	*Don't* assume that everyone thinks and behaves like you
Do believe that you are a talented, capable human being. Project self-confidence	*Don't* become obsessed with how others view you. Be and do your best
Do let go of past baggage	*Don't* keep telling everyone about a past negative experience
Do set goals in writing	*Don't* set goals that are impossible to reach
Do set long-term and short-term goals	*Don't* give up on goals
Do make your goals attainable	*Don't* wait to create goals
Do have measurable goals	*Don't* create unrealistic goals
Do set priorities. Include trade-offs and flexibility when setting goals	*Don't* give up when working to reach your goals

Concept Review and Application

Summary of Key Concepts

- How you view yourself dictates how you treat others and what type of employee you will be
- Your views of yourself, your environment, and your past experiences comprise your personality, values, attitude, and self-efficacy
- Negative past experiences create unnecessary baggage that either delays or prevents you from reaching your goals. Acknowledge and begin dealing with these negative experiences

- There are three primary learning styles: visual, auditory, and tactile/kinesthetic (sight, sound, and touch). Individuals must recognize how they best learn and also be aware that others may or may not share their same learning style
- Goal setting is important in helping you keep focused. It will increase your self-concept and help you become more successful in all areas of your life
- As goals are reached, motivation and self-confidence will increase
- Goals need to be put into writing. They need to be realistic and measurable. Know who owns the goals and who controls the goals. A time frame is needed to know when you plan on reaching these goals
- Long-term goals are set to be achieved in five to ten years
- Short-term goals are achieved within a year's time and are needed to reach long-term goals
- When creating a life plan, consider all aspects of your life, including personal, career, and education
- Flexibility and properly managing priorities are needed to successfully achieve goals
- As you begin a new job, establish a relationship with a mentor

Key Terms

attitude	extrinsic rewards	goal
human relations	intrinsic rewards	learning style
life plan	locus of control	long-term goals
mirror words	objectives	personality
priorities	professionalism	projection
self-concept	self-efficacy	self-image
short-term goals	SMART goal	trade-off
values		

If You Were the Boss

1. How would you deal with an employee who displays poor self-efficacy?
2. How would recognizing different learning styles help you be a better boss?
3. Why does an employer need to set goals?
4. Why is it important that an employer ensure that employees set personal and career goals?

Web Links

http://www.humanmetrics.com/cgi-win/JTypes1.htm
http://www.colorquiz.com
http://personality-project.org/personality.html
http://www.ncrel.org/sdrs/areas/issues/students/learning/lr2locus.htm
http://www.mindtools.com/pages/article/newHTE_06.htm
http://www.topachievement.com/goalsetting.html
http://www.mygoals.com/helpGoalsettingTips.html
http://www.gems4friends.com/goals/index.html

Activities

Activity 1–1
Apply the learning styles discussed in this chapter and complete the following statements.

In the classroom, I learn best by

_____

In the classroom, I have difficulty learning when

_____

How will you use this information to perform better?

_____

Activity 1–2
Write down four words to describe your ideal self-concept.

1. _____

2. _____

3. _____

4. _____

What steps are necessary to make your ideal self-concept a reality?

_____

_____

Activity 1–3
What outside experiences and/or influences affect your educational behavior?

Outside Experiences and/or Influences.
1.
2.
3.
4.

Activity 1–4

Share the following information to introduce yourself to your classmates.

1. What is your name?

   _____

2. Where were you born?

   _____

3. What is your major (if you don't have one, what interests are you pursuing at school)?

   _____

4. What is your favorite color?

   _____

5. What is your favorite thing about attending school?

   _____

6. If you could be any animal, what would it be and why?

   _____

7. What else would you like us to know about you?

   _____

Activity 1–5

Create three long-term goals in each section of your life plan. Make them realistic.

Personal	Career	Education
1.	1.	1.
2.	2.	2.
3.	3.	3.

Activity 1–6

Using the previous activities in this chapter, set long- and short-term goals. The star is your long-term goal. The steps are your short-term goals. Write positively and in detail. Set one personal goal and one career goal. Keep short-term goals specific, measurable, and realistic. Include what (the goal), when (specific time you plan to achieve it), and how to get there (be specific). Hint: Refer back to Cory's goal to obtain a car.

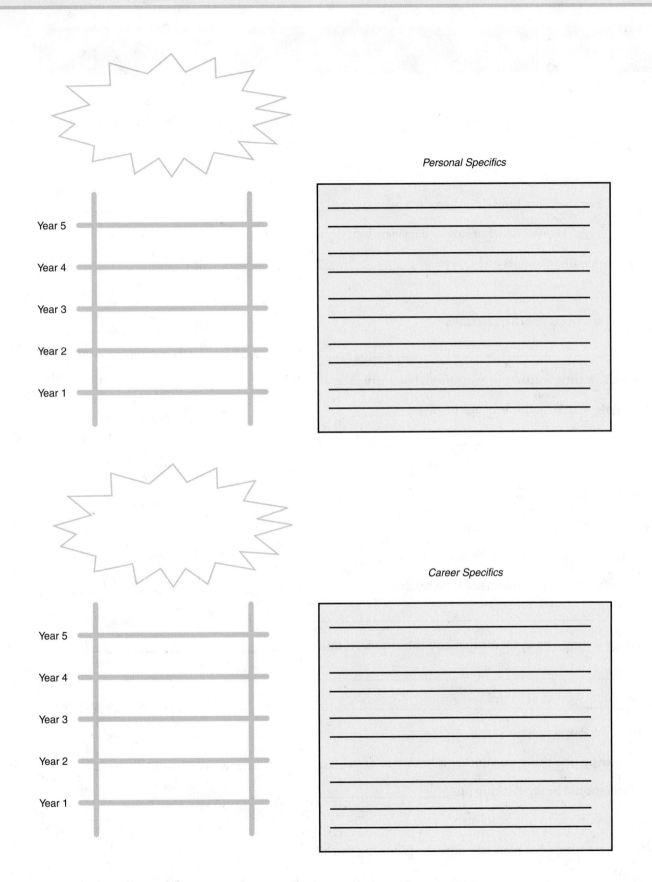

Year 5

Year 4

Year 3

Year 2

Year 1

Personal Specifics

Year 5

Year 4

Year 3

Year 2

Year 1

Career Specifics

1. The _____ identifies who you believe controls your future.

2. _____ is an individual's perception of how he or she views himself or herself, while _____ _____ is one's belief of how others view him or her.

3. When one understands one's own _____ and _____, it is much easier to understand reactions to others' actions.

4. A/An _____ affects group performance, which, in turn, impacts organizational performance.

5. Dealing with negative baggage involves _____ your past, _____, and moving _____ _____.

6. Past influences shape our _____

7. Goals need to be set so you can become _____.

8. Long-term goals are set to be reached after _____.

9. Short-term goals should usually be reached _____.

10. _____ help you reach long-term goals.

11. When setting a goal, there must be a time frame; it must be _____ _____ and _____.

12. _____ will help you decide what needs to be done and in what order.

13. To give up one thing for another is known as a/an _____.

14. Goals should be challenging but _____.

15. It is important to put goals into _____.

16. When creating a life plan, consider the following three areas:

    _____

    _____

    _____

Career Goal Setting

By (Student Name)

This writing assignment guides you through the process of creating goals. Remember that these goals must be realistic, attainable, important to you, and measurable. Be as specific as possible in every paragraph.

Identify and write your five-year and one-year career goals here. Identify what kind of job and what title you want, in what city you want to work, whom you want to work for, and why you chose this goal. Use the SMART method.

Five-Year Goal

Paragraph 1:	*In five years, I want to be . . .*

One-Year Goal(s)

Paragraph 2:	*In order to reach my five-year goal, I need to set the following short-term goals:*
	Identify necessary steps to reach your five-year goal. Be specific with activities, resources, and time frames.
Paragraph 3:	*I am currently...*
	What are you currently doing to reach these short-term goals? Be specific with activities, resources, and time frames.
Paragraph 4:	*I will know I have reached these goals when...*
	Goals must be measurable. How will you know when you have reached each short-term goal? Be specific with activities, resources, and time frames.
Paragraph 5:	*I need the following resources to reach my goal:*
	Identify physical, financial, emotional, and social resources and where they will come from.
Paragraph 6:	*My priorities for reaching my goals are:*
	Have priorities set for reaching your goals. Include your trade-offs and the areas where you may need to be flexible.

Personal Financial Management

The entire essence of America is the hope to first make money—then make money with money—then make lots of money with lots of money.

Paul Erdman (b. 1932)

How-Do-You-Rate

	How personal are you making finance?	Yes	No
1.	I have a personal budget.	❑	❑
2.	I routinely use a personal budget.	❑	❑
3.	I can tell you exactly how much money I have in my checking and/or savings account(s).	❑	❑
4.	I can tell you exactly how much I currently owe in long-term debt/credit card bills.	❑	❑
5.	I routinely pay off the entire balance of my monthly credit card bill.	❑	❑

If you answered "no" to two or more of these questions, treat this as an opportunity to get personal with your finances. Knowing and applying personal financial concepts will enable you to achieve personal goals, improve your self-concept, and provide a better understanding of business.

Financial Management

We go to work to earn a paycheck. What we do with our paycheck reveals a lot about us, including our goals and values. It is difficult to be productive and sometimes trusted at work if an individual does not have his or her personal financial affairs in order. Individuals without a personal financial plan usually have little control over spending and a lot of stress caused by financial crisis. Creating and utilizing a personal financial plan helps create positive financial habits that contribute to the realization of long-term goals and professional success. **Personal financial management** is the process of controlling personal income and expenses. **Income** is money coming in. This money may come from parents, grants, student loans, and/or a job. While you are a student, your income may be minimal. However, after finishing college, you will start a new career and your income should increase. Although you need to be careful handling your money presently, this becomes even more important as your income grows.

An **expense** is money going out. This is money spent. Examples of expenses associated with being a student include tuition, textbooks, school supplies, housing, and transportation. Expenses you have because of life needs include food, shelter, and clothes. Then there are additional expenses such as hobbies, entertainment, medical, and loans.

As you achieve your career goal and income increases, expenses also increase. This is where personal financial management becomes extremely important. Practice healthy financial management by creating good spending and saving habits.

Objectives

- Describe the importance of *personal financial management*
- Identify the significance of money management and budgeting
- Identify the difference between *gross income* and *net income*
- Create a personal *budget*
- Recognize *money wasters*
- Identify *debt* and debt management resources
- Identify wise use of credit
- Describe the importance of savings and investments
- Protect yourself from identity theft

Personal Financial Management Affects Work Performance

Personal finances impact all areas of your life. Finances are important in helping you reach the goals you identified in chapter 1. Personal financial management does not have to restrict your activities. Instead, it is a way to make your financial resources assist you in reaching goals while ensuring a healthy financial future. Now is the time to start making your money work for you by creating a personal financial plan.

Proper financial management includes managing your money and keeping your debt under control. It also involves maintaining a positive credit report by using credit wisely and beginning savings and investment plans now. It is also wise to know how to be protected against identity theft.

As explained at the start of this chapter, a lack of personal financial management can negatively affect your work situation. If you are not properly managing your finances, you will eventually have difficulty making purchases and paying your bills. You will also experience considerable stress. In turn, this stress will flow into the workplace and your performance will start to deteriorate. This will then cause stress within the workplace. Some employers require that you submit references and/or agree to a credit check prior to hiring, especially if your job requires working with money. Employers rationalize that if you cannot manage your personal finances, you may not be a responsible employee, nor can you be trusted with company resources.

For example, a coworker has been asking to borrow money for lunch from Cory. Cory has noticed that this coworker comes to work with a specialty coffee each morning and buys lunch every day. This is causing a strain on the relationship between Cory and the coworker. Cory has been on a strict budget since starting this job. Cory brings lunch from home instead of buying it and goes to the coffee shop only on special occasions. After loaning money to the coworker several times, Cory decides to confront the coworker. Cory shares with the coworker the importance of budgeting and helps the coworker create a budget of her own. After a while, the coworker stops asking Cory and others for money. The coworker starts bringing lunch from home and treats herself to a specialty coffee only once in a while. A few months later this coworker thanks Cory because now she is beginning to save money.

Your Paycheck

Many students struggle to keep up with expenses. Although you may currently have or had a job, your wages may have not been very high. Perhaps you have been low on cash and have had just enough money to get through school. Once you graduate and begin a job in your desired field, your wages will most likely increase. With the pay increase, you will have extra cash. While it may be tempting to increase spending on treats that you could not afford in the past, now is the time to start managing your money.

Chapter 1 explained how to create goals. Many goals require time and money to achieve. Therefore, create both long-term and short-term financial goals. Cory has a goal to buy a car after working for one year. Cory has to stay on a budget and save a specific amount of money to get that car when planned. In order to reach this goal, Cory needs to create a budget as soon as possible.

While it is sometimes tempting to spend money just because you have it, think about the future, learn to practice self-control and not give in to that temptation. Financial success begins with discipline and planning.

Money Management

The best way to manage your money and still be able to buy some of the extras you want is to create a budget. A **budget** is a detailed financial plan used to allocate money for a specific time period. A budget reflects goals and specifies where your money goes in order to reach these goals. Control and prioritize your spending to match these goals. Be as precise and honest as you can when you are creating and working with a budget.

Cash management is the key to good budgeting. Carry only a small amount of cash. Cash is too easy to spend, and it is hard to track where it has gone. Most individuals spend more cash when it is readily available. A good cash management practice is to track every single transaction. Many individuals forget how much money has been spent and where it has gone. Physically record all deposits and withdrawals made with your ATM card, debit card, or checking account when they occur. Physically keeping track of how much money you have in your account results in accurate accounting. Smart phones have apps designed to assist you in this practice. Reduce your trips to the ATM, as well. Prior to spending money, take time to seriously think about where your money is going and if the expense is necessary or if it is an impulse purchase. These cash management tips will help you realize when and where you are spending your money.

The first step in creating a budget is to identify goals. That is why in chapter 1 you created and identified goals for the future. Effective goals must be in writing and should provide direction for creating your budget. Attach financial goals to your personal goals. The series of exercises and activities throughout this chapter will assist you in developing financial goals.

Determine your income and expenses to put your budget into action. Remember, income is money coming in and an expense is money going out. Because it is best to establish a budget on a month-to-month basis, identify monthly income and expenses.

Start by determining all money that you receive on a monthly basis. If you know your income on a yearly basis, divide it by 12 (months) to identify monthly income. Using net income instead of **gross income** simplifies the budget process. Gross income is the amount of money in a paycheck before paying taxes or other deductions. However, to make it easier to set up the budget, use **net income.** Net income is the amount of money you have after all taxes and deductions are paid.

Exercise 2-1   Determine Your Monthly Income

Complete the following information the best you can.

Salary(ies)/wage(s) per month *(Use net income—after taxes)* $_____

Interest income per month (Savings, checking, other)   _____

Other income per month   _____

Total monthly income $_____

After you have identified your monthly income, determine your expenses. Exercise 2–2 lists categories with common expenses. Estimate how much you spend every month in each category. If you spend money in an area that is not listed, add another category to the list. Do not overuse the miscellaneous category. The idea is to track exactly where your money is being spent. Ideally, track all of your expenses over the next few months. Track every penny. Doing so will give you a true picture of where you really spend your money. At the end of this chapter, you will find additional activities and resources designed to assist you in determining your exact expenses.

Fixed expenses are more easily identified. These are expenses that do not change from month to month, such as a monthly mortgage or rent payment. **Flexible expenses** are those that change from month to month, such as food or utilities. It is better to average flexible expenses than to try to determine which months may be more or less.

Exercise 2-2   Determine Your Monthly Expenses

Complete the following information as accurately as you can. Determine what amount goes in each category. This will be an estimate. Over time, identify and update actual amounts as you become aware of them.

Category	Monthly
Housing	$
Food	
Transportation	
Education	
Health	
Clothing	
Entertainment	
Loans (debts)	
Utilities (gas, electric, etc.)	
Communications (phone, Internet)	
Daycare	
Investments/savings	
Insurance	
Donations	
Miscellaneous	
Total	$

First budgets are not perfect. Adjust your personal budget monthly as you track and identify specific income and expenses. Activity 2-4, found at the end of the chapter, provides you the opportunity to create a personal budget.

The following is an example of a partial budget.

	Estimated (what you have been receiving and paying or what you think you will receive and pay for the month)	**Actual** (this is the actual amount you received or spent)	**Difference** (this is the actual amount minus estimated amount)	**Balance** (income minus all expenses—what you have left to spend and save)
INCOME				
1. Net Income	$1,600	$1,760	$160	$1,760
EXPENSES				
2. Housing	500	500	0	1,260
3. Food	200	240	40	1,020

1. Your previous net income (take-home pay) has been $19,200 for the last year. To find your ESTIMATED monthly you calculate $19,200 ÷ 12 (months in a year) = $1,600 per month. However, assume this month you got a raise (assume you did not know about the raise) to make your yearly net salary $21,120. Your new monthly salary would be $1,760. That would be your ACTUAL net income. The DIFFER-ENCE would be $1,760 − $1,600 = + $160. The BALANCE is income minus expenses. The income for this month was $1,760.

2. Your rent has been $500 a month (estimated). This is considered a fixed expense that would not change from month to month . The balance is $1,760 − $500 = $1,260.

3. Your food usually costs about $200 a month (estimated). This month you ate out more and you spent $240 on food (actual). The difference is +$40. The balance is $1,020.

Your budget will identify where you are spending unnecessary money and will allow you to modify your spending while developing good personal financial management habits. You will be able to identify **money wasters,** which are small expenditures that you may not realize are consuming a larger portion of your income than expected.

Here is a common example of a money waster: On average, a specialty cup of coffee is about $3. If you buy a cup of coffee five days a week, over a year's time you have spent $780 ($3 × 5 days × 52 weeks) on coffee. You may have been buying coffee because you do not have a coffeemaker and think you cannot afford to purchase one. Assume a coffeemaker costs about $25 and, on average, flavored coffee runs about $8.99 a pound. This will last one person about two to three months. So the total spent for coffee for the year would be under $100 ($8.99 × 5 + $25). If you purchased the supplies and made your own coffee, you could save $680. Imagine what you could do with an extra $680 a year.

Exercise 2-3   Determine Money Wasters

Working with a partner, list at least three ways people waste money on small expenditures. What is the estimated cost? What can be done to save that money? Refer to the coffee example.

Small Expenditure Waste (Money Wasters)	Estimated Cost	Behavior Change
1.	$	
2.		
3.		

Debt Management

Debt is money owed. There is the difference between an expense and debt. An expense is money going out. A common expense is a bill. A **loan** is a large debt that is paid in smaller amounts over a period of time and has interest added to the payment. **Interest** is the cost of borrowing money and is the extra money you pay a lender. Debt includes all types of loans (car, home, school) and credit cards. You may already have some debt, such as a student loan or a credit card.

The use of credit cards is one way many people fall into uncontrollable debt. This causes individuals to file for bankruptcy, which results in long-term bad credit. Do not allow yourself to fall into a debt trap. The best way to avoid a debt trap is to purchase only what you can afford.

Keep your net worth positive. **Net worth** is the amount of money that is yours after paying off debt. Net worth is determined by comparing your assets and liabilities. Although your net worth may not be high now, in the future, as you practice sound money management, your net worth will increase. You increase net worth by decreasing your liabilities and increasing your assets.

Total assets − total liabilities = total net worth

Personal **assets** are what you own. These are items that are worth money—for example, a car, home, and furniture. A **liability** is an obligation to pay what you owe. If you have a car loan, it is a liability.

If you are in debt, now is the time to begin getting yourself out of debt. Seek advice and support from a parent, school counselor, or financial counselor. Talk with your creditor to work out a reduced payment or lower interest rate. Cancel and destroy unnecessary credit cards. There are reputable national, nonprofit credit-counseling services and credit-repair organizations that can assist you, such as the National Foundation for Consumer Credit or Myvesta Foundation.

The following are general steps to get out of debt:

1. Do not create additional debt. Avoid using an existing credit card (cut it up if necessary) or taking on additional debt.
2. Prioritize your debt. Pay off the smallest amount or the amount with the highest interest first.
3. After you have paid off one loan, apply the extra cash to the next debt on your priority list.

Talk It Out

What are warning signs that you may be getting into debt?

Exercise 2-4   Debt Repayment Goals

If you have debt, write down each loan then list the amount you pay each month and the total amount you owe. Include the amount of interest you pay annually. Identify which creditor should be paid first.

Creditor (Whom You Have the Loan With)	Amount Paid per Month	Total Amount Still Owed	Interest Percentage	Order of Payoff
1.	$	$	%	
2.				
3.				
4.				

Wise Use of Credit

The best way to stay out of a debt hole is to manage your credit. As you increase your earning power, you may receive offers from credit card companies. Do not accept every offer. Although credit can buy a lot of things, do not abuse the privilege of credit. As experienced in our nation's most recent economic downturn, many individuals received credit and made purchases they ultimately could not afford. Build good credit and maintain that good credit. Good credit aids in purchasing large items such as a car or home at a lower interest rate. If you have a credit card, use it as a tool for establishing good credit. Spend wisely and pay off the balance each month. This will assure good credit and keep you out of debt. If you know you cannot pay the balance each month, do not use a credit card. Use the credit card only for items you can afford, and always make credit payments on time. Do not take cash advances against your credit card.

If you find yourself in a credit hole, do not get in the habit of making only a minimum payment. Pay as much of the balance as you can. Do not skip a payment, and do not make a late payment, as this will show on your credit report.

If you take out a loan, it should only be for necessities such as reliable transportation, education, a home, or an emergency. Use the loan funds wisely, and do not overspend. Only purchase items you can afford based upon your income.

When applying for credit, lenders consider your character, capacity, collateral, and condition. Character reflects your past attitude toward paying your bills on time, thus telling the lender if you will be likely to repay the loan. Capacity is your ability to repay the loan; your salary will play an important role in this matter. Collateral is the assets you own that are used as security to pay the debt. Other issues to be aware of when applying for a loan are interest rates, hidden costs, the purpose of the loan or credit card, what your payments will be, and how long you will be paying on the loan. Always read and understand the fine print of loan documents prior to signing the loan agreement. Loan documents outline the lender's right to change the terms and conditions of a loan. Once you agree to the loan, you are legally obligated to abide by these terms and conditions.

For example, Cory has been receiving credit card offers and is deciding whether to apply for one. Cory knows credit cards can be dangerous and can cause financial trouble. However, Cory also realizes that good credit is needed in order to get a car loan and decides that getting a credit card would not be a bad idea as long as it was not used on frivolous items. Cory reads all the details on each credit card application, including annual fees, minimum payments, and annual percentage rates. After researching the fine print on the credit offers and identifying all hidden fees, Cory secures a good credit card but uses it only for establishing credit, and each time it is used it is paid in full each month.

Talk It Out

Identify potential terms and conditions that you should consider before getting credit from a lender.

Credit Reports

A **credit report** is a detailed credit history on an individual. Creditors look at this report to decide who is a good candidate for credit. A credit report details balances and payments on current and past credit cards and loans. It shows if you have paid these debts on time or if you don't pay them at all. Credit reports are summarized in the form of a credit score. Your credit score is a rating system that evaluates the risk of lending you money based upon your credit history. The most common credit rating is known as a **Fair Isaac Corporation (FICO) score**. The higher your FICO score, the better your credit, making you a better candidate for getting a loan at a lower interest rate. If you have a low FICO score, you have a bad credit rating and you may have difficulty securing a loan and will pay a higher interest rate if you do secure one.

The credit report contains personal identification information. This includes any previous names, addresses, and employers. Liens, foreclosures, and bankruptcies will also appear on this report. If you are denied credit because of information on your credit report, the institution is required by law to provide you a copy of your credit report.

There are three credit reporting agencies. They are Equifax, Experian, and TransUnion. Your FICO score is a combination of these agency ratings. Under federal law, you are entitled to a free copy of your credit report from these agencies once every twelve months. For details, please visit www.annualcreditreport.com. While there are many other websites that offer free credit reports, this is the only site that is sponsored by the three national credit-reporting agencies and is affiliated with the national free credit report program. Take advantage of this free benefit and regularly monitor your credit. Because you can receive one free report from each agency every year, it is recommended you request a free copy from each reporting agency at different times throughout the year. For example, request a copy from Equifax in January, a copy from TransUnion in May, and a copy from Experian in September. Doing so allows you to monitor your credit for free throughout the year. If you find an error on any of these reports, immediately notify the credit-reporting company and correct the error.

Savings and Investments

Do not wait until you have acquired your career job to start a savings plan. Begin saving today. A good rule of thumb is to have at least five months' income saved for emergencies or major expenses that you did not expect. You save this amount by spending less than you earn. Make a commitment to take a specific percentage, about 5 percent, from your paycheck and place it in a savings account. After you complete your budget, you will be able to identify unnecessary expenditures that you can convert into savings.

Keep your savings in a financial institution where it can earn interest. If your company provides an automatic deduction service, use it. An **automatic deduction plan** usually works best because the funds are automatically deducted from your paycheck and placed into your savings account so you do not have the opportunity to spend the money.

When saving, decide if you need the money to be readily available or if it can be left untouched for a specified period of time. This will help you determine if you should place your money in a traditional savings account or place it in a certificate of deposit (CD). A traditional savings account typically pays a lower interest rate than a CD. However, you can add and take out funds at any time from a traditional savings account without penalty. A CD pays a higher rate than a traditional savings account, but the funds are locked in for a specified time period. You are not allowed to add funds to the amount during the specified time period. If funds are withdrawn before the maturity date, you will pay a penalty.

There is a difference between saving and investing. Saving money means that you are setting away funds for short-term goals and/or emergencies. Investing may provide a greater opportunity to increase the value of your money and generally is a long-term endeavor. Typical investments include stocks, mutual funds, and real estate. However, investing involves risk. It is recommended that individuals first establish a traditional savings account for emergencies. Once an emergency fund is established, funds can be directed to an investment account.

Investments for the future are important to start now. If invested properly, money grows over time. There are many ways to invest money, all of which you should research to decide what level of risk you desire. Do not invest all of your money nor invest it all in one place.

Web Quiz

Be a winner and play the Smart Money Quiz Show or search for information about saving and investing.

http://www.practicalmoneyskills.com/games/

Identity Theft

Protecting yourself from identity theft has become increasingly important. Identity theft is when another individual uses your personal information to obtain credit in your name. To prevent this from happening, properly dispose of any communications (electronic or hard copy) that contain your personal information. Anything thrown in the garbage should not contain your personal information. The most popular pieces of personal information desired by identity thieves include your Social Security number, date of birth, credit card numbers, and mother's maiden name. Cut up or shred junk mail. Register to opt out from receiving credit offers. This can be done at https://www.optout prescreen.com or by calling 1-888-567-8688.

Keep track of all your credit card numbers and other important information. Make a copy of your license, Social Security number, and all credit information and store this information in a safe place. Do not share your Social Security number, birthplace, birthday, or mother's maiden name unless you have verified that this individual works for the company from whom you want to secure credit. This private information is used to verify your identity and credit history. If this information gets in the wrong hands, it provides someone easy access to your identity.

The following are tips to remember:

- Do not share your social security number over the telephone or Internet without verifying the authenticity of the company and individual requesting the information. When using the Internet, note that a secure website will use https.
- Document all important numbers, such as license, credit cards, and savings account, and keep them in a private and safe place.
- Practice good personal financial management by routinely reviewing details on your credit card bills, bank statements, credit reports, and other financial documents.
- Delete your name from credit card lists and marketing lists.
- Monitor your credit and bank accounts regularly.
- If you receive a call from a collection agency and do not have poor credit, do not ignore the call. Someone may have taken credit in your name and made you a victim of identity theft.

If you become a victim of identity theft, the first thing to do is file a police report. Immediately contact your bank, all credit card companies, and your wireless communications provider. Do not change your social security number, but do contact the Social Security Administration Fraud Department and all of the three credit report agency fraud lines. Document everyone you talk to and everything you do for future reference.

Important Telephone Numbers and Websites

The following is a list of important resources to assist you with credit and fraud issues.

Consumer Counseling Services

- The National Foundation for Consumer Credit: 1-800-388-2227 or http://www.nfcc.org
- Myvesta Foundation: http://www.myvesta.org
- Social Security Administration Fraud Department: 1-877-438-4338 or http://www.ssa.gov/oig/ifyou.htm

Credit Report Agencies and Resources

- Equifax credit report: 1-800-685-1111; fraud: 1-800-525-6285
- Experian credit report: 1-800-397-3742; fraud: 1-800-397-3742
- TransUnion credit report: 1-800-916-8800; fraud: 1-800-680-7289
- Free Credit Reports: 1-877-322-8228; www.annualcreditreport.com

Please visit the text website for online resources to build and maintain financial health.

Workplace Dos and Don'ts

Do create good financial goals	*Don't* use credit cards unwisely
Do keep a budget	*Don't* waste money
Do start saving and investing now	*Don't* ignore credit reports
Do learn to protect yourself from identity theft	*Don't* use cash for all spending

Concept Review and Application

Summary of Key Concepts

- Personal financial management is the process of controlling your income and expenses
- Income is money coming in
- Expense is money going out
- A budget is a detailed plan for finances
- The first step to creating a budget is to identify goals
- Debt (liability) is the money you owe
- Net worth is assets minus liabilities
- A credit report is a detailed credit history
- Identity theft is when another individual uses your personal information

Key Terms

assets
credit report
expense
flexible expenses
income
loan
net income

automatic deduction
  plan
Fair Isaac Corporation
  (FICO) score
interest
money wasters
net worth

budget
debt
fixed expenses
gross income
liability
personal financial
  management

If You Were the Boss

1. You need to hire a receptionist that will be handling cash. What steps would you take to make sure you hire the right person?
2. Why should you teach your employees the importance of personal financial management? What are some creative ways of doing this?

Video Case Study: Healthy Personal Financial Management

This video presents a financial professional providing expert advice on how to practice healthy personal financial management. To view these videos, visit the Student Resources: Professionalism section in www.mystudentsuccesslab.com. Then answer the following questions.

1. What specific steps can you take to improve your spending habits?
2. Share two specific pieces of advice the financial expert shared regarding saving and investing.
3. Name four methods of using credit wisely.

Web Links

http://www.betterbudgeting.com
http://www.personal-budget-planning-saving-money.com
http://financialplan.about.com/cs/budgeting/a/Budgeting101.htm
http://www.moneyadvise.com

Activity 2-1

Create a personal financial statement. List the net worth of all your *assets* (what they would be worth today if you sold them). Under *liabilities,* put the total amount you owe (not just monthly payments) to any creditors. For your *net worth*, take your total amount of assets minus your total amount of liabilities.

Assets	Amount
(Present Value)	
Cash (savings/checking)	$
Investments	
Life insurance	
House	
Automobile	
Furniture	
Jewelry	
Other assets	
Total assets	$
Liabilities	
Home loan	$
Automobile loan	
Credit card debt	
Educational loan	
Other Loans	
Total liabilities	$
Net Worth (Total Assets Minus Liabilities)	$

Activity 2-2

Create financial goals and a budget to support these goals. Write the specific goal you want to reach. Identify the amount of money needed to reach that goal. In the last column, identify when you want to reach that goal.

Goals	Amount	Time
Debt payoffs	$	
Education		
Personal (car, home)		
Miscellaneous		
Savings		
Starting a business		

Activity 2-3

Use these sheets to track your spending for two weeks to identify where you are spending your money. Record all spending. Even minor expenses (every penny) should be recorded. Include the date, amount spent, what you bought (service or product), and how you paid for the item (means).

	SPENDING RECORD SHEET WEEK 1		
Date	Amount Spent	Item Bought	Payment Method (Cash, Credit Card, Debit Card, Check)
	$		

Activity 2-4

Create a personal budget. Refer to page 25 for an example.

BUDGET FOR MONTH OF _____

Monthly Payment Category	Estimated Budget	Actual Budget	Difference + OR −	Balanced Budget
Net spendable income per month	$	$	$	$
Housing				
Food				
Insurance				
Debts				
Clothing				
Medical				
Donations				
Entertainment				
Miscellaneous				
Investments				

1. _____ is the process of controlling your income and your expenses.

2. A/An_____ is a detailed plan for a specific time period for specifying your financial goals.

3. The small expenditures that add up to larger amounts are referred to as _____.

4. When considering applications for credit, lenders consider _____, _____, _____, and _____.

5. _____ is money you owe.

6. Your _____ is the amount of money that is yours after paying off debts.

7. A detailed credit history on an individual is called a/an _____.

Time and Stress Management/ Organization Skills

Chapter 3

We must use time as a tool, not as a crutch.

John F. Kennedy (1917–1963)

	Is your life in order?	Yes	No
1.	The inside of my car is clean.	❏	❏
2.	My personal workspace is free of clutter.	❏	❏
3.	My computer files are in order and it is easy to find documents.	❏	❏
4.	I maintain an address book (electronic or traditional) to keep my professional network current.	❏	❏
5.	I make my bed every day.	❏	❏

If you answered "no" to two or more of these questions, it's time to get your life in order. Organization in all areas of your life decreases stress and improves time management—two factors that will contribute to workplace success.

The Impact of Stress on Performance

Walk into a workplace and you'll quickly form an impression of the work environment. Your first impression will most likely be based upon the demeanor of the employees and their interactions with each other. You will also notice if the work area is messy and unorganized or if it is clean and orderly. This chapter examines the influences that stress management, time management, and organization have on workplace productivity. We waste a lot of time looking for items that if arranged in an organized manner would make our jobs easier and save us time. When we fail to plan appropriately and do not have enough time to complete our work, we get stressed. Of course, there are other factors that contribute to a productive workplace, but time, stress, and organization are certainly major contributing forces. Stress management, time management, and organizational ability are personal skills that must be developed and consistently practiced. As you learned in chapter 1, positive personal habits spill into the workplace and become positive workplace behaviors.

Employers need employees who are healthy, relaxed, and well organized. Healthy employees are able to perform at their highest levels, have decreased absenteeism, and have fewer health claims than their unhealthy counterparts. Stress can impact workplace productivity, and stress is affected by factors including self-care matters such as diet and exercise and organizational issues like time management.

Stress is the body's reaction to tense situations. Stress can cause more than just a bad day. Constant stress can result in permanent mental and/or physical harm.

Although some forms of stress are beneficial and keep you mentally challenged, long-term (chronic) stress will eventually harm you in one way or another. It may start to affect your work performance and will most likely carry on to your personal life. While not all stress is within your control, try to maintain a low stress level. Stress-related losses are high and are costing organizations billions of dollars annually.

Objectives

- Describe how *stress* impacts workplace performance
- Identify the causes of stress and name methods of dealing with stress
- Deal with *procrastination* in a productive manner
- Apply *time management* techniques in the workplace
- Define the importance of organizing for optimal performance
- Apply organizational techniques in the workplace

How can stress from school impact other areas of your life?

Types of Stress

You arrive in class and your teacher announces that today students are to give impromptu presentations on the lecture material. The students who are prepared and confident may be quite excited about the activity, while those who are not prepared or not confident may suddenly flush and feel their hearts racing. As a result they will be stressed. This illustration demonstrates that stressful situations vary from individual to individual. Stress is a normal part of life. What is important is that you recognize when you are stressed and deal with the stress appropriately. There is positive and negative stress. You will experience stress at school, at work, and at home. There is no avoiding it. However, how you react to and deal with stress determines how it will affect you. Some stress is minor and affects you at a specific time. This can be **positive stress.** Positive stress is a productive stress that provides the strength to accomplish a task. However, even positive stress can become negative if it continues and becomes problematic. For example, if you have a rushed deadline for a special project, your adrenaline will increase, giving you the mental and/or physical strength to finish the project on time. However, if you consistently have rushed deadlines, your stress level could increase and will eventually start working negatively on your mind and body.

Any stress can become **negative stress.** Becoming emotional or illogical or starting to lose control of your temper is a sign that you are experiencing unproductive or negative stress. This type of stress is continuous and may affect your mental and/or physical health. Negative stress commonly results in anger, depression, and/or distrust. Other signs of negative stress may include frequent headaches, fatigue, diminished or increased appetite, a poor immune system, or other physical weakness. Negative stress can ultimately result in ulcers, heart disease, or mental disturbances.

Cory has started experiencing headaches and fatigue lately. After thinking about recent activities, Cory realizes the headaches and fatigue may be a symptom of stress. With college and work, there seems to be no time for relaxation. Cory decides that this situation needs changing or the physical symptoms could get worse. Cory takes time to write out goals, make a plan, and practice stress management techniques. Soon after, Cory starts feeling better and has more control in balancing school and work, and has found free time to relax.

What are common negative stressors students face, and what are positive responses?

Exercise 3-1   Recognize Your Stress

List at least three significant things that have happened to you in the last year that have caused you stress. Next to the stressor, include what happened to you mentally and/or physically.

Stressor	Symptoms of the Stressor (How You Respond Mentally and/or Physically)
1.	
2.	
3.	

Dealing with Stress

The first step in dealing with stress is to identify the key stressors in your life. Learning to both identify and deal with these stressors will reduce their negative effects. Be aware of them and how they affect your attitude and behavior. Life is not stress-free. The following steps will assist in not allowing stressful situations to get the best of you:

1. Identify the stressor. Find out what is causing you to be stressed.
2. Recognize why and how you are reacting to that stressor.
3. Take steps to better deal with the stress by visualizing and setting a goal for responding in a positive manner.
4. Practice positive stress relief.

The following are ways to relieve stress:

- Find an outlet to release tension. This can include daily exercise, a hobby, or some other healthy activity.
- Diminish (or ideally eliminate) the use of alcohol and/or drugs. These stimulants may cause mood swings that typically make matters worse.
- Do not become emotional. Becoming emotional means you are losing control and may become illogical in your response to the stress.
- Get organized. Take control of your workspace by eliminating unwanted clutter and prioritizing projects.
- Create and maintain a support network. Identify a few close friends and family members in whom you can confide and share concerns.
- Make time for yourself and learn to relax.
- Control your attitude and how you handle stressful situations.
- Eat a balanced diet and get plenty of sleep. Common results of sleep deprivation include anger, irritation, and exhaustion, all of which contribute to stress.
- Develop realistic goals.

Cory has been noticing that a coworker, Tammy, has been short-tempered and moody lately. Because Tammy is normally very pleasant to work with, Cory decides to ask her if something is wrong. Visiting with Tammy, Cory finds out that Tammy is being harassed by someone at work. She tells Cory how stressful this has been and that it is affecting her work and personal life. Cory encourages Tammy to take steps to stop this harassment (presented in chapter 12). Cory also gives Tammy some tips to help deal with the stress. After a few weeks, Cory notices a positive change in Tammy. Dealing with the problem, along with using stress relievers, is helping Tammy get back to her pleasant self.

The key is to become aware of what is causing stress. Ignoring stress does not make it go away. Your body responds to stress. By being aware of what causes your stress, you can change how it will affect you.

Two final and important methods of managing stress include diet and exercise. A healthy physical body leads to a healthy mental mind. Consistently eat a balanced diet, including breakfast, lunch, and dinner. At these meals, balance protein, carbohydrates, vegetables, and fruit. Do not skip meals, especially breakfast.

Along with a balanced diet, exercise is a must. While you do not have to join a gym or lift weights, you do need to have a consistent exercise plan that gets your body moving. Exercise is a good way to clear your mind of troubles and

Talk It Out

What are ways you relieve stress?

increase creativity. There are simple ways to increase physical activity. Use the stairs instead of taking the elevator, or park your car a little farther away from a building to increase your walking distance. You don't have to spend an hour or more at a time; just exercising for ten minutes several times a day will increase energy and improve your health.

Exercise 3-2   What Have You Eaten in the Past Twenty-Four Hours?

A nutritious diet can make a difference in how you perform throughout the day and how you react to stressful situations. List what you have eaten in the past twenty-four hours. Decide whether or not it was nutritious.

What Have You Eaten?	Is It Nutritional?
1.	
2.	
3.	
4.	
5.	
6.	
7.	
8.	
9.	
10.	

The following is a list of simple physical activities that relieve stress. You probably do some of these things without realizing that they relieve stress.

- Enjoy leisure time
- Listen to music
- Relax
- Meditate and do deep breathing exercises
- Use positive visualization

Recognize what situations cause stress. If you recognize stressful situations, you can better control them. The more organized you are, the better prepared you will be, thus reducing stress.

When at work, if you cannot surround yourself with positive people, then create a positive personal space. Find a private place where you can take a few minutes each day for yourself to relax. Realize that people are not always going to agree with you at the workplace. There may be annoying people, and there may be people with whom you may not have a positive relationship. You may find yourself in situations that become very stressful. Use the stress relief tools mentioned earlier in this chapter and make the best of the situation. As we discussed in chapter 1, only you can control you attitude and your response to situations.

Take time outside of work to relax. Do not bring work troubles home with you, nor take home troubles to work. When you recognize your stressors and take care of yourself, you can reduce and/or eliminate the harm stress can do to you both at home and at work.

Check if your company has an Employee Assistance Program (EAP) and use it to get professional help. Typical employee assistance programs offer help with financial, legal, and psychological issues. Additional information on employee assistance programs is provided in chapter 8.

Job burnout is a form of extreme stress where you lack motivation and no longer have the desire to work. Signs of job burnout include:

- Being frequently tardy or absent
- Continually complaining
- Exhibiting poor physical and emotional health
- Lacking concern for quality
- Clock-watching and being easily distracted
- Gossiping
- Demonstrating a desire to cause harm to the company (theft of or damage to property)

If you have seriously tried to improve the current work situation and still find yourself at a dead end, you may need to consider a job change. Continuing in a job in which you have not been motivated in for a long period of time is destructive not only to you, but also to your company and coworkers.

Web Quiz

Take the online quiz to rate your current stress level or research ways to reduce stress levels.

http://www.arc.sbc.edu/ stressquiz.html

Time Management

Recall the earlier scenario where the teacher assigned impromptu presentations on the lecture material and some students were stressed while others were not. Perhaps the stressed students were stressed because they did not study and therefore were not prepared. There is a clear link between stress and time management. There is also a link between time management and success. **Time management** is how you manage your time. Sometimes it seems there are never enough hours in the day. In business, time is money. The ability to use time wisely is a skill in itself. This skill is needed in the workplace. When you use your time efficiently, your tasks will be completed on time, and sometimes even early. Focus on tasks at hand and pay attention to details needed to do the job right the first time. If you are being more efficient and paying attention, your employer sees that you care about your job and are organized. In turn, this may lead to higher pay and/or a promotion.

Without proper time management skills, you may forget, lose, or spend more time than needed on an important project. Proper time management at work frees up more time for other activities both at work and at home. Make the effort to control your time.

You may get stressed at work because you do not have enough time to complete a project. However, many work projects are similar in nature and can therefore be managed easily. Prior to starting a project, make a plan. Set priorities and get organized. Do not wait until the last minute. If you have similar projects, create a template so you are not starting over with each project. Rushing through a job typically results in errors that will only take more time to correct. Focus on completing a job right the first time.

A common workplace interruption is that of individuals who visit your work area and stay longer than necessary. When dealing with these individuals, always be professional and polite. Inform the individual that although you would like to visit, you have work that must be completed. If you are in an office environment, do not sit down nor invite your office visitor to take a seat. Standing by the door or entry to your workspace, politely tell your visitor that you are busy and unable to visit. Avoid having items such as a candy dish on your desk that attract unwanted guests. Further discussion of the use of body language and communication will be presented in later chapters.

Use activity 3-1 at the end of this chapter to identify how you spend your time. The following tips will help you organize and control your time:

1. Make a list of tasks for each day and prioritize that list; this is commonly referred to as a *to-do list*. Many PCs and smart phones offer task applications to make electronic lists. This is the electronic version of using a sticky note.
2. Keep a calendar accessible at all times. List all appointments, meetings, and tasks on your personal calendar. The calendar can be electronic or traditional.
3. Organize your work area. Use file folders and in-boxes to organize and prioritize projects.
4. Practice a one-touch policy. After you have looked at a project, letter, memo, or other item, file it, place it in a priority folder, forward it to the appropriate individual, or throw it away. Do not pile papers on your desk.
5. Avoid time wasters. Time wasters are small activities that take up only a small amount of time but are done more frequently than you may realize. These include unnecessary visiting or inappropriate activities such as personal texting or updating your social network site.
6. If possible, set aside time each day to address all communication at once, as opposed to handling messages as they arrive (e.g., e-mail and phone messages).
7. Do not be afraid to ask for help. Asking for help is not a sign of weakness or inefficiency if you are practicing sound time management techniques.

Exercise 3-3   Avoid Time Wasters

List time wasters you have experienced in the past few weeks. How did these time wasters affect your productivity? What change should be made?

Time Waster	How Did It Affect Productivity?	What Will You Improve?
1.		
2.		
3.		

Cory has learned to save time by answering some memos in a unique way. When Cory receives a memo that requires only a short response, instead of creating a new memo, Cory writes a response on the original memo. After writing the answer and making a copy for record, Cory sends the memo back. This procedure has saved Cory time.

Some individuals procrastinate and delay performing priority tasks. **Procrastination** is putting off tasks until a later time. This poor habit severely impedes time management and contributes to stress. People procrastinate for many reasons, including fear of failure, perfectionism, disorganization, or simply not wanting to perform the task because it is not pleasant. To overcome procrastination, first visualize the completed task. Knowing your end result and how you will feel when it is completed will motivate you to get started. The next step is to make a plan for completion by identifying what information and resources are required for the end result you envisioned. List every activity and piece of information you will need. After you have made your plan, get to work. If the task appears overwhelming, break it down into smaller tasks and complete each task in priority order. Breaks and celebrations are not only essential, but encouraged when you are working on a big project.

Cory was taking a chemistry class in which the instructor assigned a semester-long research project. When the project was assigned at the start of the semester, the instructor encouraged the students to make a plan and schedule dates to complete sections of the research throughout the semester so as to produce a quality project. Cory struggled with the class material and procrastinated working on the assignment. Unfortunately, as the semester wore on, Cory became immersed with other courses, a job, and personal issues and kept delaying the research project. The more Cory thought about the project, the more stressed Cory became. Finally, two weeks before the end of the semester, the instructor reminded the class that all research projects were due the day before the final. Cory realized there was no time to properly study for exams and also complete the research project. The procrastination resulted in Cory being stressed and receiving a failing grade in the chemistry course, because Cory gave up and did not even attempt to write the paper or take the final exam.

One final issue that contributes to both stress and poor time management is the inability for individuals to say "no" to co-workers, bosses, or others. At work, our goal is to be as productive as possible by prioritizing our current workload. Overcommitting ourselves risks compromising quality for quantity.

Exercise 3-4   What Went Wrong?

Based on what you have learned so far in our discussion of stress and time management, detail what Cory could have done to produce a better outcome in the chemistry class.

When you are pressed for time and someone asks you to assist with a project, first evaluate if the project is part of your primary work duties. If you have time and it does not conflict with your priority projects, agree to take on the new project. If you do not have time and you have greater priorities, decline the project. If it is your boss that is making the request, politely inform your boss that you want to help wherever and whenever possible, but you are currently working on another priority project and ask him or her which project should take precedent. Many bosses are unaware of an individual's workload at any given time, so your goal is to communicate your current priorities.

Talk It Out

How can you apply what you just learned regarding time management to your school performance?

Organizing and Performance

Individuals who are organized operate around goals and have learned that being surrounded by clutter deters focus. Organized individuals arrange their belongings in their home and work environments in a manner that reflects their goals. In chapter 1 you established a life plan and created goals to support this plan. Your life plan details what you want to accomplish and by when. Have your personal and work environment reflect your life plan, priorities, and values. Getting organized for optimal performance is not difficult. Being organized will not only optimize performance, but will also help you use your time more efficiently and reduce stress.

Follow these steps to get organized:

1. Take inventory. If you don't need it, donate it or throw it away. If an item is necessary but not used often, store it.
2. Place items where they are required. For example, keep printer paper by the printer, notepad and paper near the phone.
3. Avoid piles and miscellaneous folders. Although the intention is to get to a pile of information or a miscellaneous file sometime in the future, this rarely happens.
4. Return a used item to its appropriate area.
5. Routinely de-clutter. Organization skills are learned habits that must be reinforced. If you create a clean space and fail to keep it clean, you end up with a messy space.

While it may take time to organize, the time you invest in cleaning and organizing your space will release much more time for you to accomplish your goals. An organized and clutter-free area is calming and allows you to focus.

Tools for getting organized in the workplace can also be used at home. Technology has made it easier to get organized with electronic devices. However, there are other common organization tools to use, including shredders, filing, and the appropriate arrangement of desk space.

One of the easiest ways to get organized is to use a calendar. There are many calendaring options, including a computerized calendar, a mobile calendar, and a traditional paper calendar. For efficiency, businesses prefer an electronic calendar for computer networking purposes. It is common to have access to a computerized information manager on the web, a communications program on a computer, and/or a mobile device. Determine which type of calendar works best for your work situation; sometimes the solution is to use more than one that can be synced. Once you have determined which option is best for you, make a commitment to record all work-related and personal meetings and important deadlines. If your personal information manager and communications program is electronic, store telephone numbers, e-mail addresses, and other important messaging data in the program for easy access. Tasks, to-do lists, and notes can also be monitored and updated. Keep data current by immediately recording changes. If you use multiple organization tools, make a habit of transferring information on a daily basis. For maximum efficiency, customize applications to suit your needs.

Other ways to keep organized and improve performance is to check and answer your phone messages and e-mails at regular intervals. It is inefficient to return each phone message or e-mail as it comes in. The only exception to this is if there is an important message or e-mail that needs to be sent or answered immediately. Also break down larger tasks into simpler, smaller ones. When you break down tasks, you can space out projects. This enables you to organize the time needed to complete each task before starting the next. Again, the exception to this is if you have a priority task that needs to be completed immediately.

If you are assigned a personal workspace, keep your work environment and desk clean and clutter-free. Having no more than two personal items on a desk will maintain a professional look. Keep frequently used work tools easily accessible, including a stapler, tape, a notepad, pens, pencils, paperclips, scissors, a ruler, a calculator, highlighters, and a computer storage device. In addition, the use of a small bulletin/whiteboard for posting important reminders will help you keep track of important tasks and appointments. Have a trash can close to your desk, and throw away supplies that have been used or do not work anymore. Shred confidential materials at least once a day.

When managing paper files, maintain these files properly in a file cabinet and keep files neatly arranged in clearly labeled file folders. Keep dated documents in chronological order (most recent first). Other files can be arranged by subject or alphabetically. Be consistent in your filing method. Routinely used files should be easily accessible. Keep files updated, and be sure to dispose of old files properly. Any unnecessary files with personal information or identification numbers are considered confidential and should be shredded. If files are not important and do not have identification, they may be thrown in the trash.

For efficiency and security purposes, keep electronic files organized. Your computer desktop should contain only shortcuts to frequently used programs and files that you are currently working with. Routinely clean your computer desktop and keep it clutter-free. Just as with paper files, electronic files should be well organized and labeled. Establish folders for major projects, committees, and other items related to your job. Place appropriate documents inside each major project folder. Whenever possible, create subfolders for large projects so that you can properly file and quickly retrieve documents when necessary. Keep both folder and file names simple and easily identifiable. Also remember to routinely back up and/or secure your files to protect confidential information. Effective organization includes the proper handling of both electronic and paper mail. Your job may include sorting and/or opening mail. Use a letter opener to open all paper mail at one time. After opening the paper mail, sort it into piles. Throw away or shred junk mail immediately after opening. Respond to the sender of the mail if needed, file the document, or forward the mail to the appropriate party within the company. Do not open mail that is marked confidential unless instructed to do so. Mail should be kept private and not shared with co-workers. If you encounter a piece of mail that should be confidential, place it in a separate envelope and mark it confidential. Company letterhead or postage is not for personal mail.

Workplace Dos and Don'ts

Do recognize your stressors	*Don't* allow stress to make you mentally or physically sick
Do deal with stress appropriately	*Don't* think that stress will just go away
Do eat a balanced diet and have an exercise plan	*Don't* skip breakfast
Do manage your time by setting priorities and getting organized	*Don't* be afraid of asking for help when getting behind
Do take time to get organized	*Don't* give in to time wasters

Concept Review and Application

Summary of Key Concepts

- Stress is a physical, chemical, or emotional factor that causes bodily or mental tension
- Stress can be positive and/or negative
- Signs of stress include becoming emotional or illogical or losing control of your temper
- The first step in dealing with stress is to identify the stressor
- A balanced diet along with exercise will help you to better manage stress
- There are many ways to reduce stress, such as setting goals, relaxing, and getting enough sleep
- Good time management comes from being organized
- Avoid procrastination
- Being organized will optimize your performance and reduce stress

Key Terms

job burnout   negative stress   positive stress

procrastination   stress   time management

If You Were the Boss

1. You have noticed that an employee frequently is calling in sick and appears agitated when at work. What do you do?
2. You have just become the supervisor for a new department. What can you do to make the department and its employees more organized? Discuss appointment tools, necessary equipment, and software.

Video Case Study: Time Management and Organization Tips

This video presents expert advice on time management and workplace organization. To view these videos, visit the Student Resources: Professionalism section in www.mystudentsuccesslab.com. Then answer the following questions.

1. Name three reasons why time management and workplace organization is important.
2. Share three time management tools.
3. Share three organization tools you should practice in your personal work area.
4. Define *time wasters* and explain how to deal with them.

Web Links

http://www.mindtools.com/smpage.html

http://www.cdc.gov/niosh/topics/stress

http://www.effective-time-management-strategies.com

http://www.studygs.net/timman.htm

Activity 3-1

Your instructor will distribute a time log, use this log to keep track of how you spend your time for the next twenty-four hours. Track exactly how your time was spent. At the end of the time period, identify specific time wasters.

Identify three time wasters from your time log.
1.
2.
3.

Activity 3-2

In addition to what was mentioned in the chapter, research physical responses generated by prolonged stress. List your findings.

1.	4.
2.	5.
3.	6.

Activity 3-3

Conduct additional research and identify tips for relieving work stress. List them and explain how they help relieve stress.

Tip for Relieving Stress at Work	How Does It Help?
1.	1.
2.	2.
3.	3.
4.	4.

Activity 3-4

Identify the workplace effects of good and bad time management.

Effects of *Good* Time Management	Effects of *Bad* Time Management
1.	1.
2.	2.
3.	3.
4.	4.
5.	5.

1. Stress is a physical, chemical, or emotional factor that causes tension and may be a factor in

   _____.

2. Stress can be positive and/or _____.

3. The first step in dealing with stress is to _____.

4. Some ways to relieve stress include (choose four): _____,

   _____, _____, and

   _____.

5. Realizing your stressors and taking care of yourself will reduce or eliminate

   _____.

6. Managing time when you do not seem to have enough hours in the day is _____.

7. Being organized can _____ your performance.

Etiquette/Dress

chapter 4

Winning is accomplished in the preparation phase, not the execution phase.

Anonymous

MyStudentSuccessLab   Visit www.mystudentsuccesslab.com for added practice, activities, assessment, and videos.

Objectives

- Describe and discuss the importance of professional behavior
- State the impact dress can have on others' perception of you
- Demonstrate a professional introduction and handshake
- Demonstrate appropriate professional behavior in business dining situations
- Recognize and apply the appropriate use of technology in business/social situations
- Utilize professional *etiquette* in appropriate business situations

How-Do-You-Rate

	How proper are you?	True	False
1.	You do not have to shake someone's hand if you already know the person.	❏	❏
2.	Visible tattoos, nose rings, or lip rings, if tasteful, are now acceptable in a professional business situation.	❏	❏
3.	If you are invited to a business meal, you may order anything on the menu.	❏	❏
4.	Sending a handwritten thank-you note is no longer necessary.	❏	❏
5.	It is now acceptable business practice to read a text message during business meetings.	❏	❏

If you answered "true" to two or more of these questions, it is time to begin actively practicing business etiquette. While business protocol may vary in some industries, it is best to lean toward a conservative, traditional approach until you are confident of acceptable industry standards.

Executive Presence

Employees represent their company. Therefore, the way you communicate, dress, and behave, both inside and outside the company, contributes to others' perception of you and your company. Consistently demonstrating proper etiquette and protocol in business, dining, and social situations results in positive business relationships. The way you look and behave is a reflection of the organization for which you work. **Executive presence** is defined as having the attitude of an executive. Projecting an executive presence demonstrates to employers that they have hired a new employee with knowledge regarding appropriate workplace behavior.

Many of our parents taught us early in life that good manners, such as smiling and saying please and thank you in social situations, create positive relationships. Those successful at work understand the basics regarding expected professional behavior on topics including attire, business protocol, social etiquette, dining, and the appropriate use of technology. You will encounter many social situations at work. Knowing how to behave in professional social situations will help you be more successful in workplace relationships. Some of this information may be new to you, and you may feel awkward when you first implement these positive behaviors. The purpose of this chapter is to prepare you for many of the social experiences you will face in the workplace.

Influences of Dress in a Professional Environment

Both your maturity and the importance you place on your job are reflected in the way you behave and dress at work. Because impressions are often made in the first few minutes of meeting someone, individuals rarely have time to even speak before an impression is formed. The majority of first impressions are made through visual **appearance,** which is how you look. Coworkers, bosses, and customers form attitudes based on appearance. Appearance also has an impact on how you perform at work. If you dress professionally, you are more apt to act in a professional manner. The more casually you dress, the more casually you tend to behave. Think of your appearance as a frame. A frame is used to highlight a picture. You do not want the frame to be too fancy, because it will take away from the picture. You want a frame to complement the picture. The frame highlights not only your physical features, including your face, but also your attitude, knowledge, and potential.

Exercise 4-1 Define Your "Frame"

What does your frame look like? Be honest.

Is it trendy, outdated, professional, or inconsistent?

_____

Does it complement your desired appearance as a professional?

_____

If your current frame is not yet professional, what changes need to occur?

_____

_____

One of the toughest transitions to make when entering the workplace is choosing appropriate dress. Dressing professionally does not have to conflict with current fashion trends. The trick is to know what is acceptable. A basic rule of thumb is to dress one position higher than your current position (i.e., dress like your boss). Doing so communicates that you are serious about your career and how you represent the company. Dressing professionally will assist you in projecting a favorable image at work and position you for job advancement.

Know your workplace dress policies, and understand that professional dress carries different meaning depending on both the industry and work environment. One of the first steps to determining appropriate attire for work is to identify your company's **dress code.** A dress code is a policy that addresses issues such as required attire, uniforms, hairstyle, undergarments, jewelry, and shoes. Dress codes vary by company depending on the industry, the specific work area, and health/safety issues. If your company has a mandatory uniform, the company dress code will be detailed. If a uniform is not required, iden-tify what is and is not acceptable attire by reading the dress code policy, by observing what is practiced in the workplace, or by asking your supervisor. Some dress codes are vague, while others are specific. Work attire should pose no safety hazards. Unstable footwear that does not provide protection are not appropriate. Dangling jewelry that could be caught in equipment is also inappropriate for work. As previously stated, organizational dress policies exist for customer service, safety, and security reasons. Frequently, these policies are included in the employee handbook. If there is no policy, ask your boss if there is a formal dress code and secure a copy. An important cue to workplace attire is to observe how managers dress. Suits are not always the preferred attire in an office environment. In some situations, pants are acceptable for women, while in other situations they are not. Note that sweats (shirts and/or pants) are not appropriate for the traditional workplace.

Once you have identified what your organization considers proper attire, begin to create a **work wardrobe.** These are clothes that you primarily wear only to work and work-related functions. You need not invest a lot of money when building a work wardrobe. Start with basic pieces and think conservative. For women working in a traditional office environment, this attire includes a simple, solid skirt or pantsuit in a dark color and a blazer. Skirt length should not be above the knee. Pants should be worn with a matching blazer. For most office environments, men should select dark slacks, a matching jacket, and a tie. If you are just starting your job and cannot afford new clothing, these items can sometimes be found inexpensively at thrift and discount stores. If these items are purchased at a thrift store, inspect them for tears or stains and take them to the dry cleaner for cleaning and pressing. You will be surprised how professional these items look after they are cleaned and pressed. Select items that are made of quality fabrics that will not wear out quickly, fit properly, and are comfortable. As you begin to earn money, continue building your wardrobe and develop a style that conforms to both company policy and your taste.

Casual Workdays and Special Events

Many companies allow **casual workdays.** These are days when companies relax their dress code. Unfortunately, some employees attempt to stretch the term casual. If your company has a casual workday, remember that you are still at work and should dress appropriately. Of course, you can wear jeans if jeans are the preferred attire; just adhere to the head-to-toe tips presented later in this chapter. Do not wear clothing that is tattered, stained, or torn (even if it is considered stylish). Avoid wearing shirts with sayings or graphics that may offend others. In general, it is best to dress modestly.

As you learn more about professional dress and expectations regarding professional attire, consider cultural and geographic differences and expectations. Globally, differing cultural expectations apply to workplace dress. In some countries, women must be completely covered from head to toe, while in other countries, women should not wear pants. "Business casual" for men on the East Coast of the United States may require a suit jacket, while "business casual" on the West Coast of the United States may allow for wearing khaki pants and a polo shirt. When conducting business in a geographic area different than yours (whether in your own country or abroad), research appropriate attire prior to your visit.

Your company may also host or invite you to attend a special function. Holiday parties and receptions are examples. In these situations, instead of daily work attire, more formal attire may be required. Just as with casual workdays, stick with the basics provided in the head-to-toe tips. Women, if appropriate, should wear something in a more formal fabric. Although you have increased freedom and flexibility regarding style and length, this is still a work-related

Talk It Out

Name local places where you can buy professional attire at a low cost.

function, so dress conservatively and not suggestively. Men, check ahead of time and see if tuxedos are preferred. For most semiformal occasions, a suit will suffice.

As a reward for being selected Employee of the Month, Cory was invited to attend a one-day conference luncheon with several managers from the company. Cory had not attended a function like this before and was a little nervous about how to dress and behave in this new business situation. Cory did some preparation and found that dress and behavior are as important in public situations as they are at work. Cory checked with others who had attended these functions and decided that dressing in formal business attire would be most appropriate. Cory made sure to shower, clean and trim fingernails, wear polished shoes, and not wear inappropriate jewelry. When entering the conference, Cory was glad to have conducted research, as nearly everyone was dressed in formal business attire.

Talk It Out

Identify people in class who are wearing something appropriate for a casual workday.

Tips from Head to Toe

Regardless of the company's dress code, practice these basic hygiene rules:

- *Shower daily.* If needed, use deodorant. Use perfume, lotion, or cologne sparingly. Scent should not be overpowering.
- *Clothes should be clean and ironed, not torn or tattered, and should fit properly.*
- *Hair should be clean, well kempt, and a natural color.* Your hairstyle should reflect your profession. Fad hairstyles and unnatural color are inappropriate in many workplaces.
- *Practice good dental hygiene.* Brushing and flossing your teeth both in the morning and at bedtime, if not more often, not only ensures clean teeth and fresh breath, it also helps prevent tooth decay. Many public health clinics provide no-cost or low-cost dental care.
- *Hands and nails should be clean, well groomed, and trimmed.* Unnaturally long nails are inappropriate. Polish or artwork if allowed, should be neat and kept conservative.
- *Jewelry should be kept to a minimum.* Jewelry should complement your outfit. Do not wear anything that is distracting or makes noise.
- *Shoes should be in good condition.* Keep shoes polished and free of scuffs. Flip-flops are not appropriate for the workplace. Men's sock color should match shoe or pant color. Women, keep heels in good condition; repair or replace them as needed. Heels should not be too high. Nylons should be free of runs and snags.

A woman's outfit should reflect her style and personality—within reason. When dressing for work, your goal is to appropriately frame yourself in a manner that draws attention to your professional qualities (i.e., your brains and inner beauty). Additional tips for women include the following:

- *Makeup should be for day wear.* Makeup is appropriate for work. Makeup that makes people think you are going to a bar after work is not. Do not wear heavy eyeliner, eyeshadow in colors that draw attention, or lipstick in bold colors.
- *It is not acceptable to wear suggestive clothing.* Visible cleavage or bare midriffs are inappropriate for work. No matter the current fashion trends, undergarments (bras and panties) should not be visible. Skirts worn at work should be no shorter than knee length.

Just like a woman's outfit, a man's outfit should reflect his style and personality. For some positions, a suit may not be appropriate. The biggest wardrobe blunder men make is wearing clothing that is not clean and/or pressed. After checking your company's dress code, heed these unspoken rules regarding professional dress at work for men:

- *Shave and/or trim facial hair, including nose and ear hair.*
- *In an office environment, dress pants are the only pants that are professional.* With the exception of casual workdays, jeans are inappropriate. Baggy pants that reveal underwear are also inappropriate. Whenever possible, wear a neutral, plain belt that does not draw attention.
- *Shirts should be tucked in.* A polo shirt or a dress shirt with a tie is best. Shirts should not display excessive wear (check around the collar line for fraying or stains). Shirts with offensive logos or offensive phrases are inappropriate at work.
- *Hats should not be worn inside buildings except for religious purposes.*

Talk It Out

When or when not is it appropriate for a woman to be sleeveless in a professional setting?

Jewelry, Body Piercing, and Tattoos

As with professional attire, you do not want to wear or display anything that brings unwanted attention to you in the workplace. While body art and piercings are becoming more common and acceptable in society, many companies have policies that prohibit visible tattoos and/or visible body piercings beyond one in each ear. Body art and piercings are offensive to some individuals. Many people get a tattoo and/or body piercing to signify a special event, individual, or symbol. If you are considering getting a tattoo or body piercing, consider the long-term consequences of doing so. Relationships and situations change. Tattoos and some piercings are difficult and painful, if not impossible, to remove. While you may currently not care how society feels about your tattoo and/or piercing, you may regret your decision in the future. If you already have body art and/or piercing, it is recommended that you cover your tattoo with clothing, makeup, or other means until you are clear on your employer's policy regarding visible body art. Many companies also have strict policies on body piercings beyond earrings. Some piercings close quickly, so it may be impossible to remove the piercing during work hours. Other forms of piercings, such as microdermal piercings, cannot be easily removed. In these cases, determine which is more important—a job, or your body art and/or piercing. In general, follow these guidelines regarding jewelry, piercings, and tattoos:

- Nose rings, lip rings, and/or tongue rings are not professional and should not be worn in a professional setting. Any other body piercing/body jewelry should not be visible at work.
- More than two earrings worn on each ear is considered unprofessional.
- Earrings, chains, and other jewelry should not draw attention. This includes symbols or words that could be considered offensive to others.
- Body art (tattoos) should not be visible at work.

Business Etiquette

In a modern workplace, human interaction is unavoidable. Our society has a standard of social behavior that is called **etiquette.** Typically, when individuals think of etiquette, they think it applies only to high society. This is not true. Socially acceptable behavior should penetrate all demographic and economic groups. Individuals wanting to succeed in the workplace need to heed this protocol and consistently utilize proper etiquette not only at work, but in all areas of their life.

Before we study common areas of business etiquette, we need to define a few terms. Understanding these terms and integrating them into your daily routine will make it much easier to carry out the desired and appropriate workplace behavior. The first word is **courtesy.** When you display courtesy, you are exercising manners, respect, and consideration toward others. The second word is **respect.** Respect is defined as holding someone in high regard. This means putting others' needs before your own needs. Displaying both courtesy and respect toward others are the keys in becoming ladies and gentlemen at work.

Some of the first words most parents teach young children are *please* and *thank you.* Although they are not used as frequently as they should be, both are extremely valuable terms that can actually create power for you at work. Think about it; when someone says "please" and "thank you" to you, you are more likely to repeat a favor or gesture because your deed was acknowledged. When someone does something nice, verbally say "thank you." Not doing so makes you appear selfish and unappreciative. When you express thanks, individuals will be more likely to continue performing kind acts for you.

Make it a habit to write a thank-you note when someone does something for you that takes more than five minutes or when someone gives you a gift. Write the note as soon as possible. Do not wait more than three days to write the thank-you note.

> **Talk It Out**
>
> Discuss ways you can be courteous and respectful in class.

Handshakes

A good handshake conveys confidence. Make a habit of greeting others in business situations with a professional handshake and friendly verbal greeting. Approach the individual you are greeting, make eye contact, smile, and extend your right hand as you verbalize a greeting. For example, "Hello Ms. Cao, my name is Talia. We met at last week's meeting. It's nice to see you again." Ms. Cao will extend her right hand. Your two hands should meet at the web (see Figure 4-1). Grip the other person's hand and gently squeeze and shake hands.

- Do not squeeze the other hand too firmly.
- Shake the entire hand and not just the other person's fingers. Doing so is insulting and implies that you feel you are better than the other person.
- Do not place your hand on top of the other person's hand or pat the hand. Doing so is insulting.
- If your palms are sweaty, discretely wipe your palm on the side of your hip prior to shaking.

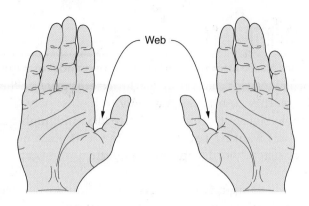

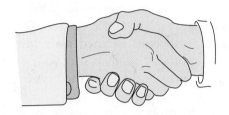

Figure 4-1

Proper Handshake

A good handshake takes practice. As mentioned earlier, get into the habit of being the first to greet and introduce yourself to others. At first you may not feel comfortable, but practice makes perfect. The more frequently you initiate a good handshake, the more comfortable and confident you will become.

Exercise 4-2   Shake Hands

With another person practice initiating an introduction, making sure to include a professional handshake. Rate the quality of the introduction and handshake on a scale of 1 to 5, with 5 being the best. Discuss what improvements should be made.

Introductions and Business Networking

An element of success in the workplace involves meeting new people. This process of meeting and developing relationships with individuals outside of one's immediate work area is referred to as **networking.** Networking is also commonly used in the job search process and will be discussed in greater depth in chapter 13. In the workplace, creating a professional network is a useful tool for collaboration. In a business situation when you do not know someone in the room, increase your confidence by being the first to initiate a conversation. After you have introduced yourself, ask your new acquaintance about himself or herself. Learn about his or her job and find something you have in common. Keep the initial conversation focused on him or her. Your goal is to meet new people and create a positive impression so that if you see them again or contact them in the future, they will remember and have a favorable impression of you.

At times, you will be with individuals who do not know each other. When you are with two people who do not know each other and you know both people, it is your responsibility to introduce the two individuals to each other. Politely introduce the lower-ranking person to the higher-ranking person. For example, "Matt, this is Ryan McClaine, the president of our company." "Ryan, this is Matt Yu, my next-door neighbor." Apply this introduction rule to all social situations, including dining, meetings, receptions, and parties. Making introductions to others is an excellent form of networking. After you have introduced the two individuals, if possible, provide a piece of information about one of the individuals that creates a foundation for a conversation. For example, "Ryan, you and Matt attended the same college."

Appointments

A daily function of business is making and keeping appointments. Appointments can occur in many forms, such as face-to-face meetings, over the phone, or through current technologies (e-mail, texting, or video chat). When setting meeting times, check regional time differences and clearly include the regional time zone abbreviation in your confirmation if you are located in different time zones. For example, "I look forward to meeting with you on Tuesday, April 21st, at 9 a.m. Pacific Standard Time (PST)."

Sometimes you will be required to work with receptionists and/or administrative assistants to schedule appointments. Be kind to the receptionist and/or administrative assistant. These individuals are the gatekeepers to their bosses; they control schedules and often wield great power in decisions. When scheduling an appointment, state your name, the purpose, and the desired date and time of the meeting. If possible, avoid scheduling appointments on Monday mornings; many people use Monday mornings to schedule their own week and are less likely to accommodate you. If you will be arriving late to an appointment, call and let the other party know you are running late. If you must cancel an appointment, do so immediately and apologize for any inconvenience. Do not just ignore an appointment.

If your meeting is to take place on the telephone, ensure you are holding the call in a quiet place where you will not have distracting background noise. Use a reliable phone connection. If your meeting requires Internet technologies, use a reliable connection and log in at least ten minutes early to ensure a proper connection. If your meeting involves video chat with a web camera, dress professionally and hold your meeting in a professional location. In general, an office or study is most appropriate. Due to confidentiality issues, problems with noise, and the need for a professional backdrop, do not use a public location. Additional information regarding communications technology is included in chapter 10.

When keeping an appointment (face-to-face or via technology), arrive or check in five minutes early. For face-to-face meetings, after you enter the office, greet the receptionist and politely introduce yourself. State whom you have an appointment with and the time of the meeting. When entering an office for a meeting, wait to be invited to sit down. At the close of any meeting, thank the other participants for their time. If you are in person, exchange business cards if appropriate and close with a final handshake. Additional information on meeting management will be presented in chapter 11.

Dining

In the workplace, you will encounter a variety of dining situations. Some dining experiences will be less formal than others. You will most likely come across some form of the table setting illustrated in Figure 4-2. Take time to study and review a common place setting to learn the proper location and use for utensils, plates, and cups. Apart from fast food, few college students are generally comfortable eating in a formal dining situation. Here are several rules of thumb regarding dining etiquette:

- As soon are you are seated, place your napkin on your lap. If you leave the table, place your napkin to the side of your plate, not on your chair.
- Do not discuss business matters until everyone has ordered. Table conversation should be positive and free of controversial subjects such as politics and religion.
- Utensils are set to be used in order of necessity. As your courses are served, start with the outside utensil and work in, toward the plate. The utensils set at the top of the plate are for your dessert.
- When serving coffee, water, tea, or any other beverage available at the table, first offer and serve others at your table.
- Do not order anything expensive or messy.
- Do not order alcohol unless others at your table first order an alcoholic beverage. Abstaining from alcohol is the most desired behavior. If you choose to drink, limit consumption to one drink.
- When bread is available, first offer bread to others at your table before taking a piece.

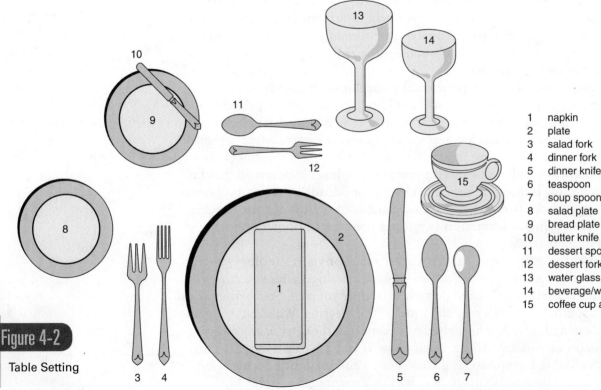

1	napkin
2	plate
3	salad fork
4	dinner fork
5	dinner knife
6	teaspoon
7	soup spoon
8	salad plate
9	bread plate
10	butter knife
11	dessert spoon
12	dessert fork
13	water glass
14	beverage/wine glass
15	coffee cup and saucer

Figure 4-2

Table Setting

- Place your bread on the bread plate (located at the top left corner of your dinner plate). Place your serving of butter on the bread plate. Do not butter the entire piece of bread at one time. Tear a piece of bread and butter only that piece of bread before eating.
- Do not take the last piece of bread or appetizer unless it is first offered to others at your table.
- When your meal arrives, do not begin eating until everyone at your table has been served. If everyone receives their meals except you (you are the last to be served), give others at your table permission to begin eating without you so that their food does not get cold. Eat your meal at the same pace as others at the table.
- Do not eat your meal with your fingers unless your main course is meant to be eaten without utensils.
- Be kind and polite to the staff and servers.
- Burping and slurping are inappropriate while dining. If you accidentally burp or slurp, immediately apologize and say "excuse me." Also, chew with your mouth closed.
- When you are finished eating, place your knife and fork together, with the blade facing in and the tines up. When you are only resting and you do not want the server to take your plate away, cross your utensils with the tines facing down.
- It is inappropriate to use a mobile communication device while dining. If you must take a call or text, excuse yourself from the table.

When Cory arrived at the conference, Cory was glad to be dressed professionally. Everyone was dressed in business attire. As Cory was introduced to others, Cory was sure to make eye contact, smile, and properly shake hands. Cory also collected many business cards while networking. During the meal, Cory was careful to follow dining etiquette. At work the next day, Cory immediately wrote a thank-you note to the managers who invited Cory to the event. At the end of the day, Cory's manager called Cory and let Cory know what a great impression Cory made at the conference. Several colleagues had mentioned to Cory's manager how impressed they were with Cory's professionalism. Cory realized that conducting a little research and being professional was well worth the effort.

A common activity in business involves attending social functions. Many invitations request an RSVP, which is French for *répondez s'il vous plaît* (i.e., please respond). As soon as you receive an invitation, send a reply—whether it is an acceptance to attend or a regret that you cannot attend. Not acknowledging the invitation and failing to respond is rude.

When you attend a social function, remember that you are attending it to meet and network with other professionals. Do not focus on the food; focus on the networking opportunities.

- As with dining situations, refrain from or limit the consumption of alcohol.
- If you choose to eat, serve yourself a small plate of hors d'oeuvres and move away from the food table.
- Hold your hors d'oeuvres in your left hand, leaving your right hand free to shake hands and greet others.
- If there are name badges, wear one placed neatly on your right shoulder. If you must handwrite your own name badge, print your first and last name clearly.
- Do not talk with food in your mouth.

Talk It Out

Share common dining and social situations that make you uncomfortable, and identify how best to deal with these situations.

Web Quiz

Rate your workplace etiquette. Use the following website, or find another etiquette web quiz.

http://www.usatoday.com/img/content/flash/getiquettequiz/flash.htm

Other Etiquette Basics

At first glance, business etiquette can be a bit overwhelming. However, with practice, business etiquette becomes habit. When in doubt, mimic what the most polished person in the room is doing. Be aware of your surroundings and watch and learn from those whom you admire. The following is a final list of etiquette tips to assist you in becoming one of the most admired and respected individuals in the workplace.

- *Have a pleasant attitude.* In addition to saying "please" and "thank you," do not underestimate the value of a simple smile and eye contact. If you have a positive attitude, it will be reflected in your demeanor. When encountering people in the hallways, elevators, and/or meeting rooms, smile, make eye contact, and greet them.

- *Knock before entering an office.* Do not enter an office or private workspace such as a cubicle until you are invited. If the individual you want to see normally has his or her door open, do not disturb the individual when the door is closed. The exception is for an emergency or urgent situation needing his or her attention—but apologize for interrupting. If the door is open but the individual is with someone else, politely wait your turn.

- *Put others first.* When you are with colleagues and you are taking turns (in line, to order, etc.), allow your colleagues to go first. Doing so shows respect and courtesy.

- *Apologize when necessary.* Everyone is human. Therefore, everyone makes mistakes. When you realize that you may have said or done something hurtful to someone, apologize immediately. As you will learn in chapter 12 relating to conflict and negotiation, apologizing is not a sign of weakness. Apologizing is a sign of strength and maturity. Even if you are not certain if you have offended someone, apologize to avoid any potential misunderstandings. However, do not unnecessarily and continually apologize. Doing so not only gives you the appearance of being needy and insecure, more importantly you are not being assertive and possibly not standing up for your rights in an unoffending manner.

- *Do not use profanity.* The use of profanity is not appropriate in the workplace. Even if others in your presence use profanity, do not assume everyone is comfortable with the bad language. Conversations should be professional, respectful, and free of profanity.

- *Avoid dominating a conversation.* There is a key to carrying on a successful conversation: listening. You will learn in chapter 9 how to become an active listener. When you are an active listener, you value the information the other individual is providing. Too frequently, individuals dominate a conversation with their own personal accounts. In general, this is not appropriate. This behavior becomes annoying to the listener when you turn the conversation to yourself. Next time you are in a conversation, listen to how many times you state the words *me, I,* and *my.* Try to minimize the use of these words in your conversation.

Workplace Dos and Don'ts

Do wear professional clothes to work	*Don't* wear sweats, flip flops, or suggestive apparel at work
Do shower and make sure you are always clean	*Don't* overdo the cologne (or any body sprays)
Do make eye contact and offer a gentle but firm handshake	*Don't* grasp just the fingers when shaking hands
Do follow formal dining etiquette at work-related functions	*Don't* reach, grab, or overload your plate at the hors d'oeuvres table
Do say "please" and "thank you" when appropriate	*Don't* assume that the other person knows you are thankful for his or her act of kindness

Concept Review and Application

Summary of Key Concepts

- Projecting an executive presence is important in demonstrating knowledge of basic workplace behavior
- The majority of first impressions are made through visual appearances
- Both your maturity and the importance you place on your job are reflected in the way you behave and dress at work
- Begin to create a work wardrobe today
- Visual body art/piercing and body rings/jewelry are offensive to some individuals and are not appropriate in a professional work environment. Consider the long-term consequences of getting a tattoo or piercing
- Follow business etiquette protocol and consistently utilize it in all areas of your life
- Make a habit of thanking individuals either verbally or in writing
- Appropriate etiquette at social functions and while dining is as important as professional behavior at work

Key Terms

appearance	casual workdays	courtesy
dress code	etiquette	executive presence
networking	respect	work wardrobe

If You Were the Boss

1. You are the manager of a bank, and one of your employees comes in on a Monday morning with a pierced tongue and purple hair. What should you do?
2. You have just hired a new employee who clearly has no concept of business etiquette. What specific steps would you take to teach your new employee how to behave professionally?

Video Case Study: Dress for Success

This video presents expert advice on how to dress professionally at work. To view these videos, visit the Student Resources: Professionalism section in www.mystudentsuccesslab.com. Then answer the following questions:

1. What specifically are Francesca and Brad wearing that makes their appearance professional?
2. What four items make Patricia's and Brian's appearance unprofessional?
3. What specific advice does the expert provide for looking professional regarding makeup, tattoos, jewelry, jeans, hair, and shoes?

Video Case Study: Business Lunch Etiquette

This video addresses a common business lunch sales meeting. To view these videos, visit the Student Resources: Professionalism section in www.mystudentsuccesslab.com. Then answer the following questions:

1. Name three things Brian did right or wrong.
2. What advice would you give Brian?
3. Midway through this lunch, how should Karen have handled this situation?

Web Links

http://www.ravenwerks.com/practices/etiquette.htm

Activities

Activity 4-1

Assume you are starting a new job as an accounting clerk next week. You need a work wardrobe and are limited to a $50 budget. Make a list of what you need and could buy to get you through your first week of work. Include the cost.

What You Need to Buy	Cost
	$
Total Cost	$50

Prior to being faced with this scenario, what items can you purchase today to begin building your professional wardrobe?

Activity 4-2

Imagine you are at a business reception and you do not know anyone else in the room. Role-play formal introductions with a classmate, and then evaluate your partner's performance by identifying strengths and weaknesses.

STUDENT NAME

Strengths	Weaknesses

STUDENT NAME

Strengths	Weaknesses

Activity 4-3

Visit a (non-fast-food) restaurant to practice proper dining etiquette. While you are doing so, identify five acts of inappropriate behavior others are exhibiting and explain why this behavior is not professional.

Inappropriate Behavior	Why Behavior Is Not Professional
1.	
2.	
3.	
4.	
5.	

1. The majority of first impressions are made by _____.

2. One of the first steps to determining appropriate attire for work is to identify

   _____.

3. Provide five tips for women for dressing professionally from head to toe.

   _____, _____, _____,

   _____,_____.

4. Provide five tips for men for dressing professionally from head to toe.

   _____,

   _____, _____, _____,

   _____.

5. A standard of social behavior is called _____.

6. When someone does something nice for you, you should _____.

7. A good handshake conveys _____.

8. Provide five rules of thumb regarding dining etiquette. _____,

   _____, _____, _____,

   _____.

Ethics, Politics, and Diversity

I hope I shall possess firmness and virtue enough to maintain what I consider the most enviable of all titles, the character of an honest man.

George Washington (1732–1799)

How-Do-You-Rate

	How strong is your moral character?	Yes	No
1.	If your new boss openly stole small office supplies, would you report him/her?	❏	❏
2.	If your coworkers bad-mouthed another coworker who is a friend, would you openly defend the friend?	❏	❏
3.	If an outside vendor incorrectly undercharged your company, would you bring the error to the vendor's attention?	❏	❏
4.	If your human resource department incorrectly overpaid you on your paycheck, would you bring the error to their attention?	❏	❏
5.	If company executives asked you to not fully disclose a product defect to customers, would you inform the customer of the defect anyway?	❏	❏

If you answered "no" to two or more of these questions, take a moment to reevaluate who guides and/or influences your personal values. Workplace ethics begin with you. How you conduct business is a reflection of your moral character.

Ethics, Politics, and Diversity at Work

Business is based on competition. Because competition sometimes clouds an individual's judgment, employees need to recognize how personal values and morals impact ethical behavior at work. Power and politics are routinely used in workplace relationships. Personal ethics govern the outcome of how you deal with power and politics. While workplace power and politics are inevitable, it is important that these control mechanisms be used appropriately. This chapter focuses on the link between ethics and power, then leads into a discussion of diversity and the influences diversity has in the workplace. Diversity comes in many forms, all of which must be respected and ideally harnessed into a competitive advantage.

Ethics Defined

Throughout our schooling, we are told to behave ethically. In education, ethics typically refers to not cheating on homework and exams. At work, cheating can occur in all areas of a job. From the time we clock in to the time we leave the office—and even extending into non-work hours—we must behave in an ethical

Objectives

- Define *ethics* and its impact both personally and professionally
- Identify the importance of maintaining *confidentiality*
- Define and identify the appropriate use of *power* and power bases
- Understand the topics of *politics* and *reciprocity* and their appropriate use in the workplace
- Understand the importance of ethical decision making
- Define *workplace diversity* and realize its impact on performance
- State the basic employee rights and legal protection available for workplace diversity issues
- Recognize the negative impact *stereotypes* and *prejudice* have in the workplace and on performance
- Identify *cultural* differences and the positive and negative impact these differences have on business

manner. Ethical behavior is a twenty-four-hour process. Personal behavior reflects ethical values. In turn, our ethical behavior reflects and represents our company.

Ethics is a moral standard of right and wrong. Although the definition of ethics is a simple statement, it is important to identify who and what determines what is morally right and wrong. Just as your personality is shaped by outside influences, so is your ethical makeup.

Ethical behavior is a reflection of the influences of friends, family, coworkers, religion, and society. For example, if you associate with people who shoplift, you most likely will not view shoplifting as an unethical act. As a result, you may shoplift without remorse. If your family routinely lies about a child's age to pay a lower admission fee to a movie theater or amusement park, the child is being taught to be dishonest. Common religions teach that lying, cheating, and stealing are wrong. Consider the influences our society and culture have on our ethical behavior. Corporate America has been bombarded with ethics-related scandals. Additionally, many of the marketing messages we receive on a daily basis influence ethical behavior.

Although the preceding factors all have an enormous influence on the makeup of one's ethics, note that ethical behavior starts with the individual. As we explore the concept of ethics at work, remember that ethics begin with you.

We often hear people state that more business leaders should have moral character; what does this really mean? As stated earlier, ethics is a moral standard of right and wrong as defined by society. While society determines an ethical standard, **morals** are a personal standard of right and wrong. An individual's **values** are the important beliefs that guide his or her behavior. Both morals and values guide and influence behavior at work and determine character. **Character** is defined as the unique qualities of an individual and is usually a reflection of personal morals and values. Therefore, if someone says an individual is of high character, they are most likely stating that the individual is honest and fair.

In chapter 1, we mentioned the link between ethics and values and how values affect character. In a competitive work setting, situations are often stressful and filled with hidden agendas and underlying politics. Do not be tempted to give in to negative behavior. How you respond to a situation reveals your character. Just as with first impressions, once someone has formed an opinion of you and your character, it is difficult to change that opinion. Therefore, ensure your character consistently projects honesty and fairness and reflects your personal morals and values.

Talk It Out

Discuss recent corporate ethics-related scandals.

Influences on Ethics at Work

At work you will be confronted with ethical issues. Many issues must be kept **confidential,** meaning they are matters that are private. These matters include client records, employee information, business reports, documentation, and files. Whether you are told or not told to keep work-related information confidential, you have an obligation to not share information with individuals for whom the business is of no concern. This is called **implied confidentiality.** An example of implied confidentiality is not sharing customers' personal information with others. Sometimes you may be tempted or even asked to share confidential information. Do not fall into this trap. If you are uncertain about sharing confidential information with someone, check with your boss. Doing so will demonstrate to your boss that you want to not only maintain the privacy of your department, but also behave in a professional manner.

Ethical behavior extends beyond the professionalism of how you deal with others. It is also reflected in your dependability and how you conduct yourself on company time. The company is paying you to work when you are on the job. Although at times it may be necessary to conduct personal business on company time, it is inappropriate to consistently spend your time on nonwork-related activities. The following activities should not be conducted during work time:

- Using the Internet for personal business such as social networking or shopping
- Taking or making personal calls or texts
- Routinely exceeding allotted break and lunch periods
- Playing computer games
- Using company supplies and equipment for nonbusiness purposes

If you must conduct personal business while at work, do so only during your break or lunch hour. Whenever possible, conduct the business before or after work hours and in a private manner.

Power and Ethics

Power is one's ability to influence another's behavior. Whether you recognize it or not, everyone at work has a form of power. Some people understand this ability to influence others' behavior and use it appropriately. Let us first review the different types of power, what they are, and how you can increase this use of power at work. There are seven bases of power: legitimate, coercive, reward, connection, charismatic, information, and expert.

Legitimate power is the power that is given to you by the company. It includes your title and any other formal authority that comes with your position at work. For example, a manager has legitimate power to assign schedules. **Coercive power** is also power that is derived from your formal position. However, the difference between legitimate and coercive power is that coercive power is always negative and uses threats and punishment. An example of coercive power is if your manager threatens to cut your hours. In contrast to coercive power is **reward power.** Reward power is the ability to influence someone with something of value. For example, a manager has offered you a bonus for meeting a goal. Those with legitimate power can reward others with promotions, pay increases, and other incentives. However, you do not have to have legitimate power to reward others in the workplace. **Connection power** is based on using someone else's legitimate power. Consider the department assistant who arranges meetings based on his or her boss's power. This power arises because the department assistant has a connection to an individual with authority.

The three remaining types of power come from within. They are often referred to as types of personal power. **Charismatic power** is a form of personal power that makes people attracted to you. We all know someone who walks into a room and immediately attracts other people's attention. This is because the individual with charismatic power or charisma shows a sincere interest in

Talk It Out

When is it appropriate to make personal calls at work?

Talk It Out

What activities done during class could be considered unethical?

Web Quiz

Test your business ethics at the following website or find a different online quiz about ethics.

http://www.careerbuilder.com/Article/CB-1382-The-Workplace-Quiz-How-Ethical-Are-You/

Exercise 5-1   Identify What Power Can Do

Identify three ways employees without legitimate power can reward others.

1.

2.

3.

others. **Information power** is based upon an individual's ability to obtain and share information. Doing so makes you more valuable to those with whom you interact. For example, a coworker is part of a committee and routinely shares information. **Expert power** is power that is earned by one's knowledge, experience, or expertise. Consider the company's computer repair technician. On the company's organization chart, he or she is not very high in the formal chain of command. However, this individual wields a lot of power because of his or her computer expertise.

Increasing Your Power Bases

As mentioned earlier, everyone possesses some form of workplace power. The trick is to recognize, utilize, and increase your power. The easiest way to increase legitimate power is to make people aware of your title and responsibilities. Because coercive power utilizes threats and/or punishment, coercive power should be used only when an individual is breaking policy or severely behaving inappropriately.

Reward power can and should be used daily. Whenever possible, dispense a sincere word or note of appreciation to a coworker who has assisted you or has performed exceptionally well. Doing so will develop and enhance relationships not only within your department, but also outside your department. Be sincere. Increase your connection power by strengthening your network. **Networking** means meeting and developing relationships with individuals outside your immediate work area. As discussed in chapter 4, network with individuals within and outside of your organization. Charismatic power is increased when you focus attention on others. Make eye contact, initiate conversation, and focus the conversation on the other individual instead of on yourself. Increasing charismatic power establishes trust, improves communication, and makes others want to work with you. Information power is developed by attending meetings, joining committees, and networking. Whenever possible and without overcommitting, join committees, attend meetings, and actively share information with appropriate individuals. Doing so exposes you to other people and issues throughout the company. You, in turn, not only learn more about what's going on within the organization, but also increase your connection and network power. Increase your expert power by practicing continual learning. Read books and business-related articles, scan reputable and applicable Internet sites, attend workshops and conferences, and learn new technology when possible. Whenever you learn something new that can assist others at work, share this information. Coworkers will see you as the expert in the respective area.

Politics and Reciprocity

When you begin to obtain and utilize your power, you are practicing politics. **Politics** is obtaining and using power. People generally get a bad taste in their mouth when someone accuses them of being political, but this is not necessarily a bad thing. As mentioned earlier, recognize, increase, and utilize the various power bases at work. It is when one expects reciprocity that politics at work gets dangerous. **Reciprocity** is when debts and obligations are created for doing something. Suppose you are on a time crunch and must complete a report in two hours but need help. You ask a coworker to help you. The coworker stops what he or she is doing and assists you with an hour to spare. You have just created a reciprocal relationship with the coworker. When this coworker is in a crunch, he or she will not only ask you, but expect you to help. The workplace is comprised of reciprocal relationships. Unfortunately, sometimes the phrase "you owe me" encroaches on our ability to behave ethically.

Cory has a coworker who helps Cory with special projects when time is short. When the coworker tells Cory she needs help with something, Cory immediately responds, "Sure, no problem." Unfortunately, there is a problem. The coworker wants Cory to attend a meeting for her and tell people at the meeting that she is home sick when Cory knows she plans to take a trip with friends. Cory tells the coworker that it would be unethical to cover for her. "But you owe me!" says the coworker. Cory is unsure what to do. After some thought, Cory tells the coworker that Cory wants to repay the favor and appreciates all the help the coworker provides but will not lie for her. Cory should expect some tension with this coworker, but in the long run, she will respect Cory.

Corporate Values/Culture

Each company has a corporate culture. A corporate culture is the way a company's employees behave. It is based upon the behavior of its leaders. This culture can be viewed from a corporate level and also from a departmental level. For example, if all the executives within the company are very laid-back and informal, most employees throughout the company will also be laid-back and informal. If a department supervisor is stressed and unprepared, the department members will most likely be stressed and unprepared, as well. This behavior also reflects an organization's ethical behavior. Companies that want to be proactive and decrease any type of unethical temptation will have and enforce an **ethics statement.** An ethics statement is a formal corporate policy that addresses the issues of ethical behavior and punishment should someone behave inappropriately. As Corporate America recovers from its scandals, more companies are placing great importance on ethics statements. Included in most corporate ethics policies will be a statement addressing **conflicts of interest.** A conflict of interest occurs when you are in a position to influence a decision from which you could benefit directly or indirectly.

Cory's company needs a flower vendor for an upcoming company event. Cory's uncle owns a local flower shop, and getting this contract would be a big financial boost to his store. Cory wonders if it would be unethical to tell his uncle about the opportunity. After some thought, Cory decides to ask the boss about the dilemma. Cory's boss explains that there is no conflict of interest if Cory does not financially benefit from the contract and encourages Cory to contact the uncle.

If there is ever a possibility that someone can accuse you of a conflict of interest, excuse yourself from the decision-making process. If you are uncertain that there is a conflict, check with your boss or the respective committee. Explain the situation and ask for your boss's or committee's opinion. To avoid a conflict of interest, many companies have strict policies on gift giving and receiving. Many companies do not allow the acceptance of gifts or have a dollar value of a gift allowed.

Exercise 5-2   Receiving a Gift at Work

Your company has a strict policy on not accepting gifts valued over $15. A key vendor for your company sends you flowers on your birthday. The arrangement is quite large, so you know it clearly exceeds the $15 limit. What do you do?

_____

_____

_____

Making Ethical Choices

As you attempt to make ethical choices at work, use the three **levels of ethical decisions.** Each level contains a question that if answered "no" deems the decision unethical.

1. First level: Is the action legal? When confronted with an ethical issue, first ask if the action is legal. If the answer is no, the action is illegal; therefore it is unethical.

2. Second level: Is the action fair to all involved? If the answer is no, it is unethical. Your actions/behavior should be fair to all parties involved. If, when making a decision, someone is clearly going to be harmed or is unable to defend him- or herself, the decision is probably not ethical. Note that the concept of "fairness" does not mean that everyone is happy with the outcome. It only means that the decision has been made in an impartial and unbiased manner. Sometimes, a behavior is legal but may be considered unethical. Just because a behavior is legal does not mean it is right. Take the case of an individual who has a romantic relationship with someone who is married to someone else. While in some states it is not illegal to have an extramarital affair, many consider this behavior unethical.

3. Third level: Does the behavior make you feel good? It is understandable that not everyone agrees on what is right and fair. If the answer to this question is no, it is unethical. This is when your conscience must be considered. This is also when an ethical decision gets personal. In the classic Disney movie *Pinocchio,* the character named Jiminy Cricket was Pinocchio's conscience. He made Pinocchio feel bad when Pinocchio behaved inappropriately. Just like Pinocchio, each individual has a

conscience. When people knowingly behave inappropriately, most will eventually feel bad about their poor behavior. Some people take a bit longer to feel bad than others, but most everyone at some point feels bad when they have wronged another. Sometimes a behavior may be legal and it may be fair to others, but it still may make us feel guilty or bad.

Cory is responsible for a petty cash box at work. Cory is planning on going to lunch with friends but does not have time to stop by the ATM until later in the afternoon. Cory struggles with the thought of temporarily borrowing $10 from the petty cash box and returning the money later in the day (after a visit to the ATM). No one would ever know. Technically, it is not stealing, it is just borrowing. As Cory debates temporarily borrowing the money, Cory begins to feel guilty. Cory decides the behavior is unethical, does not take the petty cash, and skips going out to lunch with friends.

Exercise 5-3 Legal Behavior

Based on Cory's dilemma, answer the three levels of ethical behavior.

1. Is Cory borrowing money from the petty cash box legal?

Yes ❑ No ❑

2. Is Cory borrowing the money fair?

Yes ❑ No ❑

3. Would you feel bad about borrowing the money?

Yes ❑ No ❑

Whom could it harm and why?

_____

_____

_____

_____

Exercise 5-4 Honesty: Part I

It is 9:00 P.M., it is raining, and you are hungry. You are on your way home from a long workday. You only have $5 in your wallet, so you decide to go to a fast-food drive-through to get dinner. You carefully order so as not to exceed your $5 limit. You hand the drive-through employee your $5, and he gives you change and your meal. You place it all on the passenger's seat and drive home. When you get home, you discover that the fast-food employee gave you change for $20. What do you do?

_____

_____

_____

_____

Review the scenario; apply the three levels of ethical decision making to the following questions.

Is it legal to keep the money?
Yes ❑ No ❑

Is it fair to keep the money?
Yes ❑ No ❑

Do you feel bad about keeping the money?
Yes ❑ No ❑

Exercise 5-5   Honesty: Part II

Typically, in the fast-food business, employees whose cash boxes are either short or over more than once are at risk of being fired. If you initially were going to keep the money, but now you know the employee who gave you too much cash could get fired because you decided to keep the money, would you still keep the money?

_____

_____

When Others Are Not Ethical

The previous section discussed how to behave ethically at work. But what should you do when others are not behaving ethically? Let us review the three levels of ethical decision making. Everyone must abide by the law. If someone at work is breaking the law, you have an obligation to inform your employer immediately. This can be done confidentially to either your supervisor or the human resource department. Whenever you accuse anyone of wrongdoing, present documented facts and solid evidence. Keep track of important dates, events, and copies of evidence. Your credibility is at stake. Depending on the enormity of the situation, you as an employee have three choices: (1) alert outside officials if the offense is illegal and extreme; (2) if the offense is not extreme and is accepted by management, accept management's decision; or (3) if the inappropriate behavior is accepted by management and you are still bothered, decide whether you want to continue working for the company.

Cory finds out that a certain coworker received a smart phone from a vendor for personal use. No other employee received a smartphone. The coworker said the device was an incentive for the company's good standing with the vendor and, because he was the employee who made the purchases, it was his right to keep the device. Cory thinks this is unfair and unethical. Cory politely checks with the human resource department, and they tell Cory that the coworker can keep the smartphone. Cory must accept the company's policy. Although Cory construed the situation as unethical, the company found no conflict with its policies. Cory decides the offense is not extreme, and because it was accepted by management, Cory accepts management's decision.

Another common ethical issue at work occurs in the area of company theft. Company theft is not always large items such as laptops or other equipment. More often, it is smaller items such as office supplies. Time can also be stolen from a company. If you use company time to surf the Internet, make personal texts and calls, or take extra-long breaks, you are stealing from the company. You may not realize that taking a pen or pencil home is also stealing from your company. Work supplies should be used only for work purposes. Although it is heavily influenced by the company and how others view right behavior from wrong, ethical behavior begins with the individual.

Diversity Basics

This section addresses workplace diversity, cultural differences, and employee rights regarding these differences. Diversity comes in many forms. Although most people think of diversity as a race issue, the topic goes far beyond race. People are different in many aspects, ranging from ethnicity to the way we wear our hair. As we discuss these issues, note three primary messages regarding workplace diversity:

- No matter what our differences are, everyone should be treated with respect and professionalism.
- Diversity should be viewed as an asset that utilizes our differences as ways to create, innovate, and compete.
- Workplace diversity should only be an issue when the diversity negatively affects performance.

The following is a common example of workplace diversity: One of Cory's new friends at work has a different religion than Cory's. Although Cory's friend has never openly mentioned his religious beliefs, the new friend subtly slips into his office at routine times of the day and eats a special diet. Cory really enjoys the workplace friendship with this coworker and, although Cory is confident in Cory's own beliefs, Cory wants to learn more about the friend's beliefs. Cory sometimes does not know how to behave around this friend when the topic of meals or religion comes up. Cory thinks about talking the coworker about the differences but does not want to offend him. After some thought, Cory decides that asking the coworker is not offensive and politely asks him questions regarding religious practices.

Workplace diversity refers to differences among coworkers. Whenever people address the issue of diversity at work, they primarily address cultural and racial differences. However, diversity extends well beyond culture and race. We differ in age, gender, economic status, physical makeup, intelligence, religion, and sexual orientation, among other things.

The Equal Employment Opportunity Commission (EEOC) enforces laws that protect individuals from workplace discrimination in recruiting, hiring, wages, promotions, and unlawful termination. These laws are based upon Title VII of the Civil Rights Act, which prohibits discrimination based on sex, religion, race or color, or national origin. Since that time, additional laws have been made to further protect individuals from discrimination in the areas of age (forty years and older), physical and mental disabilities, gender, sexual orientation, hate crimes, pregnancy, and military service. If you ever feel you are a victim of workplace discrimination, first contact your human resource department. If you feel you are still experiencing discrimination, contact your state's Department of Fair Employment and Housing or Department of Labor (depending on your state) or the Equal Employment Opportunity Commission.

Race is defined as people having certain physical traits. Racial differences include various ethnicities, such as Hispanic, Asian, African American, Native American, and Anglo-Saxon. **Culture** is the different behavior patterns of people. Examples of various cultures may include where you live geographically, your age, your economic status, and your religious beliefs. As the workplace becomes more diverse, it is hard to imagine a workplace that does not include various races and cultures.

Talk It Out

What does the Cory story found in the Diversity Basics section have to do with stereotypes and prejudice?

Exercise 5-6 What Do You See?

Look around the room and list at least three differences between you and your classmates.

1.

2.

3.

As we move into a global economy, recognize and respect global differences. Americans sometimes are accused of being **ethnocentric.** Ethnocentrism is when an individual believes his or her culture is superior to other cultures. It seems a bit foolish when Americans behave in an ethnocentric manner, since America is really a compilation of many cultures. No one culture is better than another. In the workplace, respect and be aware of how various cultures impact the work environment.

Understanding how race and culture impact our workplace helps us begin to recognize how these differences influence our values and behavior. In chapter 1, we discussed that not everyone thinks and behaves like you. Moreover, people look different and have different value systems. Although we may not like someone's looks or agree with others' values or religious beliefs, we must respect everyone's differences and treat them professionally.

Digging deeper into the issue of culture, we need to appreciate various generational differences and their impact on the workplace. Individuals entering the workforce (eighteen- to twenty-two-year-olds) have different needs than those preparing to retire (fifty-five and older). Moreover, these needs reflect priorities, values, and attitudes.

Stereotypes and Prejudice

In chapter 1, we discussed the differences in people's attitudes and how these attitudes form our personalities. Everyone is a product of past experience. Individuals use these past experiences to form perceptions about people and situations. A **perception** is one's understanding or interpretation of reality. If we had a positive previous experience, we will most likely have a positive perception of a person or circumstance. For example, if your boss calls you in to his or her office, you will either have a positive or negative perception of the impending conversation. If your boss is a good communicator and you frequently visit his or her office, you will have a positive perception of being called in to the office. On the other hand, if your boss calls you in to his or her office only for bad news, your perception of reality is that the boss's office solely represents reprimands and punishment.

To make situations easier to understand or perceive, we often stereotype. **Stereotyping** is making a generalized image of a particular group or situation. Often, our perceptions mold how we view groups or situations. These images can be positive or negative, but we generally apply them to similar situations and groups. At work, this can include types of meetings (situations) or members of specific departments (groups). Using the preceding example of the boss and his or her office, one could stereotype that all bosses are good communicators.

It is wise to not only know the definition of stereotyping, but also to avoid applying stereotypes in a negative manner. Let us use the example of females with blond hair. A common stereotype is that females with blond hair are not intelligent. This is not true. Prior to responding to a situation, conduct an attitude check to ensure that you are not basing your reaction on a perception or stereotype rather than responding to the current facts and situation.

Using the previous example of attitudes toward females with blond hair, if we assume that all females with blond hair are unintelligent (stereotype), we have demonstrated prejudice. **Prejudice** is a favorable or unfavorable judgment or opinion toward an individual or group based on one's perception (or understanding) of a group, individual, or situation. Typically, at work, prejudice is a negative attitude or opinion that results in discrimination. Therefore, if we do not hire females with blond hair because we believe they are not intelligent, we are guilty of discrimination. **Workplace discrimination** is acting against someone based on race, age, gender, religion, disability, or any of the other areas we have discussed in this chapter.

Many people harbor some form of prejudice. Recognize in what areas you may be harboring prejudice and begin understanding why. Once you recognize what areas need improvement, begin taking action to decrease your prejudice. One way is to learn about the individual, group, or situation that is causing the prejudice.

Exercise 5-7   Look for Prejudice

What areas of prejudice do you see on campus?

_____
_____
_____

What areas of prejudice do you see in your community?

_____
_____
_____

Labeling is when we describe an individual or group of individuals based upon past actions. We attach positive or negative labels to groups or individuals, and we frequently have the group or individuals live up or down to these standards. We then watch for supporting behaviors to see if these behaviors live up to or dispel the labels we have attached. For example, if we label a coworker as being the smartest person we know, that person may live up to this expectation by behaving as the smartest person (regardless of whether he or she really is intelligent). However, he or she may dispel the label by purposely behaving ignorantly.

Assumptions sometimes are made at work based on people's language differences and accents. These assumptions may include economic status, intelligence, and social customs. In our melting pot society, it is common for individuals to speak a different language (bilingual) when at home. At work, speaking a second language can be a means of attracting and meeting customer needs. Therefore, being bilingual can be a workplace asset.

Do not make fun of people with different cultures or lifestyles or individuals with physical and mental disabilities. Even jokes that we believe are innocent may cause deep wounds. Moreover, they may not only be offensive, but may violate someone's civil rights. Inappropriate comments can be construed as both workplace discrimination and harassment.

For example, Cory is invited to lunch with some new coworkers. During the meal, one of the coworkers tells a joke about a blind person of a certain ethnicity. Cory politely chuckles at the punch line but is actually offended. Cory wonders how to best handle the situation. Should Cory tell the joke teller that the joke was offensive? Should Cory tell the department supervisor? Cory clearly believes that this type of behavior is inappropriate. Cory decides to informally let the joke teller know that the joke was offensive. If Cory continues to see inappropriate or offensive behavior from this employee, Cory has decided to mention the behavior to the department supervisor and request diversity training for the department.

Companies are attempting to better address workplace diversity through several actions. First, they are developing **diversity statements.** These statements remind employees that diversity in the workplace is an asset and not a form of prejudice and stereotyping. Second, companies are providing **diversity training** to teach employees how to eliminate workplace discrimination and harassment. This training applies to all employees, customers, and vendors. Third, they are eliminating the **glass ceiling** and **glass walls.** These are invisible barriers that frequently make executive positions (glass ceiling) and certain work areas or work-related places, such as a golf course (glass wall), off limits to females and minorities. A glass ceiling prevents females and minorities from moving up the corporate ladder through promotions. Glass walls are barriers that exclude females and minorities from certain situations. Proactive companies offer formal mentoring programs to assist in identifying and training women and minorities for promotion opportunities. People should not receive special treatment because they are female or a minority, but they should be given an equal opportunity. The employer is responsible for hiring the most qualified candidate.

Cultural Differences

Our society is a mix of individuals from all over the world. For this reason, it is important to address cultural differences and their impact on the workplace. Cultural differences include religious influences and are related to the treatment of individuals based on age, gender, and family.

There are many different religions in the world. Although most major U.S. holidays are based around Christian holidays, not everyone who works in the United States is a Christian. Individuals who do not share your religious values are afforded the same rights as you. As mentioned earlier in this chapter, the Civil Rights Act protects individuals from discrimination based on religion. Everyone is entitled to observe his or her respective religious holidays and traditions. Once again, we must be respectful of everyone's individual religious beliefs and not condemn someone for his or her religious difference. Although an individual's religious beliefs may permeate every element of his or her life, as with other issues of diversity, if religion negatively impacts performance, the issue must be addressed.

Some countries have cultures that focus on the individual, while other countries prioritize what is best for society over personal needs. In some cultures, women and children are often not treated as equals to men. Although we may not agree with this treatment, we have to respect cultural differences. Understand these differences so you do not offend others. For example, some hand gestures commonly used in the United States may be offensive to someone who has come from another country. If you feel you may have offended someone based upon a cultural difference, find out what behavior offended the other person, apologize if necessary, and try to not repeat the offensive behavior.

Cultural differences have both a positive and negative impact on business. Learning about other cultures can provide insights into new markets and stimulate creativity. With so much diversity among employees and customers, knowing other cultures will result in improved relationships. Outcomes can be negative when companies do not properly train employees and address cultural differences; this is when prejudice and discrimination may emerge.

Workplace Dos and Don'ts

Do always behave in an ethical manner	*Don't* behave one way at work and another around your friends
Do keep information confidential	*Don't* break the company's trust
Do recognize and increase your workplace power bases	*Don't* use your workplace power in a harmful or unethical manner
Do know your rights regarding workplace diversity	*Don't* accept defeat in discriminatory situations
Do learn to respect differences in others	*Don't* use your minority status to take advantage of situations
Do be proud of your culture and heritage	*Don't* show prejudice toward others
Do take responsibility for increasing awareness about workplace diversity issues	*Don't* label people

Concept Review and Application

Summary of Key Concepts

- Personal ethical behavior is a reflection of the influences of friends, family, religion, and society
- Do not share confidential information with individuals for whom the business is of no concern
- Power and power bases are effective tools to use in the workplace
- Be cautious to not use power and reciprocity in an unethical manner
- A conflict of interest occurs when you are in a position to influence a decision from which you could benefit directly or indirectly
- No matter what our differences, treat everyone with respect and professionalism
- Title VII of the Civil Rights Act prohibits discrimination based on sex, religion, race or color, or national origin
- Diversity should be used as an asset that utilizes our differences as ways to create, innovate, and compete
- Workplace diversity should be an issue only when the diversity negatively affects performance

Key Terms

character	charismatic power	coercive power
confidential	conflict of interest	connection power
culture	diversity statements	diversity training
ethics	ethics statement	ethnocentric
expert power	glass ceiling	glass wall
implied	information power	labeling
confidentiality	legitimate power	levels of ethical
morals	networking	decisions
perception	politics	power
prejudice	race	reciprocity
reward power	stereotyping	values
workplace	workplace diversity	
discrimination		

If You Were the Boss

1. You have just been promoted to boss. What are the first five things you should do?
2. What is the best method of dealing with an ethical decision regarding the performance of an employee?
3. What would you do if you noticed an employee treating another employee in a discriminatory manner?
4. What can you do to minimize workplace discrimination and harassment?

Video Case Study: Making Ethical Choices

Two employees are having a conversation at work. This video shows two different ethical perspectives. To view these videos, visit the Student Resources: Professionalism section in www.mystudentsuccesslab.com. Then answer the following questions:

1. Are either of the characters in this video demonstrating unethical behavior? If so, what are the specific unethical behaviors?
2. Is Brian's ethical behavior Regina's business? Why or why not?
3. How does the ethics test apply to this scenario?
4. What should the company be doing to address the situation?

Web Links

http://www.discriminationattorney.com/eeocdfeh.shtml
http://www.managementhelp.org/ethics/ethics.htm
http://www.dol.gov
http://www.dol.gov/dol/topic/discrimination/index.htm
http://www.executiveplanet.com

Activities

Activity 5-1

Is it ever ethical to take paperclips, copy paper, and pens home from work?

Yes ❏ No ❏ Sometimes ❏

Support your answer.

_____

_____

Activity 5-2

List a time when you overheard confidential information that should not have been shared—for example, sitting in a physician's office or overhearing a private conversation while shopping.

_____

_____

How should this situation have been better handled?

_____

_____

Activity 5-3

Identify at least three potential areas for employee theft on a small scale.

1. _____

2. _____

3. _____

Identify at least two potential areas for employee theft on a large scale.

1. _____

_____

2. _____

Activity 5-4

In the United States, the thumbs-up symbol communicates a job well done. Research and identify what the thumbs-up symbol communicates in at least two other countries. What did this activity teach you about various cultures and hand gestures?

Country	Meaning

Conclusion: What did you learn?

_____

_____

Activity 5-5

Identify a recent experience where you observed act of prejudice. How could you have handled the situation differently?

Act of Prejudice	How You Would Handle the Situation?

Activity 5-6

With a partner, dialogue what you would say if someone offended you with a joke. Was this dialogue easy? Why or why not? Share your findings with your class.

_____

_____

1. _____ is a moral standard of right and wrong.

2. _____ is your obligation to not share information with individuals for whom the business is of no concern.

3. Everyone at work has some _____. The difference is that some people understand this ability to _____ and use it appropriately.

4. _____ means creating debts and obligations for doing something.

5. A/An _____ occurs when you are in a position to influence a decision from which you could benefit directly or indirectly.

6. The first question for ethical decision making is: Is it _____?

7. The second question for ethical decision making is: Is it _____?

8. The third question for ethical decision making is: How does it _____?

9. Differences among coworkers are referred to as _____.

10. _____ is a group of individuals with certain physical traits, while _____ are different behavior patterns of various groups.

11. Companies provide _____ to teach employees how to eliminate workplace discrimination and harassment.

Accountability and Workplace Relationships

chapter 6

You cannot escape the responsibility of tomorrow by evading it today.

Abraham Lincoln (1809–1865)

Objectives

- Define and link the concepts of *empowerment*, *responsibility*, and *accountability*
- Describe how best to deal with your boss
- Describe how to respond when a workplace relationship turns negative
- Identify appropriate and inappropriate relationships with your boss, colleagues, executives, and customers
- Identify basic workplace expectations regarding social functions and gift giving

How-Do-You-Rate

	Who cares?	True	False
1.	I should not have to clean the break room if I did not make it dirty.	❑	❑
2.	I should not have to unjam the copy machine if I was not the one who jammed it.	❑	❑
3.	I have the right to date anyone I please, including coworkers, vendors, and customers.	❑	❑
4.	I have the right to privately and discreetly share my dislike of my boss or coworker with other employees if they promise to keep the matter confidential.	❑	❑
5.	I do not have to attend company functions if I don't want to attend.	❑	❑

If you answered "true" to two or more of these questions, you are correct, you have the right to make workplace choices on these sensitive matters. However, your actions should reflect accountability and responsibility. Consistently respond to situations such as those listed above in a manner that reflects positively on both you and your employer.

Accountability and Empowerment

Employees need to be accountable, but what does that really mean? As you will learn in this discussion, accountability involves taking personal responsibility for ensuring whatever has your name attached to it (a project, a customer experience, a workplace conflict, a relationship with a vendor) reflects positively on both you and your company. In politics, business, and education, individuals need to be held accountable for their actions. Unfortunately, too many people do not demonstrate accountability. This chapter discusses the concepts of accountability and workplace relationships. The concepts of empowerment, responsibility, and accountability are all about personal choices. These personal choices not only impact how successfully you will perform at work, but have a tremendous impact on workplace relationships.

In chapter 5 we discussed power bases and how workplace power affects politics and ethical behavior. Employees in the workplace have power. Unfortunately, many people in the workplace do not use their power appropriately or at all. As companies place an increased focus on quality and performance, correct decision making by employees becomes more and more important.

Empowerment is pushing power and decision making to the individuals who are closest to the customer in an effort to increase quality, customer satisfaction, and, ultimately, profits. The foundation of this basic management concept means that if employees feel they are making a direct contribution to a company's activities, they will perform better. This will then increase quality and customer satisfaction.

Consider the case of a manager for a retail customer service counter telling his employee to make the customer happy. The manager feels he has empowered his employee. However, the next day, the manager walks by the employee's counter and notices that the employee has given all customers refunds for all returns, even when some returns did not warrant a refund. The boss immediately disciplines the employee for poor performance. Didn't the employee do exactly what the manager asked the employee to do? Did the manager truly empower his employee? The answer is no. Telling someone to do something is different than showing someone the correct behavior. The employee interpreted the phrase "make the customer happy" differently from the manager's intention. The proper way for the manager to have empowered the employee would have been to discuss the company's return policies, role-play various customer scenarios, and then monitor the employee's performance. If or when the employee made errors through the training process, the wrong behavior should have been immediately corrected, while good performance should have immediately received positive reinforcement.

When you, as an employee, demonstrate a willingness to learn, you have taken responsibility. **Responsibility** is accepting the power that is being given to you. If you are not being responsible, you are not fully utilizing power that has been entrusted to you. The concept of empowerment and responsibility is useless without accountability. **Accountability** means that you will report back to whoever gave you the power to carry out that responsibility. Employees at all levels of an organization are accountable to each other, their bosses, their customers, and the company's investors to perform their best.

One of the best ways to gain respect and credibility at work is to begin asking for and assuming new tasks. If you are interested in learning new skills, speak up and ask your boss to teach or provide you opportunities to increase your value to the company. Assume responsibility for these new tasks and report back (become accountable) on your performance. Worthwhile activities support the company's overall mission. Each project for which you assume responsibility must have a measurable goal. If it lacks a goal, it will be difficult to be accountable for your performance.

As you increase your workplace responsibilities, do not be afraid to seek assistance. Learning and success come from others and from past experiences. When you make mistakes, do not blame others. Determine what went wrong and why. Learn from mistakes and view them as opportunities to do better in the future.

Cory is rapidly becoming more confident on the job. Cory wanted to be of more value to the company and began studying the concept of personal responsibility and accountability. Cory was excited about the new concepts that were learned and began requesting extra projects at work. Cory gladly kept the boss informed on the status of each project and reported when each project was successfully completed. The boss noticed how Cory took responsibility not only for personal growth, but also for the success of the department. As a result, the boss informed Cory that he was impressed with Cory's willingness to improve and is considering Cory for a promotion.

Personal Accountability

In today's uncertain economy, it is even more important that employees show up to work with a positive attitude and give 100 percent effort when at work. All companies are continuously exploring methods to increase efficiencies and decrease waste. Each employee must take personal responsibility for his or her performance and be accountable for his or her actions and workplace choices. Good employees contribute to this effort by taking personal accountability for their actions while at work. Be on time and do what is expected of you. Do not miss work, and do not call in sick unless you truly are ill. Reserve personal leave days for emergencies, funerals, or other such situations. During work hours, work. Do not surf the Internet or waste company time on personal activities. When an employee is constantly late, absent, or not completing his or her duties, other employees must assume the responsibilities of this employee. Not being accountable to your coworkers leads to poor workplace relationships and negatively affects productivity.

Workplace Relationships

People who are mature and confident behave consistently around others, while those who are not as secure frequently behave differently around the boss or selected colleagues. Some could argue in favor of this behavior, but it is wrong and immature to behave inconsistently at work. Consistently behave professionally and respectfully, no matter who is around or watching. This section explains the dynamics of workplace relationships and their impact on performance.

Because many people spend more time at work than at home, workplace relationships have a profound impact on productivity. Treat everyone respectfully and professionally. It is easy to be respectful and professional to those we like; it is much more difficult doing so with those with whom we do not get along. Chapter 12, regarding the topic of conflict at work, addresses the sensitive issue of working productively with those we do not like. Unfortunately, having strong friendships at work can sometimes be equally as damaging as having workplace enemies if we fail to keep professional relationships separate from our personal lives. Socializing with our coworkers is both expected and acceptable to a degree, but do not make workplace relationships your only circle of friends. Doing so is dangerous because it becomes difficult to separate personal issues from work issues. It also has the potential to create distrust among employees who are not included in your circle of workplace friends. Finally, it creates the potential for you to unknowingly or subconsciously show favoritism toward your friends. Even if you are not showing favoritism, those who are not within the circle of friends may perceive favoritism and may become distrustful of you.

As you become more comfortable with your job and company, you will be in various situations that provide opportunities to strengthen workplace relationships with coworkers, executives, investors, vendors, and customers. The following section addresses selected situations and how best to behave in these circumstances.

Executives/Senior Officials

It is often difficult for new employees to know how to behave in a roomful of executives or board members. There may be occasions when you are in the presence of executives and board members. These may include meetings, corporate events, and social functions. While it is tempting to pull a senior official aside and tell him or her stories about your boss or how perfect you would be for an advanced position, be aware that some may view this behavior as both inappropriate and unacceptable. Do not draw attention to yourself by appearing overly assertive. Project a positive, professional image. Highlight the successes of your department instead of personal accomplishments.

If you are in a meeting that you do not normally attend, do not dominate the discussion. If it is convenient, before or after the meeting, network by introducing yourself to senior officials. When networking, do not interrupt when others are engaged in conversation. Be confident, extend a hand, and state, "Hello, Mrs. Jones, my name is Tim Brandon. I work in the accounting department. It's nice to meet you." Keep your comments brief and positive. Your objective is to create a favorable and memorable impression with the executive. When introducing yourself, make eye contact when talking so that the executive can connect a face, name, and department. Do not speak poorly of anyone or a situation. It is also inappropriate to discuss specific work-related issues, such as wanting to change positions, unless you are in a meeting specifically to discuss that issue. Allow the executive to guide the conversation. During the conversation read the executive's body language. If the executive's body language includes a nodding head and his or her body is facing you, continue visiting. If the executive is glancing away or his or her body is turning away from you, that body language is communicating the executive's desire to be elsewhere. Therefore, politely end the conversation, excuse yourself, and leave. Use networking encounters with executives as opportunities to create favorable impressions for you and your department.

Talk It Out

Why should you not speak poorly of others when networking?

Your Boss

Typically, there is no middle ground when it comes to workers and their feelings for their bosses. Many employees have strong emotions for their bosses (sometimes favorable, sometimes unfavorable). Prior to discussing how to professionally work with various types of bosses, we must remember that bosses are human. Like us, they are continually learning and developing their skills. Although they are not perfect, we should assume they are doing their best.

If you have a **good boss,** be thankful. A good boss is one who is respectful and fair and will groom you for a promotion. It frequently becomes tempting to develop a personal friendship with a good boss. Keep the relationship professional. While it is okay to share important activities occurring in your personal life with your boss (e.g., spouse and child accomplishments, vacation plans), do not divulge too much personal information. Take advantage of your boss by turning the relationship into a mentoring opportunity. Mentoring will be explained in greater detail in chapter 8. Identify what management qualities make your boss valued, and begin integrating these qualities in your own workplace behavior.

Web Quiz

Rate your relationship with your boss by taking the web quiz or find a similar quiz online.

http://www.officearrow.com/oa-quiz/quiz-how-is-your-relationship-with-your-boss-oaiur-373/view.html

There may be other situations where we feel our boss is incompetent and appears to not know how to do his or her job. As with any work situation, no matter how bad we perceive our boss to be, we need to remain professional and respectful. Make it your mission to make your boss look good. Doing so demonstrates maturity and diminishes any potential tension between you and your boss. Do not worry about your boss receiving credit for your hard work. If your boss is a poor performer, others in the company will discover that your boss is not producing the quality work being presented. If you are producing quality work, it will get noticed by others in the company. If you and your boss have a personality conflict, do not allow your personal feelings to affect your performance. Focus on staying positive and productive, consistently being of value to your company. Even when coworkers want to bad-mouth the boss, do not give in to temptation. Remain professional and respectful. If you have a less-than-perfect boss, use the experience as a time to learn what not to do when you become a boss.

Sometime in your career, you may experience an **abusive boss.** The abusive boss is one who is constantly belittling or intimidating his or her employees. Abusive bosses generally behave this way because they have low self-esteem. Therefore, they utilize their legitimate and coercive power to make themselves feel better by knocking someone else down. There are several ways to deal with an abusive boss. If the abuse is tolerable, do your best to work with the situation. Do not speak poorly of your boss in public. If the situation becomes intolerable and is negatively affecting your performance, seek confidential advice from someone in the human resource management department. This expert can begin observing, investigating, and documenting the situation and take corrective action or provide needed management training to your boss if necessary. Be factual in reporting inappropriate incidents. Human resource managers want only facts, not emotions. While it may be tempting, do not go to your boss's boss. Doing so implies secrecy and distrust. Finally, if it looks as if your boss's behavior and work situation is not going to improve, begin quietly searching for another job in a different department within the company or at a new company. As an employee, you have rights. If your boss ever discriminates against you or harasses you, document and report the behavior immediately. Your boss should not make you perform functions that do not reasonably support those identified in your job description. Some bosses ask employees to run personal errands or perform duties not appropriate for your job. If you are asked to perform unreasonable functions, politely decline. Regardless of what type of boss you have, consistently give your personal best.

Colleagues

Having friends at work is nice. Unfortunately, when workplace friendships go awry, it affects your job. Be cautious about close friendships developed at work. A close friend is someone whom you trust and who knows your strengths and weaknesses. While you should be able to trust coworkers, they should not know everything about you. While it is important to be friendly to everyone at work, there will be some with whom you want to develop a friendship outside of work, but beware. If there is a misunderstanding either at work or away from work, the relationship can go sour and affect both areas. If one of you gets promoted and suddenly becomes the boss of the other, it also creates an awkward situation for both parties. Even if both you and your friend can get beyond this issue, others at work may feel like outsiders or feel you are playing favorites with your friend. If you socialize only with friends developed at work, you risk getting too absorbed in work issues. The one common thread that binds your friendship is work. Therefore, it is work that you will most likely discuss when you are away from work. This can be unhealthy and could potentially create a conflict of interest in work-related decisions.

Others Within the Organization

The topic of friendships in the workplace extends to those throughout the organization. Increase your professional network by meeting others within your company. As discussed in chapter 5, as we build our connection power, we gain additional knowledge and contacts to assist us in performing our jobs and perhaps earning future promotions. When interacting with others in the organization, keep conversations positive and respectful. Even if another individual steers the conversation in a negative direction, respond with a positive comment. Defend coworkers when another employee is talking negatively about them, and do not contribute to gossip and rumors.

One day, Cory and a friend are sitting in the break room when Vicki, the department's unhappy coworker, walks in. "I just can't stand John!" declares Vicki. "That's too bad. John's a friend of mine," responds Cory's friend, Dee. Vicki stands there red-faced, turns around, and leaves the room. Cory tells Dee that Cory never knew she and John were close. "Well," responds Dee, "we're not personal friends, but we all work together." Dee goes on to explain that it is easy to eliminate negative conversation when you immediately communicate that you will not tolerate bad-mouthing others. Cory thinks that this is pretty good advice.

Each company has a **corporate culture (organizational culture).** Corporate culture is the company's personality being reflected through its employees' behavior. The company's culture is its shared values and beliefs. For example, if the company's management team openly communicates and promotes teamwork, the company will most likely have excellent communication and successful teams. In contrast, executives who are stressed and reacting to crisis situations will create a workplace atmosphere based on stress and crisis management. A company's corporate culture has an enormous impact on **employee morale.** Employee morale is the attitude employees have toward the company.

Exercise 6-1   Improving Morale

What can you do to help improve employee morale in your workplace?

_____

_____

_____

What workplace relationships contribute to poor employee morale?

_____

_____

_____

When Relationships Turn Negative

Unresolved conflict happens in the best of relationships. Due to a conflict or misunderstanding, a relationship may go bad. Unfortunately, this happens at work. Sometimes you have no idea what you have done wrong. In other cases, you may be the one who wants to end the relationship. As stated earlier in the text, you do not have to like everyone at work, but no one should know whom you dislike. Show everyone respect and behave professionally, even toward your adversaries.

If you are part of a bad workplace relationship, take the following steps in dealing with the situation:

- If you harmed the other person (intentionally or unintentionally), apologize immediately.
- If the other person accepts your apology, demonstrate your regret by changing your behavior.
- If the other person does not accept your apology and your apology was sincere, move on. Continue demonstrating your regret by your improved behavior.
- If you lose the relationship, do not hold a grudge. Continue being polite, respectful, and professional to the offended coworker.
- If the offended coworker acts rude or inappropriately (either directly and indirectly), do not retaliate by returning the poor behavior. Respond in a professional manner.
- If the rude and inappropriate behavior negatively impacts your performance or is hostile or harassing, document the situation and inform your boss if necessary.

Josh had been one of Cory's favorite coworkers since Cory's first day at work. They took breaks together and at least once a week went out for lunch. One day Cory was working on a project with a short deadline. Josh invited Cory out to lunch and Cory politely declined, explaining why. The next day, Cory asked Josh to lunch and Josh gave Cory a funny look and turned away. "Josh, what's wrong?" Cory asked. Josh shook his head and left the room. Cory left Josh alone for a few days, hoping whatever was bothering him would blow over and things would be better. After a week of Josh ignoring Cory, things only got worse. Cory decided to try one last time to save the relationship. As Cory approached Josh, Cory said, "Josh, I'm sorry for whatever I've done to upset you, and I'd like for us to talk about it." Unfortunately, Josh again gave Cory a hollow look and walked away.

The toughest step when addressing a broken relationship is when the other individual does not accept your apology. Most of us have grown up believing that we must like everyone and that everyone must like us. Because of human nature, this simply is not possible. We cannot be friends with everyone at work. People's feelings get hurt, and some find it hard to forgive. Behavior that is not respectful and professional interferes with performance. Your focus at work should be, first and foremost, performing your job in a quality manner. The company is paying you to perform. Therefore, if a sour relationship begins to impact performance, you must respond. Ask yourself if your behavior is contributing to the unresolved conflict. If it is, change your behavior immediately. If your wronged coworker is upset or hurt, it is common for the coworker to begin bad-mouthing you. Do not retaliate by speaking negatively about your coworker. This only makes both of you look petty and immature. Document the facts of the incident, and be mature. If the bad behavior continues for a reasonable period of time and negatively affects your performance, it is time to seek assistance. This is why documentation is important.

At this point, contact your immediate supervisor for an intervention. When you meet with your supervisor, explain the situation in a factual and unemotional manner, making sure to communicate how the situation is negatively impacting the workplace and productivity. Provide specific examples of the offensive behavior and share your documentation, including any witnesses. Do not approach your supervisor to get the other individual in trouble. Your objective is to secure your boss's assistance in creating a mutually respectful and professional working relationship with your coworker. The boss may call you and the coworker into the boss's office to discuss the situation. Do not become emotional during this meeting. Your objective is to come to an agreement on behaving respectfully and professionally at work.

Dating at Work

A sticky but common workplace relationship issue is that of dating other employees, vendors, or customers of your place of employment. Because we spend so much time at work, it is natural for coworkers to look for companionship in the workplace. While a company cannot prevent you from dating coworkers who are in your immediate work area, many companies discourage the practice. Some companies go as far as having employees who are romantically involved sign statements releasing the company from any liability should the relationship turn sour. It is inappropriate for you to date coworkers and bosses, or, if you are a supervisor, for you to date your employees. Doing so exposes you, your romantic interest, and your company to potential sexual harassment charges, which is addressed in greater detail in chapter 12. Your romantic actions will most likely negatively impact your entire department and make everyone uncomfortable.

If you date customers and vendors/suppliers of your company, use caution. In dating either customers or vendors, ask yourself how the changed relationship can potentially impact your job. You are representing your company 24/7. Therefore, do not share confidential information or speak poorly of your colleagues or employer. Be careful to not put yourself in a situation in which you could be accused of a conflict of interest. It is best to keep your romantic life separate from that of the workplace.

Socializing

Work-related social activities such as company picnics, potlucks, and birthday celebrations are common. While some individuals enjoy attending these social functions, others do not. You do not have to attend a work-related social function outside of your required work hours. However, it is often considered rude if you do not attend social functions that occur at the workplace during work hours. If you are working on an important deadline and simply cannot attend, briefly stop by the function and apologize to whoever is hosting the event. If you are invited to attend a work-related social function, check to see if guests are requested to bring items to the event. If you plan on attending, bring an item if one is requested. It is considered impolite to show up to a potluck empty-handed. It is also considered rude to take home a plate of leftovers unless they are offered. Alcohol should not be served on work premises.

Attendance at work-related social events occurring outside the work site is considered optional but provides an opportunity to network. As discussed in chapter 4, if the invitation requires an RSVP, send your reservation or regrets in a timely manner. If you choose not to attend an off-site activity, thank whoever invited you in order to maintain a positive work relationship. If you do attend an off-site social function, check to see if guests are requested to bring something. If the function is at someone's home, a host or hostess gift is also appropriate. Thank the host for the invitation when arriving and when leaving. If alcohol is served at an off-site work-related function, use caution if you choose to consume. It is best to not consume at all, but if you consume, limit yourself to one drink.

Shared Work Areas

Talk It Out

What are distractions that employees should avoid doing in a common work area?

In an effort to facilitate teamwork and fully utilize workspace, many work sites utilize cubicles. While cubicles open up a work area, respect the privacy of each shared workspace as if it were an individual office. When working or conducting business in a shared work area, avoid making loud noises, smells, or distractions that may interrupt or annoy others. Speak quietly. Imagine that each cubicle has a door. Just as you would not walk into someone's office unannounced or without knocking, avoid walking into someone's cubicle space without permission. Stand at the entrance of the cubicle and quietly knock or say, "Excuse me." Wait for the individual to invite you into his or her work area. If you are conducting business and the discussion is lengthy, utilize a nearby conference/meeting room so as to not disrupt others. Respect the privacy of others' workspace. Do not take or use items from someone's desk without permission.

Breaks and the Break Room

It is a common practice for offices to make coffee available. In most cases, the company does not pay for this benefit. The coffee, snacks, and other supplies are typically provided by the boss or someone else in the office. If you routinely drink coffee or eat the office snacks, contribute funds to help pay for these items. The same goes for office treats such as donuts, cookies, or birthday cakes. If you partake, offer to share the cost or take your turn bringing treats one day. Many offices also have a refrigerator available for employees to store meals. Do not help yourself to food stored in a community refrigerator. If you store your food in this area, throw out unused or spoiled food at the end of each work week. Finally, clean up after yourself. If you use a coffee cup, wash it and put it away when you are finished. Throw away your trash, and leave the break room clean for the next person.

Miscellaneous Workplace Issues

While it is tempting to sell fund-raising items at work, the practice is questionable. Some companies have policies prohibiting this practice. If the practice is acceptable, do not pester people nor make them feel guilty if they decline to make a purchase.

It is common and acceptable to give a gift to a friend commemorating special days such as birthdays and holidays. However, you do not have to give gifts to anyone at work. If you are a gift giver, do so discreetly so as to not offend others who do not receive gifts from you. When you advance into a management position, do not give a gift to just one employee. Managers who choose to give gifts must give gifts to all of their employees and treat everyone equally.

It is also common for employees to pitch in and purchase a group gift for special days such as Boss's Day, Administrative Assistant's Day, and retirements. While it is not mandatory to contribute to these gifts, it is generally expected that you contribute. If you strongly object or cannot afford to participate, politely decline without attaching a negative comment. If price is the issue, contribute whatever amount you deem reasonable and explain that you are on a budget. If you are the receiver of a gift, verbally thank the gift giver immediately and follow up with a handwritten thank-you note.

Good employees take ownership of common work areas and practice common courtesy with such issues as refilling a coffee pot when it is empty and/or filling the copy machine when it is low on paper. If a piece of office machinery is broken or a copy machine is jammed, do not leave the problem for someone else to solve. Take responsibility and solve the problem yourself. If you are unable to solve the problem, alert someone who knows how to fix the problem.

Workplace Dos and Don'ts

Do take responsibility for your performance and success at work	*Don't* wait for someone to tell you what to do
Do display consistent, professional behavior	*Don't* behave appropriately only when the boss is around
Do make your boss look good	*Don't* speak poorly of your boss
Do create positive relationships with coworkers	*Don't* make your workplace friendships your primary friendships away from work
Do practice business etiquette at work-related social functions	*Don't* ignore the importance of behaving professionally at work-related social functions

Concept Review and Application

Summary of Key Concepts

- Take responsibility for the job you perform by being accountable for your actions
- Keep workplace friendships positive, but be cautious that these relationships are not your only friendships away from the workplace
- If a workplace relationship turns negative, remain professional and respectful
- It is best to refrain from dating anyone at work
- Practice good etiquette at social functions that occur within the office

Key Terms

abusive boss	accountability	corporate culture
employee morale	empowerment	(organizational
good boss	responsibility	culture)

If You Were the Boss

1. How can you get employees excited about assuming additional responsibilities?
2. If you were to notice employee morale dropping in your department, how would you respond?
3. How would you handle two employees whose friendship had turned negative?
4. You never give your employees gifts, but one of your employees always gives you gifts for holidays, birthdays, and Boss's Day. Is it wrong for you to accept these gifts?

Video Case Study: Workplace Etiquette

This video addresses business etiquette in a shared workspace. To view these videos, visit the Student Resources: Professionalism section in www. mystudentsuccesslab.com. Then answer the following question:

1. Were Brian, John, and Joe acting appropriately at the start of the video? Why or why not?
2. When is it appropriate to borrow another person's desk items?
3. Is Brian dressed appropriately? Why or why not?

Web Links

http://www.librarysupportstaff.com/coworkers.html#principles
www.themeetingmagazines.com/index/Default.aspx?tabid=439

Activities

Activity 6-1

You are supposed to attend a meeting tomorrow. Overnight, you have a family emergency. What should you do? Explain your answer.

_____

_____

_____

_____

Activity 6-2

Your boss bad-mouths or belittles coworkers. You do not like it, and you wonder what he or she says about you when you are not around. What should you do?

_____

_____

_____

_____

Activity 6-3

The company that services your office equipment has hired a new salesperson. This person does not wear a wedding ring and flirts with you. If you go out on a date with this person, what are three potential problems that could occur (work-related)?

1. _____

2. _____

3. _____

Activity 6-4

Is it appropriate to discuss the following company information with individuals outside of the company? Why or why not?

Information	Yes or No	Why or Why Not?
1. Key clients/customers		
2. Financial information		
3. Boss's work style		
4. Company mission statement		
5. Names of members of the company board of directors		

1. _____ is the attitude employees have toward the company.

2. If you ever harm another, immediately _____.

3. Any behavior that is not _____ or professional interferes with _____.

4. Be cautious in engaging in _____ with coworkers, customers, vendors, or your boss.

5. You _____ have to attend any work-related social function outside of your normal work hours.

6. If _____ is being served at a work-related function off of the work site, use caution when consuming, or better yet, do not _____.

7. If you partake of office treats, it is good manners to _____.

8. Just like at home, _____ in the break room.

9. It is best to not sell _____ items at work.responsibility

Quality Organizations and Service

There are only two qualities in the world: efficiency and inefficiency, and only two sorts of people: the efficient and the inefficient.

George Bernard Shaw (1856–1950)

How-Do-You-Rate

	Are You Providing Quality Service?	True	False
1.	Providing excellent service to coworkers is not as important as providing excellent service to customers.	❑	❑
2.	A company's mission statement and strategy are important only to company executives.	❑	❑
3.	Entry-level employees do not have a big influence on product quality.	❑	❑
4.	Creativity and innovation have little influence on customer service.	❑	❑
5.	When it comes to customer service, the customer is always right.	❑	❑

If you answered "true" to two or more of these questions, use this as an opportunity to improve your understanding of customer service and its influence on a company's profits.

Productivity in the Workplace

Nearly every employee knows the importance of providing excellent customer service. However, many do not make the connection between how an understanding of the organization as a whole, the concept of productivity, and how each employee's commitment to quality creates the foundation for providing this excellent service. Whether you work for a for-profit or a not-for-profit, organizations need to make a profit to stay in business. A key element of profitability is productivity. Each employee is hired to perform a job that in some way contributes to the company's profitability. When an employee understands the basics of how a business is structured and how it operates, the employee is better able to perform his or her job. Part of your workplace success will be based upon your understanding of the business, the way it is organized, and its overall purpose. Without an understanding of the business as a whole, it may be difficult for you to be a good employee. This chapter addresses these issues.

As stated earlier, the purpose of a business is to make a profit. When you secure a job, the company has hired you to be productive. Workplace **productivity** means you are performing a function that adds value to the company. Your productivity should assist the company in achieving its mission. It is each employee's responsibility to help the company be successful. There are several ways of doing this. First and foremost, behave ethically. Make ethical choices that serve the best interests of the company. Take care of company resources that have been entrusted to you. This includes eliminating waste and producing quality products. As you learned in chapter 1, your attitude assists the company with becoming successful because your attitude affects the attitudes of those around you. Maintain a positive attitude. Work to create positive workplace relationships and be open to learning new skills.

Objectives

- Define *productivity* and its impact on organizational success
- Identify and define *directional statements*
- Know the various types of plans used in an organization
- Define the primary business functions and their purpose in an organization
- Define *quality* and its importance in business
- State the differences between a *product*, a *good*, and a *service*
- Define *creativity* and *innovation*
- Identify and describe the importance of *customers* and *customer service*
- Describe how to handle a difficult customer

A company's **mission statement** is its statement of purpose. It identifies why each employee comes to work. An example of a college's mission statement is to contribute to student success. This means not only providing a solid education, but also preparing students to succeed on the job or with their continuing education. If all college employees know that their ultimate purpose is to contribute to student success, each activity they perform on the job should contribute to student success. Either prior to starting your job or within your first week at work, secure a copy of your company's mission statement. If possible, memorize it. A company's mission statement is typically included in the employee handbook and/or provided to you during the employee orientation. If this information is not provided, check the company's website or ask your supervisor or the human resource department for a copy.

A company will not survive without being profitable. However, a company is not successful just because it turns a profit. Several important elements contribute to a company's success. These include satisfying customers who have purchased a quality product produced by motivated employees. Successful companies are accountable to various stakeholders, including investors, their employees, the community at large, and the environment. Factors within the business environment change, so companies should constantly monitor changes and be proactive in meeting the needs of their various stakeholders.

Once a company has identified why it exists, it determines where it wants to be in the future. This is called a **vision statement.** A company's vision statement is its viable view of the future. For example, a college may want to be the top-ranked college in the nation. This goal will take work, but it is achievable. In addition to the company's mission and vision statements, each company should have a values statement. The **values statement** defines what is important to (or what the priorities are for) the company. This could include providing a healthy return to investors, taking care of the environment, taking care of its employees, and keeping customers satisfied. An important element of the company values statement is the company's code of conduct or ethics statement. These statements discuss the importance of behaving ethically in all areas of business.

Together, the company's mission, vision, and values statements constitute the organization's **directional statements.** These statements create the foundation for why the company exists and how it will operate. These are important elements of a company's strategy. The company's **strategy** outlines major goals and objectives and is its road map for success. A **strategic plan** is a formal document that identifies how the company will secure, organize, utilize, and monitor its resources.

Cory's company was updating its strategic plan and was asking for volunteers to sit on various committees. Cory wondered if new employees were able to sit on these committees. Cory decided to ask a coworker. The coworker encouraged Cory to participate and said it would be a great way for Cory to learn more about the company, get to know people throughout the organization, and help make positive changes for the company's overall success. Cory's coworker then showed Cory the back side of Cory's name badge. On it was printed the company's mission statement. "This," Cory's coworker proudly said, "is why we come to work every day." Cory signed up for a committee that afternoon.

Company resources include financial (fiscal), human (employees), and capital (long-term investments) resources. Many companies provide summaries or overviews of the strategic plan to all employees to keep everyone focused on priorities and goals. This information is often found on the company website.

Just as you created a personal plan earlier in this text, each area of the company will have smaller plans with stated **goals** and **objectives** that identify how their respective areas will assist in achieving the company's strategy. As defined in chapter 1, a goal is a broad statement, while an objective supports a goal. Objectives are also referred to as *short-term goals*. An objective must have a deadline and be measurable. Each area of the company will utilize its respective resources and have its performance monitored based upon the company's strategy and goals.

Exercise 7-1   Create Job Goals

Assume today is your first day as a receptionist for a law firm. Write one goal and two objectives for your new job.

Goal

Objective 1

Objective 2

Lines of Authority

Functions and resources within a business are organized according to the company's mission and strategy. The way a company is organized is called its **organizational structure.** The graphic visual display of this structure is called the company **organizational chart.** This chart not only identifies key functions within the company, but also shows the formal lines of authority for employees. These formal lines of authority are also referred to as the **chain of command.** The chain of command identifies who reports to whom within the company. Respect and follow the formal lines of authority within your company. For example, based on the organizational chart in Figure 7-1, it is inappropriate for the accounts payable supervisor to directly approach the marketing vice president for a request without prior approval from the accounting director.

This story is a good example of why you should know your organizational structure and identify your superiors. One day Cory was left alone in the department while everyone was away at an important meeting. A tall man walked through the door and asked to see the boss. Cory explained that the boss was currently out. The gentleman asked how Cory felt about the company, including how long Cory had worked for the company and what could be done to improve the company. Cory found the questions strange but interesting. Cory was honest in the answers provided, always keeping the conversation polite and positive but constructive. The gentleman thanked Cory for the input and left. Two weeks later, Cory's boss returned from a meeting and told Cory that the CEO of the company had shared Cory's ideas on how to improve the company with key executives. It was then that Cory realized that the earlier conversation was with the CEO of the company. Cory was relieved to have been polite and positive in the CEO conversation but regretted not recognizing the CEO when he first walked into the office.

Each company has a leader (see Figure 7-2). The leader is typically called the **president or chief executive officer (CEO).** The president or CEO

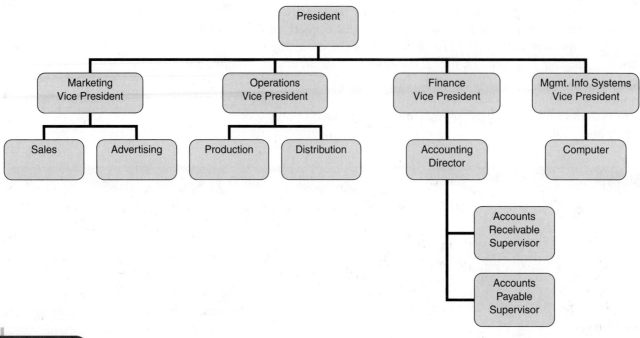

Figure 7-1

Organizational Chart

implements company strategy and reports to the company **board of directors.** This group of individuals is responsible for developing the company's over-all strategy and major policies. The company's board of directors are elected by shareholders or investors. Smaller companies may not have such a formal structure and/or titles, but each business has an investor(s) (owner[s]) and a leader (president). Become familiar with your leaders' names and titles and the formal lines of authority. This will allow you to determine who is in the organization's formal chain of command. If possible, try to view updated photos of these individuals so that, if the appropriate opportunity arises, as with Cory's experience, you can introduce yourself to them.

Within a typical company structure are three different levels of management (see Figure 7-3). These levels include senior management, middle management,

Figure 7-2

Formal Corporate Structure

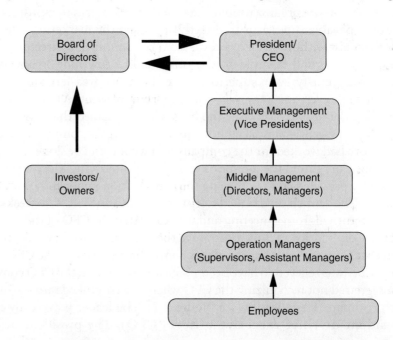

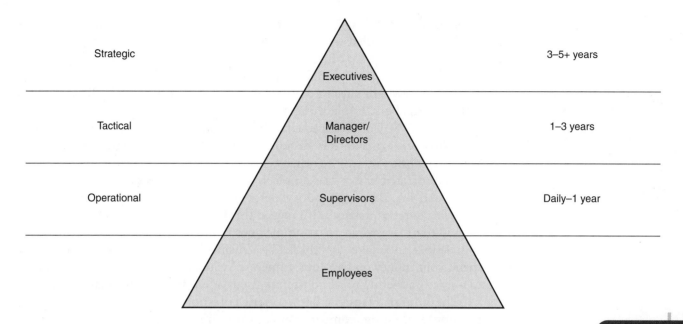

Figure 7-3

Management Levels

and operations management. **Senior managers or executives** typically have the title of *Vice President* or *Chief Executive*. These individuals work with the president in identifying and implementing the company strategy. The time line for **strategic issues** typically ranges from three to five years or more. **Middle managers** typically have the title of *Director* or *Manager*. These individuals work on tactical issues. **Tactical issues** identify how to link the strategy into the reality of day-to-day operations. The time line for tactical issues is typically one to three years. **Operations managers,** typically called *Supervisors* and *Assistant Managers*, work on **operational issues.** These are issues within the company that typically occur on a daily basis and/or no longer than one year. As you begin to develop your career, you may have the opportunity to advance into a leadership position. Your first step into a management position will be that of a **supervisor.** And, although supervisors primarily concern themselves with operational issues, successful employees and supervisors understand the bigger picture of the company's overall tactics and strategy.

As displayed in a typical organizational chart, companies are typically arranged by major functions. These major functions are frequently referred to as **divisions.** Within these divisions are **departments.** The departments carry out specific functions respective of their division. A number of major functions (divisions) are necessary in business. These include finance and accounting, human resources, operations, information systems, marketing, and legal counsel.

The **finance and accounting department** is responsible for the securing, distribution, and growth of the company's financial assets. Any invoices, incoming cash, or checks must be recorded through the accounting department. The accounting department will work with the human resource department on payroll issues regarding your paycheck. Just as you have a personal budget (refer to chapter 2), companies utilize **budgets.** A budget is a plan used to allocate money. There are several types of budgets, including a **capital budget** and an **operational budget.** The capital budget is used for long-term investments, including land and large pieces of equipment. An operational budget is used for short-term items including payroll and the day-to-day costs associated with running a business. Because the primary purpose of every company is to make a profit, you as an employee are accountable for how you utilize the company's financial resources.

One of Cory's coworkers went on vacation. Before leaving, the coworker showed Cory how to order office supplies online and asked Cory to order supplies if needed. Cory noticed that the department was running low on a few items and decided to place an order. As Cory clicked through the online catalog, Cory saw a lot of items that would be nice to have around the office, including a hole punch, a label maker, and a portable hard drive. Cory also thought it would be nice to have a pair of new scissors and a USB flash drive. As Cory was about to place the order, Cory was shocked to see that the total was over $1,000. Cory realized that the coworker never gave Cory a budget but knew that one existed. Cory decided to order only the necessities and wait to ask the coworker about the other items.

As illustrated in Cory's example, frequently, employees do not think before they spend the company's money. Before you spend the company's money, ask yourself a simple question: "If I owned this company, would I spend my money on this item?" Answering that simple question makes you more accountable for your actions and makes you think like a business owner. You most likely will not spend your money on frivolous, unnecessary items and will pay more attention to not only adhering to a budget, but also to identifying ways to save money.

The **human resource department** is responsible for recruiting, hiring, training, evaluating, compensating, promoting, and terminating employees. This department deals with the employee (people) side of business. Your first contact with this function will be when you apply and interview for a job. You will also interact with the human resource department concerning any issue about company policy, complaints and grievances, and your terms of employment. The human resource function is discussed in greater detail in chapter 8.

The **operations** function deals with the production and distribution of the company's product. It is the core of the business. Even if your position does not directly contribute to the production of a company product, your job does support individuals who produce, sell, and distribute the product.

The **information systems (IS) department** deals with the electronic management of information within the organization. This division is responsible for ensuring that the company appropriately utilizes its computer/technology resources. As an employee, you assist and support the information systems department by utilizing company technology only for work-related business. Responsible employees know and practice computer basics such as routinely backing up files, emptying the electronic trash bin, and conducting routine virus checks.

Marketing is responsible for creating, pricing, selling, distributing, and promoting the company's product. The company's **legal counsel** handles all legal matters relating to the business. Check with the company's legal department prior to engaging in a contract on behalf of the company. Large companies may have separate divisions for each of these functions, while smaller companies combine several functions into a single division, department, or position. Additionally, not all companies have the formal departments, titles, or organizational charts described in this chapter. Most small businesses will not have such formal structures. However, to be successful, they will have someone who performs these important functions for the business.

Quality and the Company

If someone asked you to describe a company, you would most likely describe a building, its employees, and the product produced. These are major elements that define a company, but a company needs customers to succeed.

Excellent service, quality, and innovation are what will persuade customers to purchase a company's product. More important, a successful company's employees and products must make customers want to make a repeat purchase.

Each employee performs a job that is necessary to help the company achieve its goal. As an employee, you are an important part of the company, so perform your best at all times. **Quality** is a predetermined standard that defines how a product is to be provided. Customers demand quality. If customers do not perceive that they have received a quality product, they will not make a repeat purchase.

Customer loyalty is another important element that contributes to the success of a company. If a customer perceives he or she has received value and a quality product, he or she will display loyalty to your company by making a repeat purchase. Companies want to build brand loyalty with customers and want customers to not substitute their product with a competing product. Customers will be loyal to a company and its products when quality products are consistently provided.

Employee loyalty is an employee's obligation to consistently support a company and its mission. Displaying loyalty contributes to a company's success. Employees show loyalty in several ways. The most obvious is for you to do your job and do it well. Another way to show loyalty to the company is to show respect for company policies, your coworkers, and the company's customers. Make every effort to promote the company and its products. To do this, understand your company, including its mission, strategy, and business structure. Regardless of your position, it is your job to contribute to producing a high-quality, high-value product. You are a walking billboard for your company. Your behavior both at and away from work represents the company. Do not speak poorly of your company, your coworkers, or the company's product.

The success of a company depends on a company consistently making a profit. **Profit** is revenue (money coming in) minus expenses (the costs involved in running the business). Help create profit for your company by monitoring and decreasing expenses and identifying ways to increase sales. Be aware of expenses you incur at work and make every effort to eliminate waste. Find ways to be involved with and take responsibility for better knowing your customers. As profits increase, the company can grow. This means a company can expand into a larger space, add more sites, offer more services and/or goods, increase your pay and benefits, and/or hire additional employees. For an employee, this growth could result in raises or promotions.

All companies offer or sell a **product.** A product is what is produced by a company. Products come in the form of goods and services. A **good** is a tangible item, something that you can physically touch. Appliances, toys, or equipment are examples of tangible products. A **service** is an intangible product. Examples of services include haircuts, banking, golf courses, and medical services.

> **Talk It Out**
>
> Identify common money wasters in the workplace.

Who Is the Customer?

A company cannot survive without customers. This makes it extremely important to know who your customers are and how to treat them.

A company has internal and external customers. **Internal customers** are fellow employees and departments that exist within a company. **External customers** are individuals outside of the company. These include vendors, and the individuals or businesses that purchase a company's product. You may have a job where you do not directly interact with the company's external customers. If such is the case, you still have an obligation to serve and treat internal customers as well as the company expects its employees to treat its external customers. Doing so makes it easier for employees who interact with external customers to do so successfully.

Exercise 7-2   Identify Professional Treatment in the Workplace

As a customer, how do you expect to be treated?

_____

_____

How do you expect your co-worker to treat you?

_____

_____

A satisfied customer will make a repeat purchase. Maintaining satisfied customers is one of the best ways to sell your product, because satisfied customers will encourage others to also purchase your product. In contrast, unsatisfied customers will spread the word about their dissatisfaction even faster than satisfied customers spread the word about their satisfaction. Think about how many times you have been satisfied or unsatisfied with a good or service. When others ask you if you know about a particular product, you will tell them whether your experience was favorable or unfavorable. Customer satisfaction is important because unhappy customers will tell others about their bad experiences without anyone asking. Given the increased use of social media to share customer experiences, both favorable and unfavorable experiences can quickly go viral over the Internet through chat sites, social networks, and blogs. No company wants people bad-mouthing it or its product.

To create a satisfied customer, a high-quality product and excellent customer service are necessary. These can exist only with quality employees producing their product with quality materials (inputs). This concept is illustrated in the quality equation found in Figure 7-4.

Figure 7-4

The Quality Equation

Quality Employees + Quality Inputs
= Quality Products = Satisfied, Loyal Customers =
Profits

Quality

When it comes to quality, customer expectations are high. With increased technology and global competition, customers demand high-quality products. Customers expect products to last. They also expect **value,** which means customers believe they are getting a good deal for the price they have paid. Companies that cannot compete on this issue will not experience long-term success.

If your job is to help produce a product, keep in mind that if you do your job well and the product is of high quality, customers will be happy and keep purchasing the product. High-quality products can be produced only if you, as an employee, are doing your job well by taking personal responsibility for your work.

Exercise 7-3   Taking Responsibility for Quality

As an employee, list three ways you can take personal responsibility for quality at work.

1. _____

2. _____

3. _____

Customers measure quality by comparing your company's product to similar products. They also measure quality by how satisfied they are after using a product. Successful companies include performance monitors in their strategies. Performance monitors identify how quality will be measured. Monitors, or standards, may include defect rates, expenses, or sales quotas. Another example of measuring quality is an employee evaluation. The evaluation can identify how an employee's performance contributes to customer quality. Performance monitors assess areas of quality and service that are performed well and those that need improvement. Quality-focused evaluation criteria address areas such as response time, attitude toward customers, and the proper use of resources. An expanded discussion on employee evaluations is presented in chapter 8.

As mentioned earlier in this chapter, the marketing department is responsible for the price, development, distribution, and promotion of a product. Although these functions are the primary responsibility of the marketing department, projecting a positive image and selling the company's product are the jobs of every employee within the organization.

Creativity and Innovation

As our economy becomes increasingly competitive, it is necessary for individuals to enhance their creativity. **Creativity** is coming up with a new and unique good, service, or system. Creativity is achieved when an individual looks at an object or situation differently than its intended use, then identifies a new use or application to that object or situation. Creativity can occur only when an individual is not restrained by traditional thinking. A creative person will always ask, "What if?" instead of being constrained by the barrier of the item or services' original use.

Consider one of America's greatest inventors, Thomas Edison. He developed the phonograph when he was trying to improve the efficiency of the

Web Quiz

Test your customer service skills using the web address below, or find another Internet site with a quiz or article related to customer service.

http://www.donnaearl training.com/Articles/ CustomerServiceQuiz.html

telegraph. Through the creativity of others, the phonograph evolved into a record player, which evolved into a portable music device, which evolved into a mobile communication device that includes a phone, Internet access, and nearly unlimited music storage. If Edison had not developed the phonograph, imagine how life would be without mobile devices.

Employees need to enhance their workplace creativity. This is done by looking at situations differently and by consistently identifying how to improve current systems and/or methods in an effort to improve quality and customer service. Doing so opens doors for new products and increased efficiencies. While creativity is important in the workplace, it is not useful if the new ideas are not acted upon. **Innovation** is the process of turning a creative idea into reality. Continually identify new uses and applications for items and/or situations and then act upon those new ideas. Work on improving your creative and innovative skills in an effort to improve and/or contribute to your company's success.

Excellent Customer Service Defined

An important business concept relating to workplace quality is customer service. **Customer service** is the treatment an employee provides the customer.

Customers expect excellent customer service. They want to be treated with respect and kindness and also expect employees to be competent, dependable, and responsive. Customers expect the business environment to be clean, safe, and organized.

A **competent** employee is an employee who knows the product(s) his or her company offers and is able to answer a customer's question. Customers expect employees to assist them by providing correct information about a product. If you cannot answer a question, direct the customer to another employee who can assist the customer.

Dependable employees are reliable and take responsibility in assisting a customer. Do not pretend to know something when you do not know the answer to a customer's question. Customers expect employees to help them solve their problem. Admit when you do not know an answer. You will gain customer respect when you admit that you do not know all the answers but are willing to find someone who can assist the customer. If there is a situation that requires you to seek assistance from another employee when helping a customer, do not just hand the customer over to the other employee without explaining the situation. Whenever possible, stay with the customer and learn from your coworker so that you will know the answer the next time someone asks.

A **responsive** employee provides a customer personal attention. Being responsive means that you are aware of the customer's need, often before the customer even realizes that need. Some customers like to be left alone to shop for a product but want you near if questions arise. Other customers would like you to guide them step by step when purchasing a product. When a customer approaches your area, make every effort to acknowledge the customer as soon as possible. Greet him or her and ask the customer if he or she needs assistance. Watch the customer's body language. The customer will let you know if he or she wants to be left alone or wants you to stay nearby. Use the customer's name if you know it. Using the customer's name creates a more personal and friendly atmosphere. Customers are different from one another and need to be treated differently according to their needs. Learn how to satisfy these needs. Many companies provide customer service and sales training specific to their industry.

A customer also expects a welcoming, convenient, and safe environment. This includes the appearance of the building, as well as the appearance of the employees. As soon as a customer comes in contact with a business, an opinion is formed about that business. There is only one first impression, so it must be positive. The appearance of the building and/or employees can be the reason a customer visits your company in the first place. Regardless of if you work directly or indirectly with customers, you have an obligation to keep your workplace clean and immediately address potential safety hazards. If there is trash on the floor or a spill of water, clean it up immediately. Take responsibility for keeping your workplace clean and safe. Your attitude, language, and attire are a total package that creates an image of your company that is reflected to its customers.

Talk It Out

What customer body language would indicate a customer needs help, and what body language would indicate a customer wants to be left alone?

The Impact of Customer Service

Know your customers. Good customers will keep returning to purchase your product if you have a high-quality product and make customers feel valued. These customers will tell others about your business. Excellent customer service is the biggest reason customers return. With so many choices and increased competition, the same product can be purchased at many different places. Often, the only thing that keeps customers coming back to your business may be the personal service that you have provided them. Your goal is to build a long-term relationship with customers that will make them loyal to you and your business. This is why so many businesses now keep electronic records of their customers. The more information businesses maintain on their customers, the more they are able to provide personal service. With the increased use of technology, many companies maintain databases of information including past purchases, preferred payment methods, birthdays, special interests, and return/exchange practices. This allows the company to establish a more personal relationship with the customer and anticipate future needs. By connecting with customers through e-mail and various social networking sites, it is common to notify customers of upcoming sales of frequently purchased products, send notification of upcoming events, or disperse discounts and coupons. Customer information and records should be kept confidential and should be used only for business purposes.

When Cory moved to a new neighborhood and wanted to order pizza, Cory found there were many different pizza parlors. The way to determine which one to try was to ask others for a recommendation or randomly try each one. Because Cory was new to the area and did not know many people, Cory called one of the pizza shops. When Cory called, the employee was friendly and sounded happy to assist with the order. Cory automatically formed a good impression about the pizza shop. When Cory went to pick up the pizza, the inside of the shop was clean, as were the employees. The pizza also tasted good. So the next time Cory wanted a pizza, Cory called the same place. Cory was really impressed when an employee at the pizza shop remembered what was previously ordered and called Cory by name. Cory experienced excellent customer service.

The success and profitability of a company depend on how you treat your customers. The happier customers are, the more likely they are to return. A business needs satisfied customers to not only make repeat purchases, but also tell others about their positive experience. As mentioned earlier, unhappy customers will go out of their way to tell others to avoid your business.

Talk It Out

Discuss the difference between a service and customer service.

The Difficult Customer

Customers can sometimes be difficult to deal with. Historically, companies have had the motto "The customer is always right." But, in many instances, the customer may not be right. Although the customer may be wrong, adopt the attitude that the customer is unhappy and do all you can to help the customer solve his or her problem. Have patience and sympathize with the customer.

Many times, a difficult customer will be unfriendly and may even begin yelling at you. If this occurs, stay calm and do not take the customer's inappropriate behavior personally. By remaining calm, you are better able to identify the real problem and logically get the problem solved as quickly as possible in a manner that is fair to both the customer and your company.

In order to successfully resolve a difficult customer's complaint, do the following:

1. *Stay calm, let the customer talk, and listen for facts.* This may mean allowing the customer vent for a few minutes. This is not easy when someone is yelling at you. However, do not interrupt or say, "Please calm down." This will only increase the anger. Pay attention, nod your head, and take notes if it helps you keep focused. As stated earlier, although the person may be yelling at you, do not take the harsh words personally.

2. *Watch body language.* This may include the tone of voice, eye contact, and arm movement. If a customer avoids eye contact, he or she may be lying to you or not fully conveying his or her side of the story. Do not allow a customer to touch you, especially in a threatening manner. If you feel a difficult customer has the potential to become violent or physically abusive, immediately seek assistance.

3. *Acknowledge the customer's frustration.* Say, "I can understand why you are upset." Let the person know you have been listening to his or her concern by paraphrasing what you have understood the problem to be. Do not repeat everything; summarize the concern to ensure an understanding of the situation.

4. *Make sure the problem gets solved.* Whenever possible, take care of the problem yourself. Sending the customer to another person may only fuel the customer's frustration. While it is tempting to call your supervisor or a coworker, stay with him or her until you know the problem is resolved.

5. *Know company policy.* Some difficult customers are dishonest customers and attempt to frazzle employees by intimidation and rude behavior. Know company policies and do not be afraid to enforce them consistently. If a customer challenges a policy, calmly and politely explain the purpose of the policy.

6. *Expect conflict, but do not accept abuse.* Difficult customers are a fact of life. Although customers may occasionally yell, you do not have to take the abuse. If a customer shows aggressiveness or is cursing, politely tell him or her that you cannot help him or her until he or she is able to treat you in a respectable manner. If the customer continues the inappropriate behavior, immediately call a supervisor.

Talk It Out

If a customer is angry with a raised voice, what would you say to that customer?

Workplace Dos and Don'ts

Do read the company mission statement so you remember why the company pays you to come to work each day	*Don't* ignore the company's directional statements and their application to your job
Do know your internal and external customers. Also know what role you play in ensuring quality and how you contribute to your company's success	*Don't* assume that your only customer is outside of the company and that you have no influence on the company's overall success
Do take responsibility for producing and/or providing quality. Be a role model for other employees by eliminating waste and showing constant concern for quality	*Don't* ignore quality by allowing wasted materials, and *don't* allow the bad attitudes of others to negatively affect your performance
Do display competence by knowing your company products and policies	*Don't* lie to customers and make up information you don't know regarding company products and policies
Do make every effort to build a professional relationship with your customers by learning their likes and dislikes	*Don't* become overbearing or intrusive when gathering or recording customer data
Do remain calm when dealing with a difficult customer, and seek assistance immediately if a customer becomes abusive	*Don't* tolerate foul language or violence

Concept Review and Application

Summary of Key Concepts

- Directional statements include the company's mission, vision, and values statements
- The company's strategic plan identifies how a company will secure, utilize, and monitor resources for success
- A company's organizational chart is a graphic display of the major functions and formal lines of authority within an organization

- Major functions (divisions) that are necessary within a business include finance and accounting, human resource management, operations, information systems, marketing, and legal counsel
- Excellent service, quality, and innovation are what will persuade customers to purchase a company's product or service
- Employees should work on improving their creative and innovative skills in an effort to contribute to a company's success
- Customers can be internal customers (other employees) or external customers (individuals outside of your company). A successful company has concern for both internal and external customers
- Employees who provide excellent customer service are competent, dependable, and responsive
- The customer is not always right, but you need to adopt the attitude that if the customer is unhappy, you must do all you can to help the customer solve his or her problem

Key Terms

board of directors	budget	capital budget
chain of command	company resources	competent
creativity	customer service	departments
dependable	directional statements	divisions
employee loyalty	external customer	finance and accounting
goals	good	department
human resource	information systems	innovation
department	department	internal customer
legal counsel	marketing	middle managers
mission statement	objectives	operational budget
operational issues	operations	operations managers
organizational chart	organizational structure	president or chief
product	productivity	executive officer
profit	quality	(CEO)
responsive	senior managers or	service
strategic issues	executive	strategic plan
strategy	supervisor	tactical issues
value	values statement	vision statement

If You Were the Boss

1. You are the supervisor for a team of employees who have a high number of product defects. They also waste materials. You recognize that product defects and wasted materials impact your department's budget. You have told your team to decrease the amount of wasted materials, but your employees do not seem to care. How can you get them to increase their quality and decrease waste?

2. One of your best customers verbally abuses two of your employees every time she visits your store. Your employees have complained to you several times about this customer. What should you do?

Video Case Study: Customer Service Dialog

This video addresses an employee taking a service call from an unhappy customer. To view these videos, visit the Student Resources: Professionalism section in www.mystudentsuccesslab.com. Then answer the following questions:

1. If you were Frank Hallady, what would you have done differently? Explain your answer.
2. If you were the manager, what specific employee training would you implement based upon Mr. Rollins's experience?

Web Links

http://www.inc.com/resources/startup/articles/20050201/missionstatement.html
http://www.smartdraw.com/tutorials/orgcharts/tutorial1.htm
http://www.personnelinsights.com/customer_service_profile.htm

Activities

Activity 7-1

Review the following organizational chart and answer these questions.

1. Whom should Linda go to if there is a question about employee benefits?

   _____

2. Who is Joyce's immediate supervisor?

   _____

3. If Joyce's immediate supervisor is not available, whom should she seek assistance from?

   _____

4. Who is ultimately responsible for creating, pricing, selling, distributing, and promoting the company's product?

   _____

5. What is Brandon's title?

   _____

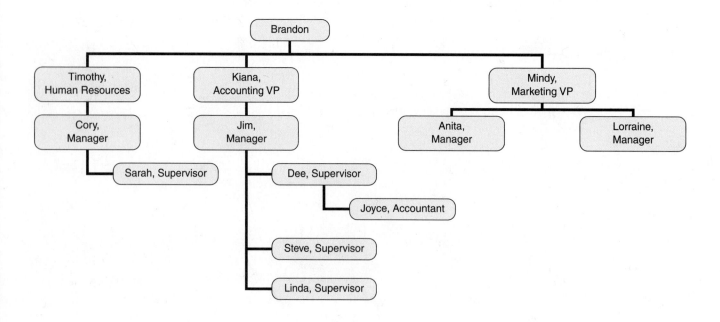

Activity 7-2

How would you measure performance in the following jobs?

Job	Performance Measures
Receptionist	
Customer service clerk	
Forklift driver	
Janitor	
Manager trainee	

Activity 7-3

What could you specifically do to communicate to your coworkers the impact customer service has on performance and profits?

_____

_____

Activity 7-4

When is it appropriate to ask your boss to assist you with a difficult customer?

_____

_____

Activity 7-5

Describe two different times when you received exemplary customer service. Be specific in identifying how employees behaved toward you.

Exemplary Service Act	Behavior Toward You
1.	
2.	

1. A company's _____ is its statement of purpose and identifies why everyone comes to work.

2. The _____ identifies how the company will secure, organize, utilize, and monitor its resources.

3. The _____ department is responsible for the securing, distribution, and growth of the company's financial assets.

4. _____ is a predetermined standard that defines how a product is to be produced or a service is to be provided. Customers demand _____ not just in the product they purchase, but also from company employees.

5. Profit is _____ (money coming in from sales) minus _____ (the costs involved in running the business).

6. A/An _____ is one who buys a service or product.

7. Quality employees + quality inputs = _____ = satisfied, loyal _____ = _____.

8. _____ is when customers believe they received a good deal for the price they paid.

9. _____ is the treatment an employee provides the customer.

10. When dealing with a difficult customer, the first step is to _____, let the _____, and _____ for facts.

Human Resources and Policies

Eighty percent of success is showing up.

Woody Allen (b. 1935)

MyStudentSuccessLab Visit www.mystudentsuccesslab.com for added practice, activities, assessment, and videos.

Objectives

- Identify the primary functions performed by the *human resource department*
- State the primary components of an *employee orientation* program
- Describe the purpose and use of an *employee handbook*
- Explain the concept of *employment-at-will* and *right-to-revise* clauses
- Identify the various types of employment status
- Name the primary types and appropriate use of employee benefits
- Explain the importance and appropriate use of an *open-door policy*

How-Do-You-Rate

	What do you know about employee rights?	True	False
1.	All full-time employees are entitled to at least two weeks' paid vacation.	❏	❏
2.	All full-time employees are entitled to vision and dental benefits.	❏	❏
3.	Employers do not have the legal right to change policies once they are printed in the employee handbook/listed on employer website.	❏	❏
4.	Employers cannot legally fire an employee without two weeks' notice.	❏	❏
5.	Employees cannot legally quit without providing the employer two weeks' notice.	❏	❏

If you answered "true" to two or more of these questions, take this opportunity to learn more about employee and employer rights. Doing so makes you a better employee and future boss.

Human Resource Department

One of the first departments you will interact with at a new job is the **human resource department (HR).** This department is responsible for hiring, training, compensation, benefits, performance evaluations, complaints, promotions, and changes in your work status. Apart from the boss, the human resource department is an employee's primary link to the employer. Being informed and utilizing the resources provided by this department makes you a more productive and valued employee. The purpose of this chapter is to share common resources and policies that exist within the human resource department that assist employees with work-related matters.

Employee Orientation

Typically within the first few days of employment, you will receive an **employee orientation.** This is a meeting where the company's purpose, structure, major policies, procedures, benefits, and other important matters will be explained. You may also be issued company property at this time, including a name badge and keys.

When you studied the concept of quality customer service, you learned that understanding your new company includes knowing the major products the company provides as well as the key people in charge. This is reflected in the company's mission statement and the company's organization chart. During your orientation, pay attention to the names of key executives and their titles, including the company president, CEO, and/or vice presidents. Through the company's materials, its website, or an Internet search, view current photos of these individuals if possible, so that if you ever have the opportunity to meet these executives, you will know who they are.

Begin meeting coworkers and identifying potential mentors. A **mentor** is someone who can help you develop leadership skills, provide support, and help you grow in your career. Mentors also provide the opportunity to improve job skills and increase potential for career advancement. A mentor will help you understand the culture of the company. The **corporate culture** includes the values, expectations, and behaviors of people at work. By understanding a company's corporate culture, you will learn about its politics, its policies, and how people expect you to act on the job.

Finding a mentor can be a formal or informal process. Some companies have formal mentoring programs. In this instance, you will be assigned a mentor who is able to help you succeed on the job. Your mentor may be paid by the company to help you succeed at work. This arrangement allows more time for the mentor to work with you.

If your company does not offer a formal mentoring program, try to establish an informal mentoring relationship with someone within your company who can help you learn about your new job and career. Your mentor should be someone you trust, who knows the company and industry, and who is willing to spend time to help you succeed. You do not have to be employed to have a mentor. If you are not employed, select someone whom you consider a leader, knows your career plans, and works in your targeted industry.

Exercise 8-1 Finding a Mentor

Name at least three qualities you desire in someone you would want to mentor you.

_____

_____

_____

List three individuals you would consider serving as a mentor.

_____

_____

_____

Employee Handbook

After a general overview of the company, you will be given a hard copy of or a web link to the electronic version of the **employee handbook.** The employee handbook outlines an employee's agreement with the employer regarding work conditions, policies, and benefits. Some of these policies are legally required, while others address rules of conduct and/or benefits from the company. Keep this information accessible and use it as a reference for major workplace issues. A representative of the company will review important sections of the handbook with you. Ask questions on topics that you do not fully understand. After the handbook is reviewed, you will usually be asked to sign a statement affirming that you have received the handbook, have read it, and agree to its contents. This is a legal agreement. Therefore, do not sign the statement until you have completely read the handbook and fully understand its contents. Most employers will provide the employee a day or two to return the signed agreement.

During Cory's employee orientation, Cory received the Internet link to the employee handbook. With all new employees present, a representative from the human resource department explained the handbook. Unfortunately, Cory was so overwhelmed with new terms, policies, and signing forms that Cory was not confident that all information was truly understood. After the orientation, Cory placed the orientation paperwork with the Internet link in a drawer at home. About three weeks later, Cory's friends wanted to take a mini-vacation on an upcoming holiday and invited Cory. Cory was not sure the company gave that day as a holiday but remembered that holidays were mentioned in the orientation meeting. Unsure of whom to ask without appearing foolish, Cory suddenly remembered the orientation documents. With the orientation information, Cory easily logged into the corporate website and immediately identified company holidays. Cory was thankful to not have thrown the orientation materials away.

Employment-at-Will and Right to Revise

Legally required in many states, a major policy statement that is usually placed at the beginning of an employee handbook is called **employment-at-will.** Employment-at-will employees are not contractually obligated to work for the company for a specified period. You may quit anytime you want. By the same token, your employer may terminate your employment at any time. This policy applies to any employee who is not hired as a contract employee for a stated period of time. Contract employees literally have contracts outlining the terms, start dates, and end dates of employment.

An employer also has the **right to revise** meaning they can change employment policies. You may be asked to sign separate statements affirming that you understand both the employment-at-will and right-to-revise policies if they are applicable.

There should also be statements in the employee handbook regarding equal employment opportunity and discrimination. These policies state that the company does not discriminate nor allow unlawful harassment of any kind, including sexual harassment, hostile workplace, or hate crimes. Harassment and discrimination are addressed in greater detail in chapters 12 and 15, respectively.

Employment Status

Another important section in most employee handbooks addresses employment status definitions, including the difference between an introductory employee, part-time employee, full-time employee, and temporary employee. These classifications are typically determined by the number of hours worked per week and/or the length of employment with a company.

Web Quiz

Visit the Department of Labor web site and create a four question quiz based upon the topic of your choice found on the FAQs page.

http://www.dol.gov/dolfaq/dolfaq.asp

Part-time employees work fewer than forty hours a week. Depending on your employer, part-time work hours can vary based upon workload. **Full-time employees** work forty or more hours per week. Depending on the position, most entry-level employees who work more than forty hours per week are entitled to overtime pay. **Temporary employees** are hired for only a specified period of time, typically to assist with heavy work periods or to temporarily replace an employee on leave.

For most companies, new employees who are hired for full-time positions are first considered **introductory employees.** Historically, this was called a "probationary period." There will be a period (typically one to three months) in which the employer will evaluate your performance and decide if you should continue as a regular employee. On that same note, you have that period to determine if you want to continue working for the employer. Near the end of this period, you may be given a performance evaluation. If the employer is satisfied with your performance, you become a regular employee and begin receiving benefits and/or other entitlements due to full-time permanent employees. If the employer is not satisfied with your performance, he or she can terminate you without cause. No excuses need to be given. If your performance is not yet acceptable but the employer thinks you demonstrate potential, the introductory period may be extended for one to three additional months.

As a new employee, identify

- Whether your company has an introductory period
- The length of your introductory period
- If and when you become eligible for benefits (if offered)
- Factors that will be used to evaluate job performance

After determining the length of your introductory period, secure a copy of your job description and performance evaluation. A **job description** outlines job duties and responsibilities (i.e., why a company is paying you to come to work). A **performance evaluation** identifies how work performance will be measured. Performance evaluations contain various criteria that measure an employee's daily productivity, efficiency, and behavior. Common factors used to evaluate performance reflect the duties and responsibilities included in a job description. Additionally, your involvement in work-related activities, ongoing education, ability to work with both internal and external customers, and your ability to assume new responsibilities may be reflected in the evaluation. Both your job description and your performance evaluation will assist you in becoming a better employee and in moving from the introductory period into that of a full-time, permanent employee.

> **Talk It Out**
>
> What performance criteria would you use to evaluate a customer-service employee?

How to Behave at Performance Evaluations

As previously mentioned, most employers typically provide performance evaluations immediately after completing an introductory period and once a year thereafter. Although the prospect of someone providing feedback on your performance can be a bit intimidating, this is a time for you to obtain information on how to become a better employee. Performance evaluations provide a time not only for your supervisor to provide feedback on your performance, but also for you to share your desire for additional training and responsibilities. Each employee should receive advance notice of an impending evaluation and performance criteria. Based upon the established criteria, keep a historical record of your past performance. This may include notes and letters from customers, coworkers, and vendors. It may also include personal documentation of events detailing when you displayed excellent judgment and/or behavior. On occasion, a supervisor provides the employee a blank copy of the upcoming evaluation form and asks the employee to complete a self-assessment. Use this opportunity to provide an honest review of your performance. Do not be overly favorable or overly critical in your self-assessment. Be honest. Refer to the evidence and documentation you collected to support your assessment. After you have completed your self-assessment, make a photocopy of your document and return the original to your supervisor.

During your formal evaluation, sit quietly and listen to your supervisor's assessment of your performance. If there is anything regarding your performance that is included in the evaluation that you do not agree with, take notes but do not interrupt your supervisor. Share your concerns only when your supervisor is finished talking or asks for feedback. Support your comments with facts. Even if you do not agree with your supervisor's response after you have presented your evidence, do not argue or challenge your supervisor during the assessment. At the end of each appraisal form is an area for the employee's signature. Immediately under the signature area should be a sentence stating that the employee's signature does not constitute agreement with everything contained in the assessment but only that the employee received an evaluation. If you do not agree with any statement included in your evaluation and the appraisal form does not contain the preceding statement, do not sign the evaluation. If you do not agree with any comments included in your evaluation and the appraisal form does include the statement, sign the evaluation but attach a written response regarding what areas you specifically do not agree with and state why. Provide supporting documentation and evidence to your attached statement. Do not write an emotional response. Make your written response factual and professional and do not verbally attack your supervisor or anyone else. Employers usually allow employees one day to provide a written response. Both your original evaluation and your written response will be forwarded to the human resource department and will become a permanent part of your personnel file. Keep photocopies of your evaluations. They serve as legal documentation of your performance. If your evaluations are favorable, they also serve as excellent reference material for future employers.

Benefits

Most employees relate employee benefits with health care. Fortunately, employee benefits extend well beyond health benefits and vacations. If your company offers paid or discounted benefits, during your orientation you will learn when and if you qualify for benefits. Benefits may be **direct benefits** (monetary) and/or **indirect benefits** (nonmonetary), such as health care and paid vacations. At the time of this book's publication, employers do not have to offer health benefits. They do so as an incentive to attract a qualified workforce. Typically, only full-time, permanent employees are entitled to major benefits. Some employers allow employees to select which benefits best meet their

Chapter 8 Human Resources and Policies   **129**

lifestyle needs. Providing employees their choice of benefits is called a "cafeteria plan." Most benefits become effective immediately, while others may become effective after employees have successfully passed the introductory period. If you are not certain of when your benefits become effective, check with your human resource department.

If you qualify for benefits, you will be given paperwork to complete. Provide accurate information and keep copies of these forms in a secure place for easy reference. Personal medical information is confidential. Not even your boss should have access to this information. The only people within your company who will know your medical information will be those who are administering your health benefits.

While there is pending legislation to make health care a mandatory employee benefit, employers currently offer health benefits as an incentive to attract and keep good employees. Common health-related benefits include medical, vision, and dental insurance. **Medical benefits** include coverage for physician and hospital visits. Physician coverage sometimes includes psychological (therapy), chiropractic (bone alignment/massage), and physical therapy (rehabilitation) services. If you or someone in your family utilizes these services, make sure you understand the coverage and stipulations. Check for emergency room access and coverage, as well as coverage for pharmaceuticals (prescription drugs). **Vision benefits** include care for your eyes. Some plans pay for eyeglasses only, while others pay for contact lenses and/or corrective surgery. Once again, be familiar with your plan and its coverage. **Dental benefits** provide care for your teeth. Check to see how frequently you are allowed to see your dentist for routine checkups. Typically, this is twice a year. Identify if your plan pays for cosmetic dental care such as teeth whitening or braces.

Exercise 8-2   Choosing Benefits

Assume you are in a cafeteria plan and qualify for only four benefits from the following list. Which four would you choose and why?

Chiropractic	Medical	Dental
Vision	Emergency	Company car
Well child care	Day care	Prescriptions
Paid vacation	Life insurance	Retail discounts
Paid holiday	Free parking	Personal days
Paid training	Tuition reimbursement	Mobile communication devices
Family medical	Bonuses	Flexible scheduling

Benefit	Why This Benefit Is Important to You
1.	
2.	
3.	
4.	

Most people utilize health benefits only when faced with an obvious health issue. While it is easy to ignore routine checkups, it is in your best interest to practice preventive care. As soon as you become eligible for benefits, schedule an appointment with a physician for a routine physical. Get your vision checked, and see your dentist. This is important not only for preventive purposes, but also for establishing relationships with medical professionals. Take advantage of the benefits for which you are eligible, because both you and your employer are paying for them. Finally, this may be a good time to evaluate personal health habits. If you need to shed a few pounds or eliminate a poor habit such as smoking or drinking, now is a good time to change your behavior.

Employers may provide you several choices for health policies. Few if any policies pay 100 percent of health expenses. Employees typically pay a copayment, or small percentage of the total fee. Many health insurance programs provide a list of medical professionals and health facilities that accept their insurance. Any time you do not use one of these preferred providers, the health insurance will not pay for your care, or it will pay only a percentage of the total. You are responsible for the rest of your bill. When selecting a health program, carefully review the list of providers and facilities for familiarity and convenience. Check emergency access, well child care, preventive care, or any other medical care you may need now or in the future.

Talk It Out

Identify health concerns and how they affect the workplace.

Exercise 8-3 Health Care Considerations

What are important considerations when selecting health care providers for you and your dependents?

Provider	Major Considerations
Physician	
Hospital	
Dentist	
Eye Doctor	
Pharmaceuticals	

As your benefits are being explained in detail, identify who else in your family may be entitled to these benefits. Frequently, benefits are available to an employee's spouse/partner and/or children. You may have to pay a bit more if you add people to your coverage, but it may be worth the extra cost. As health-care costs continue to increase, you and your family need security and access to quality health care.

Ask if your company offers a **retirement plan.** This is a savings plan for when you retire. If your company offers a retirement plan, join it and start saving. By having funds automatically deducted from your earnings prior to receiving your paycheck, you will most likely not miss the money. Many company-sponsored retirement savings plans are tax deferred, which means you do not pay taxes on these funds until you retire. This provides an added incentive to begin planning for your future.

Payroll, paydays, accrued vacation, and sick days or sick leave are terms used to discuss monetary benefits. Your employee handbook identifies when you are paid. Typically, payday is every two weeks or on the fifteenth and last day of each month. Employees have the option of receiving payment by a traditional paycheck or by having wages electronically deposited into a bank account. A traditional paycheck is in two parts. One part is the actual check, and the second part of your paycheck is called a pay stub. If you have funds transferred electronically to your bank account, you will receive only a pay stub. This pay stub contains information including hours worked, total pay, taxes paid, and any other deductions that were taken from your paycheck. Any money taken from your original earnings is documented on your pay stub. Keep payroll stubs in a file for tax purposes and future reference. The Internal Revenue Service (IRS) recommends you keep these records on file for three years.

Identify what vacations and holidays your new employer provides. Though not required to do so, some employers pay extra wages for working on a holiday. Identify how many days of vacation you will receive and when they will become available to you. Some companies also provide a personal day. This is one day that an employee can take off without explanation. However, when you take a personal day, provide your employer ample notice prior to taking this time off. Information regarding vacations and holidays should be clearly communicated in the employee handbook or on the company website. If it is not, obtain this information from either your supervisor or the human resource department.

Cory's best friend has a family cabin and invited Cory to spend a long weekend at the lake. Unfortunately, Cory had been on the job for only two months and had not accumulated any vacation time. Cory really wanted to go to the cabin. Cory remembered that the company provides sick leave and one personal day a year. Having been on the job for such a short period of time, Cory wondered if it would be okay to either call in sick or take a personal day. After some thought, Cory realized that it would be unethical to lie by calling in sick. Cory also thought it would not be responsible to take a personal day so early on the job. As a result, Cory called the friend and suggested that perhaps they could meet up at the cabin later in the year. As difficult as Cory's decision was, Cory valued the new job and did not want to do anything to risk losing credibility at work.

If you have a family, are planning a family, or care for an elderly or terminally ill family member, identify company policies regarding pregnancy and family leave. There are laws to protect you from pregnancy discrimination and/or provide relief in these situations. Some employers even provide additional benefits beyond those required by law.

Open-Door Policy

An **open-door policy** is a common practice for managers to communicate that they are available to listen to employees' ideas or concerns. Think of this policy as more of a "we're here to listen and help" policy. The purpose of an open-door policy is to communicate to employees that management and the human resource department is available to listen should the employee need to discuss a workplace concern. As will be discussed in chapter 12, the easiest way to deal with conflict is immediately, openly, and honestly. Dealing with conflict will help keep problems from becoming larger or reoccurring. Do not be afraid to speak with your supervisor or the human resource department regarding any workplace issue that causes you concern.

Unions

Depending on the size and nature of your company's business, you may have the opportunity to join a union. A **union** is an organization whose purpose is to protect the rights of employees. This organization is a third party that represents you and your colleagues' interests to your employer. Unions negotiate on behalf of employees and typically negotiate fair salaries, better benefits, and improved working conditions. This comes with a cost. Employees pay a fee to a union for this representation. As a union member, you are trusting that the union will act in your best interests. Employees have the right to unionize (become members of a union), and they also have the right to choose not to join a union. However, depending on the union contract, employees who choose not to be a union member may still have to pay dues. Union membership is only for non-management employees.

If your company's employees are represented by a union, the union will contact you and invite you to become a member when you begin employment. Employees who are covered by the union must abide by the union contract. The **union contract** is a document that states the rights of employees. The union contract and the employee handbook are equally important documents. The union contract addresses specific work-related issues that your employer and the union agree upon. These issues include work schedules, benefits, pay, performance measures, and a grievance procedure. A grievance is a formal complaint filed by the union when the union contract is not being enforced. Take time to carefully read the contract and keep it in a place where you can easily use it for later reference. Know the names of and how to contact union officials who can assist you with work-related issues.

Your primary union contact will be the shop steward or union representative. This individual is an employee of your company but has agreed to serve as a primary contact between company employees and the union. The shop steward or union representative knows the union contract in great detail and will make every effort to assist you with a work-related issue. Do not hesitate to contact the shop steward or union representative.

Once a new contract is presented, union members vote on approving the contract. It is imperative that you exercise your right to vote on a new contract or any union-related issue. The union contract dictates work rules, benefits, and other issues important to your work environment. Take an active role in knowing what services are available to you through the union, the names of union officials who can assist you, and what value and services the union provides through its representation.

Workplace Dos and Don'ts

Do read and keep your employee handbook for future reference	*Don't* ask your boss questions if you have not already referred to your employee handbook
Do utilize the employee handbook to identify paydays and company holidays	*Don't* demonstrate poor planning and be unaware of important days at work
Do maintain documentation for your performance evaluations	*Don't* interrupt during a performance evaluation
Do ask for clarification if you have questions regarding appropriate dress in the workplace	*Don't* dress in a manner that brings attention to you or does not professionally represent your company
Do immediately speak with your boss if there is a conflict regarding your work	*Don't* wait until a workplace issue gets out of control to share your concerns with your boss

Concept Review and Application

Summary of Key Concepts

- The human resource department is responsible for hiring, training, compensation, benefits, performance evaluations, complaints, promotions, and changes in your work status
- An employee orientation is the time to learn all about a company, its major policies, and employee services
- The employee handbook is an important document that outlines an employee's agreement with his or her employer regarding work conditions, policies, and benefits
- Employee benefits may include direct (monetary) benefits and indirect (nonmonetary) benefits such as health care and paid vacations
- Be aware of and take advantage of benefits that are available to you
- Be aware of paydays, paid holidays, and sick leave policies
- Unions are designed to protect the rights of employees

Key Terms

corporate culture
employee handbook
full-time employee
introductory
   employee
open-door policy
retirement plan
temporary
   employee

dental benefits
employment-at-will
human resource
   department
medical benefits
part-time employee
right to revise
union
vision benefits

direct benefits
employee orientation
indirect benefits
job description
mentor
performance
   evaluation
union contract

If You Were the Boss

1. How should you handle an employee who keeps coming to you asking for information regarding major policies, vacations, and benefits?
2. How can a boss consistently communicate an open-door policy?

Video Case Study: Performance Evaluations

This video addresses how to behave during performance evaluations. To view these videos, visit the Student Resources: Professionalism section in www.mystudentsuccesslab.com. Then answer the following questions:

1. What advice would you give Patricia regarding her behavior and conversation with Karen?
2. What can Patricia do in the future to improve her performance?
3. Did Karen handle the situation appropriately? Why or why not?
4. Was Regina's response appropriate? Why or why not?

Web Links

http://www.dol.gov/ebsa/publications/10working4you.html
http://www.ehow.com/how_138961_choose-health-insurance.html

Activities

Activity 8-1

Identify and discuss three typical areas that employers consider in performance evaluations.

1. _____

2. _____

3. _____

Activity 8-2

Using the information from Exercise 8-2, Health Care Considerations, assume you are now eligible for health benefits and must choose specific health care providers. Identify a local physician, eye doctor, dentist, and hospital that you would utilize. Why did you select these providers? How did you go about selecting them?

	Name	Why Selected	How Selected
Physician			
Eye doctor			
Dentist			
Hospital			

Sample Exam Questions

1. During a/an _____, the company's purpose, structure, major policies, procedures, benefits, and other important matters are explained.

2. Many companies offer _____ savings plans that are tax deferred for use at a later date.

3. A paycheck has two parts: the _____ and the _____.

4. What you wear to work should never pose a _____.

5. A/an _____ communicates to employees that management and the human resource department are always available to listen should the employee have a concern or complaint.

6. _____ exist to protect the rights of employees.

Communication

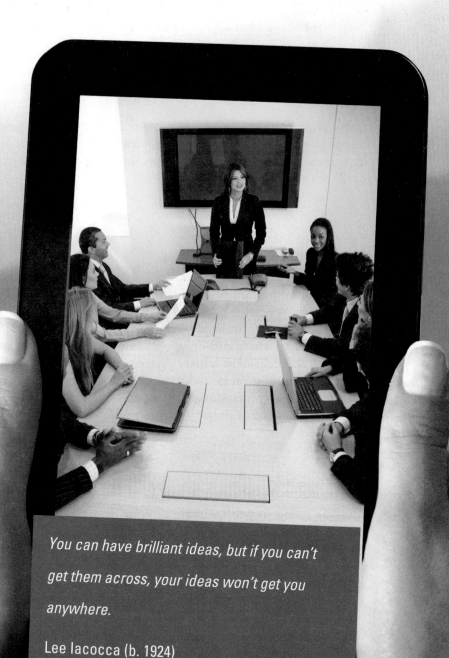

You can have brilliant ideas, but if you can't get them across, your ideas won't get you anywhere.

Lee Iacocca (b. 1924)

Objectives

- Define the impact effective *communication* has in the workplace
- Name the key elements of the communication process
- Name the three types of communication media
- Describe the dangers of becoming emotional at work
- Demonstrate proper formatting for *business letters* and *memos*
- Demonstrate basic telecommunication etiquette

How-Do-You-Rate

	Have you mastered workplace communication?	Yes	No
1.	I do not use foul language.	❑	❑
2.	I respect people's personal space.	❑	❑
3.	I do not allow emotions to influence my communication.	❑	❑
4.	I believe I am a good listener.	❑	❑
5.	When appropriate, I send handwritten notes to coworkers.	❑	❑

If you answered "yes" to four or more of these questions, you are well on your way to mastering workplace communication. Communication success begins by presenting your message in a professional manner and focusing on the needs of the receiver.

Communication at Work

Meetings, e-mails, texts, presentations, and informal discussions in the hallway play an important role in business and require proper attention and protocol. Employees who have a basic understanding of how to effectively and appropriately communicate in the workplace are at a significant advantage. Knowing what, when, and how to communicate creates a positive impression on others and helps you achieve your objective. Effective professional and electronic communication is vital to workplace success. This chapter presents the fundamentals of professional communication, while chapter 10 will focus on the appropriate use of electronic communication tools, practices, and protocol.

Workplace Communication and Its Channels

Imagine going to work, sitting at your desk, and for one day sending and receiving no communication. If there were no face-to-face contact, no phones, no e-mails, no text messages, no meetings, and no memos to receive or write, business would come to a complete standstill. Even if you are talented at your job, if you cannot communicate with others, you will not succeed, much less keep a job. This chapter discusses the process and importance of effective communication in the workplace and provides information on how to improve workplace communication skills.

At work, you have an obligation to share appropriate, timely, and accurate information with your boss, your coworkers, and your customers. Improving communication skills is an ongoing process. As explained in chapter 5, information is power. In regard to workplace communication, your goal is to be known as an overcommunicator.

While eating lunch with employees from other departments, Cory listened to others complain about how their bosses did such a poor job communicating with them. The employees complained that they never knew what was going on within the company. Cory had no reason to complain, because Cory has a manager who makes every effort to share whatever information he knows within the department. After each managers' meeting, Cory receives an e-mail outlining major topics that were discussed. During Cory's department meeting, Cory's manager reviews the information a second time and asks his employees if there are any additional questions. Cory appreciates the fact that the manager enjoys and values communicating important information with his employees.

In the workplace, there are two primary communication channels: formal and informal. Whether it is formal or informal communication, you have a professional obligation to share timely and relevant information with the appropriate people. **Formal communication** occurs through the formal (official) lines of authority. This includes communication within your immediate department, division, or throughout the company. Formal communication occurs either vertically or horizontally within an organization. Formal vertical communication flows down an organizational structure (via written correspondence, policies/procedures, and directives and announcements from management) or flows up an organizational structure (most commonly through reports, budgets, and requests). Formal horizontal communication occurs among individuals or departments at the same or close organizational levels.

The second type of communication channel is informal. **Informal communication** occurs among individuals without regard to the formal lines of authority. For example, while eating lunch with friends, you may learn of a new policy. A major element of the informal communication network is called the **grapevine.** The grapevine is an informal network where employees discuss workplace issues of importance. Although the grapevine is an informal source of communication, it usually is not 100 percent accurate. While it is important to know about current events at work, do not contribute negative or inaccurate information to the grapevine. Do not make assumptions if the information is incomplete. If you are aware of the facts, clarify the information. If someone shares information that is harmful to the company or is particularly disturbing to you, you have a responsibility to approach your boss and ask him or her to verify the rumor.

When the grapevine is targeting individuals and their personal lives, it is called **gossip.** Gossip is personal information about individuals that is hurtful and inappropriate. Any time you contribute to negative conversation, you lose credibility with others. Spreading gossip reflects immaturity and unprofessional behavior. Should someone begin sharing gossip with you, politely interrupt and clarify the misinformation when necessary. Tell the individual that you do not want to hear gossip and/or transition the conversation to a more positive subject. You have a right to defend your coworkers from slander (individuals bad-mouthing others), just as you would expect coworkers to defend you. After a while, your colleagues will learn that you do not tolerate gossip at work and they will reconsider approaching you with gossip.

Refrain from speaking poorly of your coworkers and boss. As a result of human nature, you may not enjoy working with all of your colleagues and bosses. You do not have to like everyone at work, but everyone needs to be treated with respect. Even if someone speaks poorly of you, do not reciprocate the bad behavior. It only displays immaturity on your part and communicates distrust to your colleagues.

The Communication Process

Communication is the process of a sender transmitting a message to a receiver with the purpose of creating mutual understanding. As simple as this definition is, a lot of barriers hinder the process of creating mutual understanding and successful communication. Communication is important for maintaining good human relations. Without basic communication skills, processes break down and an organization may collapse. This is why you need to know and understand the communication process (see Figure 9-1).

Communication begins with a **sender** wanting to convey a message. The sender must identify what message needs to be sent and how best to transmit this message. The sender has several options for sending the message. The message can be sent verbally, in written form, or nonverbally. Identifying the message and how it will be sent is called **encoding.**

Once the sender encodes the message, the message is sent to a receiver. **Decoding** is when the receiver interprets the message. The receiver then sends **feedback** on the sender's message based upon the receiver's interpretation of the original message.

Several barriers may cause the communication process to break down. The first barrier to overcome is clearly identifying the message to be sent. Once the message is identified, the sender needs to determine how best to send (encode) the message in a manner that will be properly interpreted (decoded) by the receiver. If the sender is not a strong communicator, his or her verbal, written, or nonverbal communication may be misinterpreted by the receiver because the message was doomed before it was even sent. The receiver contributes to the communication breakdown if he or she incorrectly interprets the message.

Another barrier to effective communication is **noise.** Noise is anything that interrupts or interferes with the communication process. The noise can be audible (you can actually hear it with your ears), or the noise can occur through

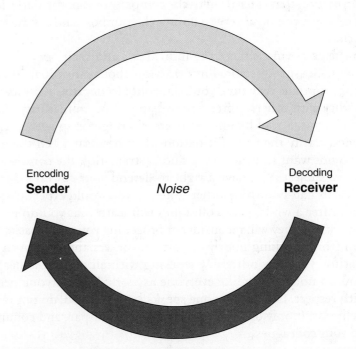

Encoding
Sender
Noise
Decoding
Receiver

Figure 9-1

Communication
Process

other means, such as visual, mental, touch, or smell. Noise may also include emotions such as hurt, anger, joy, sadness, or surprise.

A supervisor in another department really irritates Cory. Cory has never shared this annoyance with anyone. One day, Cory was asked to attend a meeting led by the irritating supervisor. As Cory sat in the meeting, Cory had a hard time focusing on the message. Cory's mind was wandering through mental noise. At the end of the meeting, Cory was embarrassed that there were no notes to share. Dislike for the irritating supervisor affected Cory's ability to listen and be a good receiver. Cory learned a hard lesson that day and made a commitment to be open to every communication, regardless of liking or disliking the sender.

Communication can be complete only if all of the components of the communication process work together to effectively send the message as they are intended to be sent. In order for this to occur, the sender must choose the right medium and overcome noise. The receiver must then be willing to accept the message and provide feedback to acknowledge that the message has been received correctly.

As previously stated, a key element of effective communication is the communication medium (how the message will be sent). Communication media include verbal, nonverbal, and written communication. Let us further explore these three types of communication media.

Web Quiz

Use the web link below, or find another online quiz to identify if you are an effective communicator.

http://ezinearticles.com/? Communication-Quiz:— Are-You-a-Great-Communi- cator? & id = 32908

Verbal Communication and Listening

Verbal communication is the process of using words to send a message. The words you select are extremely important. If you use only basic words in your communications, you may appear uneducated or inexperienced. In contrast, if you use a highly developed vocabulary, you may appear intimidating or arrogant. If others do not know the definitions of the words you are using, they will most likely not ask for clarification for fear of appearing ignorant. Therefore, your intended message will fail. When selecting words for your message, identify whether these words are appropriate or if the words can be misinterpreted. Use proper English and grammar. Be as clear as possible in your intent and how you verbally convey your message. When people are nervous or excited, they frequently speak at a rapid pace. When you increase the speed of your speech, you increase the probability that your message will be misinterpreted. Your tone of voice also conveys or creates images. It adds to others' perception of you, which either enforces or detracts from your message.

Successful verbal communication involves listening. **Listening** is the act of hearing attentively. Learn to stop and listen. Too frequently, a person will have so much to say that he or she does not stop to provide the receiver time to respond. The receiver's response is the only way a sender can verify that a message has been properly received. Listening occurs not only with our ears, but also through our nonverbal responses. The three primary levels of listening are active listing, passive listening, and not listening at all. **Active listening** is when the receiver provides full attention to the sender without distraction. When the listener focuses his or her attention on the sender, an active listener will provide frequent positive feedback to the sender through nonverbal gestures such as nodding, eye contact, or other favorable body language. Favorable verbal feedback may also include rephrasing the message to ensure or clarify

Talk It Out

In what situations is it easy to be in "nonlistening" mode? What can an individual do to improve his or her listening skills in such a situation?

understanding. With **passive listening,** the receiver is selectively hearing parts of the message and is more focused on responding to what is being said instead of truly listening to the entire message being sent. Passive listening is sometimes called conversational listening. In today's society, we have so many inputs trying to attract our attention. As a result, we often get anxious to share our point of view in a conversation and fail to allow others in the conversation to complete their sentences by interrupting the sender. Interrupting is rude and disrespectful. Show others respect by not interrupting conversations. If you accidentally interrupt someone, immediately apologize and ask him or her to continue his or her statement. When a receiver fails to make any effort to hear or understand the sender's message, he or she is in the **nonlistening** mode and is allowing emotions, noise, or preconceptions to impede communication. Sometimes it is obvious the listener is not listening, because he or she either responds inappropriately or does not respond at all. While the ideal is to consistently be an active listener, we know this is not always possible. However, every effort should be made to strive toward active listening.

Silence is also an effective tool used in communication. Silence often makes individuals uncomfortable because our society is used to filling up silence with (sometimes useless) noise. Active listeners need time to digest what is being said and time to formulate a thoughtful response. Active listeners should wait at least three to five seconds before responding. At first, this may feel awkward, but you will quickly discover that you are becoming a better communicator because you are taking time to respond appropriately. Recognize that there are times when it is appropriate to not speak. In chapter 12 we will discuss how silence is also a powerful tool when dealing with both conflict and negotiation. As discussed in chapter 4, recognize and respect cultural differences in verbal communication in regard to word use and meaning.

Nonverbal Communication

Nonverbal communication is what you communicate through body language. Even without uttering a word, you can still send a very strong message. Body language includes eye contact, facial expressions, tone of voice, and the positioning of your body. Nonverbal communication also includes the use of silence and space.

An obvious form of body language is eye contact. When you look someone in the eye, you are generally communicating honesty and sincerity. At other times, looking someone in the eye and coupling that look with a harsh tone of voice and an unfriendly facial expression may imply intimidation. In the United States, those who fail to look someone in the eye risk conveying to their receiver that they are not confident or, worse, are being dishonest. Make eye contact with your audience (individual or group), but do not stare. Staring is considered rude and intimidating. Actively work at making appropriate eye contact with your receiver. If your direct eye contact is making the receiver uncomfortable, he or she will look away. Be aware of his or her response and adapt your behavior appropriately.

Eye contact is part of the larger communication package of a facial expression. A receiver will find it difficult to interpret your eye contact as sincere and friendly when your message is accompanied by a frown. A smile has immense power and value. On the other hand, make sure you don't smile when listening to someone who is angry or upset. He or she may misinterpret your smile as condescending or as laughing at their distress. As explained previously, when actively listening, a nod implies that you are listening or agreeing with a sender's message. Even the positioning of your head can convey disagreement, confusion, or attentiveness.

Another element of nonverbal communication is the use and positioning of your body. Having your arms crossed in front of your body may be interpreted in several ways. You could be physically cold, angry, or uninterested. When you are not physically cold, having your arms crossed implies that you are creating a barrier between yourself and the other person. To eliminate any miscommunication, it is best to have your arms at your sides. Do not hide your hands in your pockets. In speaking with others, be aware of the positioning of your arms and those of your audience. Also, be aware of the positioning of your entire body. Turn your body toward those to whom you are speaking. It is considered rude to turn your back to or ignore someone when he or she is speaking. In this case, you are using your entire body to create a barrier. Avoid this type of rude behavior. This only communicates immaturity on your part.

Exercise 9-1   Body Language

With a partner, take turns communicating the following emotions through body language.

Emotion	Signal
1. Concern	
2. Distrust	
3. Eagerness	
4. Boredom	
5. Self-importance	

The use of your hands is extremely important in effective communication. Through varied positioning, you can use your hands to nonverbally ask someone to stop a behavior, be quiet, or reprimand him or her. Be aware of the positioning of your hands and fingers. In the United States, it is considered rude to point at someone with one finger. Many finger and hand gestures commonly used in the United States are quite offensive in other countries. If you have nervous gestures such as popping your knuckles, biting your nails, or continually tapping your fingers, take steps to eliminate these habits.

Apart from a professional handshake, touching another person at work is not acceptable. People in our society frequently place a hand on another's shoulder as a show of support. However, others could interpret that hand on the shoulder as a threat or sexual advance. Therefore, keep your hands to yourself.

Proxemics is the study of distance (space) between individuals and is also an important factor in body language. An individual's personal space is about one and one-half feet around him or her. The appropriate social space is four feet from an individual. Standing too close may be interpreted as intimidation or may imply intimacy. Neither is appropriate for the workplace. However, distancing yourself too far from someone may imply your unwillingness to communicate. Be aware of the space you allow between you and your receiver.

Another element that affects nonverbal communication is emotion. Make every attempt to not become emotional at work. However, reality may cause you to express emotions that oftentimes cannot be controlled. Try to control your emotions in public. If you feel you are beginning to cry or have an outburst of anger, excuse yourself. Find a private area and deal with your emotion. If you are crying or distraught, splash water on your face and regain control of your emotions. If you are getting angry, assess why you are angry, control your anger, and then create a strategy to regain control of how best to handle the situation in a professional manner. Any overt display of anger in the workplace is inappropriate, can damage workplace relationships, and could potentially jeopardize your job. When you become emotional at work, you lose your ability to logically deal with situations and risk losing your credibility and the trust of others. Practice effective stress management and think before you respond. Finally, recall our earlier discussion on the appropriate use of silence. Silence is perhaps one of the most important communication tools you have. Silence communicates to your audience that you are listening and are allowing the other party consideration. Not immediately responding to a message provides the sender time to clarify or rephrase a message.

There are many variables involved in effective nonverbal communication. Interpret body language within its entire context. For example, if you are communicating with a colleague with whom you have a positive working relationship and your coworker crosses his or her arms, your coworker is most likely cold. Consider the entire package: environment, relationship, and situation.

Written Communication

Writing is an important element of effective workplace communication. **Written communication** is a form of business communication that is printed, handwritten, or sent electronically. Because the receiver of your message will not have verbal and nonverbal assistance in interpreting your written message, take great care to ensure that the correct message is being communicated. You are normally not present when a written message is received; therefore, the receiver will be drawing additional conclusions about you based upon the grammar, vocabulary, and presentation used in your written communication.

As you advance in responsibility within an organization, you will be required to conduct an increasing amount of written communication, including formal business letters, memos, and e-mail messages. You may also have the opportunity to communicate through instant messaging, texting, blogs, or wikis, discussed more in chapter 10. Written business correspondence represents not only your professionalism and intelligence, but also your organizational abilities. Consistently present written correspondence in a professional manner. Make all written communication error-free by proofreading the message prior to sending. Choose words that clearly and concisely communicate your message. The three most common forms of written communication in the workplace are letters, memos, and electronic messages. Written communication in a professional workplace should be keyboarded and not handwritten. An exception to this rule is when you are sending a handwritten note conveying a personal message.

Plan your message for successful written communication. Identify what you want to communicate, to whom you need to communicate, and what desired action you want the reader to take after reading your message. After you have determined what you want to communicate, write a draft message that is free of negative emotion. Written communication should begin with a professional greeting and end with a complimentary closing. If the purpose of your correspondence is to address a negative situation (e.g., complaint), begin with a positive note and then factually address the situation, but do not negatively attack an individual. With all written forms of communication, do not send or write any message conveying anger. A good rule of thumb is to always put good news in writing and be cautious when sending negative information in writing. Put negative information in writing only when necessary.

After you have drafted your message and eliminated negative emotions, review your correspondence and delete unnecessary words. Keep written correspondence short and simple. Do not be wordy, and minimize personalization words (*I, my*) as much as possible. Well-written correspondence not only communicates a core message, but also clearly communicates how the sender wants the reader to respond to the communication. Include contact information and a deadline in your written communication if relevant.

Keep the correspondence simple. Identify and use words that project a more professional image. Know the definitions of the words you are using, and use these words appropriately. A thesaurus is an excellent tool to expand one's vocabulary. When utilizing a thesaurus, do not overdo it, and use words in the correct context.

After you have finished writing your message, identify who should receive the message. Share your correspondence only with individuals who need to know the information. However, make sure you have shared the information with individuals whom the correspondence affects. The remainder of this chapter focuses on common written business correspondence, including a business letter, a memo, and a handwritten note. Chapter 10 addresses written communication that occurs through electronic technologies, including e-mail, texting, instant messaging, blogging, and wikis.

The Business Letter

A **business letter** is a formal, written form of communication used when your message is being sent to an individual outside of your organization. External audiences may include customers, vendors, suppliers, or members of the community. While it is still common for formal business letters to be sent through traditional mail, with reliance on electronic communication, many businesses now send formal business letters as e-mail attachments. Letters are to be written in proper business format. Clearly communicate your message and expected follow-up activity to the receiver in a professional and concise manner. Letters sent should be error-free. Proofread, sign, and date the letter before mailing.

Business letters are written on company letterhead. Company **letterhead** is paper that has the company logo and contact information imprinted on quality paper. Companies will have a template of its letterhead for letters sent electronically. Figure 9-2 shows the correct business letter format. Figure 9-3 provides an example of a business letter. Please note that a business letter can have various styles, and an employee should follow the company-preferred style.

If a business letter is not being sent electronically, most companies have matching mailing envelopes that accompany the letterhead. Address the envelope with the same information that is in the inside address. The letter should be folded properly. Fold the letter in thirds, starting at the bottom and folding up one-third of the way. Then fold the top over the bottom and place it in the envelope with the opening on top. Number 10 envelopes are normally used for business letters.

(Do not type QS and DS, these are shown for correct spacing.)	
Since most business letters will be on letterhead (preprinted business address), you need about a two-inch top margin before entering the current *date*.	August 1, 2015
	QS (4 enters or returns)
The *inside address* should include the title, first and, last name of receiver.	Ms. Suzie Student Word Processing Fun 42 Learn Avenue Fresno, CA 93225
	DS (2 enters or returns)
The *salutation* should have title and last name only.	Dear Ms. Student: *DS*
	The first paragraph of a letter should state the reason for the letter. If you had any previous contact with the receiver, mention it in this paragraph. *DS*
For the *body,* all lines begin at the left margin. Use a colon after the salutation and a comma after the complementary closing.	The second (and possibly a third) paragraph should contain details. All information needing to be communicated should be included here. *DS*
	The last paragraph is used to close the letter. Add information that is needed to clarify anything you said in the letter. Also, add any follow-up or contact information. *DS*
Keep the *closing* simple.	Sincerely, *QS*
	Sarah S. Quirrel
The writer's first and last name should be four enters or returns after the closing to give the *writer* room to sign (remember to have the writer sign).	Sarah S. Quirrel Instructor *DS*
Typist's initials *Enclosure* is used only if you add something in the envelope with the letter.	bt Enclosure

Figure 9-2

Letter Format

August 1, 2015

Ms. Suzie Student
Word Processing Fun
42 Learn Avenue
Fresno, CA 93225

Dear Ms. Student:

It was a pleasure speaking with you over the telephone earlier today. I am delighted that you have agreed to serve as a guest speaker in my Communications class. The purpose of this letter is to confirm the details of the upcoming speaking engagement.

As I mentioned in our conversation, the date for your scheduled lecture is Wednesday, October 14, 2015. The class meets from 6:00 p.m.–8:30 p.m. You may take as much time as you need, but if possible please allow a student question and answer period. There are approximately sixty students, and the classroom contains state-of-the-art technology. If you have specific technology requests, do not hesitate to contact me. Enclosed is a parking permit and map of the campus directing you to the appropriate classroom.

Once again, thank you for continued support of our students. I and my students are looking forward to you sharing your communications insight and expertise with us on October 14. If you have any additional information, please do not hesitate to contact me via e-mail at S.Quirrel@teaching.com or call me at 123-456-7890.

Sincerely,

Sarah S. Quirrel

Sarah S. Quirrel
Instructor

bt
Enclosure

Figure 9-3

Letter Example

The Business Memo

Business memos (sometimes called interoffice memorandums) are used internally—that is, when the written communication is being sent to a receiver within an organization. While e-mail is the most common form of internal communication, a traditional business memorandum is still used for internal formal documentation and announcements. A memo includes the receiver's name, sender's name, date, and subject. As with a business letter, include all facts needed to properly communicate the message, but be brief and to the point. Ideally, memos should be no longer than one page. Most word processing software has templates for creating memos. Figures 9-4 and 9-5 illustrate one way to format and write a business memo if you are not using a template. As with business letters, many companies have a preferred memo style. Check with your employer to ensure you are utilizing the proper format. An enhanced discussion on business e-mail is presented in chapter 10.

(Do not type DS, these are shown for correct spacing.)	
Start the memo two inches from the top of the page.	**MEMO TO:** Loretta Howerton, Office Manager *DS* **FROM:** Lawrence Schmidt, OA/CIS Trainer *DS*
Double-space after each *heading*. Bold and capitalize only headings, not the information.	**DATE:** January 6, 2015 *DS*
Use initial caps in the *subject line*.	**SUBJECT:** Memo Format for Internal Correspondence *DS*
Body—single-space, no tabs, left align. Double-space between paragraphs.	A memorandum is an internal communication that is sent within the organization. It is often the means by which managers correspond with employees, and vice versa. Memos provide written records of announcements, requests for action, and policies and procedures.Use first and last names and include the job title. *DS* Templates, or preformatted forms, often are used for creating memos. Templates provide a uniform look for company correspondence and save the employee the time of having to design a memo. Word processing software has memo templates that can be customized. Customize the template so it has the company name and your department name at the top. Make sure you change the date format (month, day, year). It should be as it is seen at the beginning of this memo. *DS*
Reference initials (typist's initials) *Attachment notation*, only if needed (if you attach something)	bt Attachment

Figure 9-4

Memo Format

MEMO TO: Loretta Howerton, Office Manager

FROM: Lawrence Schmidt, OA/CIS Trainer

DATE: January 6, 2015

SUBJECT: Accounting Department Computer Training

This memo is to confirm that the computer training for the accounting department will occur on February 1, 2015 in the large conference room. Although the training is scheduled from 9:00 a.m.–11:30 a.m., I have reserved the room for the entire morning, beginning at 7:00 a.m.

As we discussed last week, this may be a good opportunity to offer breakfast to the department prior to the training. If this is something you would like to pursue, please let me know by next Tuesday, and I will make the proper arrangements. Thank you again for the opportunity to provide computer training to your team.

bt

Figure 9-5

Memo Example

Handwritten Notes

A handwritten note is a personal form of communication. In a professional workplace, it is appropriate to send a handwritten note to acknowledge special events in careers or personal lives (e.g., promotion, birthday, or birth of a child). It is also acceptable to send a handwritten note to encourage a colleague or offer condolences for the loss of a loved one. A common purpose for a handwritten note is when you are writing a note of thanks. Handwritten notes are written in pen, on a note card. However, it is also acceptable to acknowledge an occasion with an appropriate greeting card. In some situations it is acceptable to send an electronic thank-you or personal message. Handwritten notes do not need to be lengthy; generally, just a few sentences are sufficient. Acknowledge or encourage coworkers, bosses, and others with whom you work by sending handwritten notes when appropriate.

As mentioned in chapter 4, a thank-you note is a powerful tool for building relationships. When you express thanks, individuals are more likely to continue performing kind acts for you. Send a thank-you note when someone does something for you that takes more than five minutes or when someone gives you a gift. Deliver the note as soon as possible. Figure 9-6 shows the correct format and key elements of a handwritten note.

Talk It Out

When is it appropriate to send a handwritten message? And to whom?

Include the date.	*June 3, 2015*
Start your note with a salutation and the receiver's name.	*Dear Ms. McCombs,*
Be brief but specific about why you are thanking the person. Include how you benefited from the person's kindness. Do not begin every sentence with *I*.	*Thank-you for loaning me your book on business etiquette. I especially liked the chapter on social events and dining. Your constant encouragement and mentoring mean so much to me.*
	Sincerely,
Use a complementary closing, and do not forget to sign your name.	*Mason Yang*

Figure 9-6

Thank-You Note

Documentation

One final element of effective communication is documentation. **Documentation** is a formal record of events or activities. Some industries require documentation to track a project's progress or an employee's time for client billing. Documentation may be necessary for an employee evaluation, for advancement, in an instance in which a policy is not enforced, or when an abnormal event has occurred that has the potential to evolve into conflict at a later date. These events may support performance issues, business relationships, and business operations. However, it is not necessary to record every event that occurs at work. Employees should identify a method of recording relevant business situations, such as a workplace injury, an angry customer, or an employee conflict, if needed for future reference to protect themselves and/or the employer. Although there are numerous methods of documenting and retaining important information and events, the basic elements to be recorded remain the same.

Depending on the purpose of your documentation, effective documentation records the *who, what, when, where,* and *why* of a situation. Effective documentation essentials include the date, time, and location of the event. Note the event itself (e.g., who said what or did what). Also note who was present when the event occurred and how witnesses to the event behaved or responded. Documentation can be kept electronically, in a journal, or through minimal notations on a calendar. If the documentation is for billing or client purposes, your employer will provide the documentation format. Whatever system you choose, keep your documentation in a secure, private location. Also, keep copies of supporting memos, letters, or other communications, in a secure location. If you are ever called upon to defend your actions, you will have the ability to easily gather pertinent information.

Presentations

Both formal and informal presentations are a normal workplace event, and sometime in your career you will most likely be asked to give a presentation. As with meeting etiquette, be prepared and professional. Presentations are very rich in media, in that they include written, verbal, visual, and nonverbal communication. A successful presentation begins with a goal. Identify the purpose of your presentation, and ensure that every word, visual aid, activity, and/or handout will support the overall goal of the presentation. After the purpose of the presentation has been identified, an outline of key points should be identified to reinforce the message you want individuals to respond to or remember.

Formal presentations include three elements: the verbal content, the visual content, and support content. Verbal content includes the detailed information you wish to share with the audience. When presenting, do not read directly from the visual content. Summarize and add information pertaining to the content. Speak clearly and at a normal pace using professional and appropriate language. Face your audience. If you are using a screen, keep your back toward the screen. Beware of both verbal and nonverbal physical gestures. Nothing will distract an audience quicker than an overuse of "um," "like," and "you know." Hands in pockets, crossed arms, or tapping feet are examples of distracting physical gestures. Dress professionally, and do not wear anything that may distract from your message. Visual content includes anything the audience will view or any activity the audience will perform during your presentation. Oftentimes, this involves some type of technology, including presentation software, videos, or music. When using presentation software, do not overdo the use of graphics, color, or animations. Test all equipment and software prior to the actual presentation to ensure the equipment is working and the software is a compatible version. Preparation and practice ensure that your visual content and/or activities are the appropriate length. If you are including your audience in an activity (e.g., game), make directions simple and the activity brief. Keep your audience focused, and do not allow the activity to serve as a distraction from your message.

Support content normally comes in the form of a handout. This is a good way to reinforce your verbal and visual message in writing. A popular format for a handout allows the audience to fill in the blanks as you present your message. Without creating distractions, add professional and visual appeal to your handout. As you create your handout, follow the same order as the presentation outline. Check your visual presentation and support materials for spelling and grammatical errors. When you are certain your support content is error-free and professional, make enough copies for each member of your audience.

Formal presentations are an excellent way to increase workplace credibility and individual confidence. With regard to workplace presentations, remember that success is in the planning and practice makes perfect.

Slang and Foul Language

Different generations, cultures, and technology use some form of slang. **Slang** is an informal language used among a particular group. Although slang is not always inappropriate. Slang can be easily misinterpreted by others. Slang such as "cool" or "dude" when speaking in the business environment should be avoided. When sending e-mails and text messages to friends, it is common to use slang; however, slang should be avoided in both verbal and written workplace communications, including e-mails and text messages. Become a more effective communicator in the workplace by eliminating the use of slang.

Your words reflect what is going on in your heart and mind. There is no appropriate time to use profane and offensive language at work. Even in times of stress or at social functions, you are representing your company and must do so in a professional manner. Practice self-control. Attempt to eliminate foul or offensive language from your personal and professional vocabulary. Doing so will rid your heart and mind of negativity. If you utilize inappropriate language at work, immediately apologize. Make a mental note of what situation caused you to behave poorly and learn from the experience. Ask yourself how you could have better handled the situation, and mentally rehearse a proper, more acceptable method of verbally handling a challenging situation.

Potentially Offensive Names

Names that could be considered sexist and offensive are inappropriate in a business setting. Using inappropriate names toward coworkers could expose you and your company to a potential sexual harassment lawsuit. These include names such as *honey, sweetie,* and *sexy.* Even if the individual being called these names acts as if he or she is not offended, the person may actually be offended or insulted but afraid to tell you. Eliminate potentially offensive names from your workplace vocabulary. In addition, do not use gender-specific titles when referring to certain jobs. For example:

Instead of	Use
Postman	Postal carrier
Policeman	Police officer
Waitress	Server
Stewardess	Flight attendant
Maid	Housekeeper

Not Always About You

Closing our discussion on communication, we address one word that often dominates written and verbal communication. This word frequently turns listeners off. Unfortunately, too often, the sender is unaware of its overuse. The word is *I*. Be cautious with the use of this word. Self-centered people use it to draw attention, while others who lack self-confidence may subconsciously use the word to protect themselves. They may not know how to turn the conversation to others, so they choose to stay in a safety zone. When you are using verbal communication, think before you speak. If your initial sentence includes *I*, try to rephrase your message. Prior to sending written correspondence, review your message and reduce the number of sentences that begin with the word *I*.

Exercise 9-2   Checking for *I*

Take five minutes and interview a classmate about college and his or her career choice. While you are getting to know each other, keep track of how many times your new friend says the word *I*.

Workplace Dos and Don'ts

Do carefully think through your message and the appropriate medium	*Don't* be in such a hurry to send your message that an incorrect message is sent
Do demonstrate professionalism in the formatting, word choice, and grammar in your written communication	*Don't* write and send messages when you are angry
Do express kindness to others with both your words and body language	*Don't* utilize foul language at work or at home

Concept Review and Application

Summary of Key Concepts

- Effective communication is necessary for workplace success
- The goal of communication is to create a mutual understanding between the sender and the receiver
- There are appropriate times to utilize both the formal and informal communication channels
- The communication process involves a sender, a receiver, noise, and feedback
- Listening and silence are effective tools for effective communication
- Thoughtfully consider the right words to increase the chance of successful written and verbal communication
- Because the receiver of your message will not have verbal and nonverbal assistance in interpreting your message, take great care with all written messages

Key Terms

active listening	business letter	business memos
communication	decoding	documentation
encoding	feedback	formal communication

gossip	grapevine	informal communication
letterhead	listening	noise
nonlistening	nonverbal communication	passive listening
proxemics	sender	slang
verbal communication	written communication	

If You Were the Boss

1. One of your employees uses bad grammar that is reflecting poorly on your department. How can you correct the situation?
2. Employees keep saying they do not know what is going on at work. What steps would you take to increase workplace communication?

Video Case Study: Language in the Office

This video addresses language in the office. To view these videos, visit the Student Resources: Professionalism section in www.mystudentsuccesslab.com. Then answer the following questions:

1. In the opening dialog between John and Regina, what specific advice would you give John? Why? What advice would you give Regina? Why?
2. Did Regina appropriately handle her telephone call? Please explain your answer.
3. Is the dialog between John and Brian appropriate? Provide specific examples.
4. Name two examples of how Brian could improve his language when speaking with Gerald.

Web Links

http://owl.english.purdue.edu/handouts/pw/p_memo.html
http://blog.justjobs.com/using-foul-language-in-the-workplace-can-get-you-fired/

Activities

Activity 9-1

Without infringing on someone's privacy, discreetly observe a stranger's body language for approximately five minutes. Stay far enough away to not hear him or her speak. Name at least two assumptions you can make by simply watching the person's gestures, movements, and expressions.

Gesture, Movement, or Expression	Assumption
1.	
2.	
3.	

Activity 9-2

Watch a television news show for a half hour. Document at least two facial expressions of an individual being interviewed. Did the individual's facial expressions match his or her statements?

Facial Expression	Match Statements: Yes or No
1.	
2.	

Activity 9-3

Review the following letter and identify five formatting errors. How should they be corrected?

April

Sandra Wong, Vice President
Human Resource Department
Robinson Enterprises
55123 W. Robinson Lane
Prosperity, CA 99923

Dear Sandra Wong

It was a pleasure speaking with you this afternoon regarding the average salary you pay your receptionists. This data will be useful as our company begins creating a new receptionist position for our California site.

I am most appreciative of your offer to mail me a copy of your most recent salary guide for all production positions. I look forward to receiving that guide in the mail. As a thank-you for your kindness, I am enclosing coupons for our company product.

If there is any information I can provide to assist you, please let me know. Thank-you again for your cooperation.

Sincerely,

Cory Kringle

List Errors	Correct Errors
1.	
2.	
3.	
4.	
5.	

Activity 9-4

Review the following memo and identify five errors. How should they be corrected?

MEMORANDUM

[handwritten: ↓ 2 inches]

[handwritten: Bold + capital]

[handwritten: pg. 148]

Re: Budget Meeting

To: Mason Jared

From: Cory Kringle

Date: May 1   *[handwritten: year]*

[handwritten: Double space]

Hey Mason. I wanted to remind you that we have a meeting next week to talk about next year's budget. Bring some numbers and we'll work through them. Bye.

[handwritten: Double space]

-Cory   *[handwritten: typist initials]*

List Errors	Correct Errors
1.	
2.	
3.	
4.	
5.	

Sample Exam Questions

1. The two types of workplace communication include _____ and _____ communication.

2. A major form of the informal communication network is called _____.

3. When the _____ is targeting individuals and their personal lives, it is called _____.

4. When _____ are displayed at work, it becomes difficult to think and behave in a logical manner.

5. Nonverbal communication is what we communicate through our _____.

6. _____ communicates to your audience that you are listening and are allowing the other party consideration.

7. Check that all _____ is error-free by proofreading prior to sending.

Electronic Communications

Be a yardstick of quality. Some people aren't used to an environment where excellence is expected.

Steve Jobs (1955–2011)

MyStudentSuccessLab Visit www.mystudentsuccesslab.com for added practice, activities, assessment, and videos.

Objectives

- Explain the basics of utilizing modern workplace telecommunication tools
- Demonstrate proper business e-mail etiquette
- Display professionalism when utilizing both the telephone and mobile communication devices (including texting and call behaviors)
- Demonstrate professionalism when utilizing social media tools
- Demonstrate proper behaviors when participating in *video- and teleconferences*

How-Do-You-Rate

	Are you addicted to your smart phone?	Yes	No
1.	Within five minutes of waking, do you check your device for messages?	❑	❑
2.	Do you have to view/check your device at least once every hour?	❑	❑
3.	Do you use/view your device in locations/situations where you know it is not appropriate to use/view your device?	❑	❑
4.	Do you always have your device visible or easily accessible?	❑	❑
5.	Are you unable to go an entire day without access to your smart phone?	❑	❑

If you answered "yes" to two or more of these questions, you may be addicted to your smart phone.

Electronic Communications at Work

We live in a multitasking, fast-paced world that has resulted in technology addiction. The traditional workplace of the past has evolved into a virtual workplace where most people are connected electronically. Today's workplace communicates through venues including e-mail, mobile devices, texting, instant messaging, blogs, wikis, and audio and video conferencing. The more we are connected technologically, the greater the opportunity for disconnected messages. As a complement to chapter 9, this chapter focuses on electronic communications in the workplace. Due to the frequency and speed of message transmission, those who communicate through today's virtual workplace need to take great care to ensure all electronic communications are sent in a clear and professional manner.

Telecommunication Basics

With the increase of technology in the workplace, the proper use of electronic communication tools, devices, and equipment becomes increasingly important. Common communication tools include various forms of computers, software, e-mail, Internet, and mobile (smart) devices. Employers may provide these tools to employees free of charge. If you utilize company-provided tools (including a computer, company server, or e-mail address), the tools, equipment, and messages are company property. Use these items only for company business. This includes the use of the Internet and electronic messaging. Many organizations have technology-use policies that outline expectations including privacy, liability, and potential misconduct issues. Ensure the messages you send and receive do not violate confidentiality and that they represent the company in a favorable light.

With a wide variety of electronic device options, keep in mind that there are proper times and places for their use. In some work situations, it is perfectly appropriate to utilize a laptop, tablet, or mobile device. In other situations, it is highly inappropriate. Only utilize the communication tool when it is relevant to the discussion or issue you are addressing. The communication tool should not distract from the conversation at hand. When in doubt, ask permission to use the device and explain why you want to use it to assist in the discussion.

Cory was in a company meeting. During the meeting, there was disagreement on whether the company's competitor had specific information on its website. Cory quickly pulled out a smart phone and began pulling up the competitor's website. One of the company executives glared at Cory, assuming Cory was being rude by texting or tending to personal business. Catching the executive's glare, Cory immediately held up the device and said, "I don't want to appear rude. I am quickly checking our competitor's site." Cory quickly retrieved and reported on the site and was able to contribute valuable information to the discussion.

Practice good computer hygiene. If possible, routinely scan your equipment for viruses, cookies, and other malicious coding that can be potentially harmful. Just as you would not show up to work when you are sick, you do not want to be responsible for contaminating others' communication tools when sharing information electronically. Regularly back up documents for preservation should a storage device fail.

Talk It Out

How might Cory have better handled the situation of using a smart phone during a meeting?

The Business E-mail

Electronic mail (e-mail) is the most common form of internal and external electronic communications in the workplace. With e-mail messages, you can directly type a message or attach a business document to your e-mail. E-mail creates more efficient communication within an organization and with individuals outside of the organization.

When sending an e-mail, ensure the subject line clearly describes the purpose of the e-mail message to let the reader know your message is not spam or a virus. Include a descriptive subject in the subject line that makes the receiver want to read the message. Do not leave the subject line blank nor use the words "Hi" or "Hello." It is also inappropriate to use the words "Urgent," "Important," or "Test" in a subject line. Most e-mail software contains a command that tags a message as important or urgent. The common tag is an exclamation point (!). Tag only important messages. A proper business e-mail subject line is formatted the same as a hard-copy memo subject line, which uses initial capitalization of words and no abbreviations.

As with all workplace equipment, business e-mail should be used only for business purposes. When composing or responding to e-mails, emoticons (faces made and embedded in e-mail messages) are inappropriate in business messages. Including emoticons in business messages reduces your professional image. Refrain from forwarding messages that are not work-related. These non-business-related messages clutter up company servers and may contain viruses and cookies. Maintain an organized and updated electronic address book and make every attempt to preserve the confidentiality of your address book.

When you receive a work-related message that requires a reply, respond to the message. Ignoring a message is rude and communicates to the sender that you do not care. You also run the risk of being excluded from future messages.

Writing E-mail Messages

E-mail is a necessary technology in nearly every workplace and can be easily misused. As with formal correspondence written on company letterhead, an e-mail should utilize proper layout, spelling, and grammar. Just like writing a business letter, composing a successful e-mail message involves planning and identifying the purpose of your message. Include what specifically needs to be communicated and what action you want the receiver(s) to take. Your message may be informational, or it may be a topic for discussion, or the message may require a decision.

Identify who should receive your e-mail message and include only individuals who need to know the information you are sharing. When sending an e-mail message, you have the option of sending the message directly to individuals on the "To:" line to the main recipient. You can also copy (cc:) the message to individuals by listing them in the "cc:" line. Any individual to whom the message is directed should be listed in the "To" line. Individuals who are named in the message and are not included in the "To:" line should be listed in the "cc:" line, as well as individuals who may be affected by the message. It is not necessary to include your boss in every e-mail. E-mail software has the option of blind copying (bcc:) your message to others through the use of "bcc:"; when an individual is blind copied on an e-mail, the bcc: recipient can see the main and cc: recipients, but the main and cc: recipients do not see the bcc: recipient. Not all recipients are aware of who is included in the message, and this creates a sense of mistrust. The use of blind copying (bcc:) is discouraged, except in the case of sending an e-mail to a mailing list where you do not want the recipients to see the other names due to privacy issues.

Exercise 10-1   Create an E-mail

Your boss (Austin@workspace.star) asks you to send a copy of a meeting memo to your coworkers: Charlie@workspace.star, Ben@workspace.star, and Audrey@workspace.star. Fill in the proper entries.

To:

Cc:

Bcc:

Subject:

After you have planned your message, begin writing a draft message. As you write your draft, clearly communicate your primary message early in the e-mail so as to capture and keep the reader's attention. Include the key points you want to communicate and the specific action you are requesting from the reader(s). Consider the reader's perspective and communicate the message in a positive manner. If your message contains several points, bullet or number each item and/or use subheadings to make it easier for the reader to follow and properly respond to your message. After you have finished composing your message, edit the message. Delete unnecessary words, and review the message for clarity and conciseness. People often judge others' professionalism based upon their writing skills. When you are satisfied, proofread the entire message. Most business e-mail software contains both spelling and grammar check—use them. If your message refers to an attachment, do not forget to include the attachment. Before sending your e-mail, give your message one final review, ensure the proper file is attached (if relevant), and check that you are sending the message to the appropriate parties. Also, review that the subject line concisely summarizes your message. After you have taken these steps, send your e-mail.

When sending e-mail messages practice positive e-mail habits:

- Mark only important time-sensitive messages "Urgent" (!). Marking all outgoing messages as urgent weakens your credibility, as it becomes hard for individuals to identify which of your messages truly are urgent. People may stop reading your messages immediately or altogether.
- Check all outgoing messages for proper spelling and grammar. Nothing lessens credibility faster than receiving a message filled with spelling and grammatical errors, especially since the majority of e-mail software comes with tools to correct them.
- E-mail messages written in all capital letters or with large and colorful letters are interpreted as yelling and are considered rude.
- Business e-mail should not have decorative backgrounds or use emoticons.
- If your e-mail software has the ability to embed a permanent signature, use it. Include your first and last name, title, company, business address, contact phone, and e-mail address.
- Some software has the capability of requesting a "return receipt" whenever a message is read and received. Some individuals consider this an invasion of privacy. Use this function only when necessary.
- If you will be out of the office and unable to access and/or respond to your e-mail message within a reasonable time, utilize an automated response to all e-mail messages informing the senders that you are unavailable. Remember to retract the automated response when you return.

> **Talk It Out**
>
> When is an appropriate time to use the return receipt feature in an e-mail message?

A common practice when utilizing workplace e-mail is that of forwarding business messages. If misused, this practice can cause conflict and/or embarrassment. Forwarding messages saves time and brings parties into the loop on a subject they may have not originally been involved with. When forwarding messages, include only individuals for whom the information is relevant. Prior to forwarding a message, ensure that none of the earlier information in the string of e-mails could embarrass anyone and does not contain information that should not be shared with others. If you are unsure the information has the potential to embarrass someone, do not forward the message. Simply summarize the situation in a new e-mail with (potentially) new recipients and copy (cc:) the original parties if appropriate.

Using business e-mail was a common activity for Cory. Cory was careful to always include an appropriate subject line, ensured that the content was professionally and concisely written, requested an action or follow-up activity, and sent it to the appropriate people. Cory was taken aback one day when a coworker sent Cory a negative e-mail for including inappropriate recipients in an e-mail message. The individual scolding Cory had sent his negative e-mail to everyone in the department, which embarrassed Cory. Cory reviewed the e-mail in question and did not see anything wrong with the message or the recipient list. As Cory reflected on how best to respond, Cory decided that the individual

Talk It Out

Did Cory appropriately handle the negative e-mail sent by the coworker? Why or why not?

who sent the negative message acted on emotion and embarrassed himself to all of his coworkers in the process of trying to embarrass Cory. Therefore, Cory felt it best to not respond.

Mobile (Portable) Communication Devices

Today's business environment relies on current technologies to improve communication. This is achieved through the use of mobile (portable) communication devices. Common devices include cell phones, smart phones, personal digital assistants (PDAs), portable music/entertainment devices, and wireless computers. While the use of these tools is acceptable in most business situations, employees need to be aware of the proper etiquette regarding the use of these devices. Just as it is impolite to verbally interrupt someone who is talking, it is also impolite to interrupt a conversation or meeting with incoming or outgoing electronic communications. There are two basic guidelines for using electronic communication devices. First, you may use your communication device if you are alone, in a private area, and its use is permitted at your workplace. Second, you may use your device when attending a meeting or business activity and it is necessary for communication. If the use of the device is not relevant to the activity, silence your device and place it screen down on the table, or turn it off and put it away. Do not answer calls. If you are expecting and receive an important call, politely excuse yourself from the room and take the call in private. If you forget to turn off the sound and it rings, apologize and immediately silence the device or turn it off. Although these guidelines are for business purposes, they should pertain to personal use, as well. Please review the information regarding telecommunication etiquette detailed in chapter 4.

In some situations, texting is a valuable communication tool. When you are in the presence of others, a general rule of thumb is to text only if the texting is related to the business at hand. For example, if you are negotiating a deal, you may text your boss to identify terms to present. Prior to texting, inform those present of your activity. Just as with all written communication, when texting for business purposes, the use of proper spelling and grammar is essential. Constant texting and utilizing a mobile device has become a habit for many. If you give in to the temptation to utilize your device as a distraction, you will display unprofessional behavior. Therefore, when in meetings, turn off or silence and put your communication device away unless it is explicitly necessary for the meeting. If not, the mere presence of the device may be tempting and will divert your attention from the business at hand. If you are anticipating an important message, if possible, inform the leader of the meeting and explain the situation and apologize ahead of time for the potential interruption. When the message is received, quietly step out of the meeting to respond to the message. It is rude to use your communication device while dining or attending meetings or performances. It is also not polite to take calls in front of others. Doing so implies that the individuals you are with are not important. When taking a call, apologize for the interruption, excuse yourself, and step away for privacy. Many people utilize text slang, text shorthand, acronyms, and codes in personal e-mails and texts. The use of these styles is not appropriate for business communications. In the workplace, texting should be used only for brief, informal communications, always utilizing proper spelling. Just as with other portable communication devices, it is not appropriate and is considered rude behavior to view and send text messages while with others (including discreetly during meetings).

It is inappropriate to use or display portable music/entertainment devices in the workplace unless the device provides quiet background music appropriate for a professional workplace and it does not disturb others.

Phone Etiquette

The phone is one of the most common workplace communication tools. Phone etiquette, whether land-line or wireless, is something every individual must practice to create and maintain a professional image for his or her company. Because the individual(s) on the other end of the phone cannot see you, it is important to communicate properly through the words you choose, your tone of voice, the pitch of your voice, and your rate of speech.

When answering a call, try to answer on the first or second ring. Start with a salutation such as "Good morning," and identify yourself and the company. Convey a positive, professional attitude when speaking on the phone. Smile when you speak, to create a friendly tone. Speak clearly and slowly, and do not speak too softly or too loudly. If you take a call and need to place the first caller on hold, politely tell the individual on the phone that you are placing him or her on hold. If an individual is placed on hold for more than one minute, get back on the line and ask if you can return the call at a later time.

Taking a call without explanation in the presence of others implies that the individual in your presence is not important. When with others, let the call go into voice mail. If you are expecting an important call and are in the presence of others, inform those you are with that you are expecting an important call and will need to take it when it arrives. When the call is received, politely excuse yourself. If you are in your office, politely ask your office guest to excuse you for one moment while you quickly take the call.

When making a phone call, identify yourself to the receiver. The call should be for a brief interaction unless you make sure the receiver has time to talk. If you expect the discussion to be lengthy, ask the individual on the other end of the line if he or she has time to talk or if there is a more convenient time. When you are having a phone conversation, do not eat or tend to personal matters.

Speaker phones are useful communication tools for specific situations and also require proper etiquette. A speaker phone should be used only when you are on a conference call with other participants in the same room or when you require a hands-free device. Use a speaker phone only when you are in a private room where your call will not be distracting to others in your work area. When you use a speaker phone, ask individuals included in the call for permission to use the speaker phone. Alert those included in the call that others are in the room with you and make introductions. This ensures confidentiality and open communication between all parties. Those using a speaker phone should be aware that any small noise they make may be heard and distracting to those on the other end of the line.

Voice mail messages are a part of business communication. A voice mail impression is equally as important as communicating in person. When leaving a voice mail message, keep the message brief and professional. State your name and the purpose of the call, and leave a return number at the beginning of the message. Speak slowly and clearly and leave a short but concise message. After you have left your message, repeat your name and return number a second time before ending the call. When you receive voice mail messages, it is proper and important to promptly return messages left for you. Routinely check and empty your voice mail box.

On both portable and land-line phones, keep your voice mail greeting professional. Include your name and the company name in the message. Clever voice mail greetings are not professional. Musical introductions or bad jokes do not form favorable impressions when employers or customers are attempting to contact you.

Exercise 10-2   Create a Professional Voice Mail Greeting

You are the account clerk at Garret and Danielle Accounting Firm. Create a professional voice mail greeting for your work phone.

_____

_____

Social Media Tools

Web Quiz

Are you addicted to social media? Use the following quiz to identify if you are addicted to social media, or find another online quiz related to social media addiction.

http://www.blueglass.com/widgets/social-media-expert.php

Companies commonly use social media tools such as Facebook, video/photo file sharing, blogs, and micro-blogs for marketing purposes. Some companies hire professionals to maintain and manage their image through social media outlets. While it may be tempting to post a video or vent about an irate customer, coworker, or administrator online, such behavior is not only unprofessional, but could be a violation of the company's technology-use policy. The behavior could also pose potential legal issues for both you and your employer. An increasing number of employers consider any employee use of social media that reflects poorly on the employer as a violation of its technology-use policy. Individuals using social media for personal reasons need to separate personal sharing from professional sharing. Many organizations regard the posting of company-related information by employees as divulging confidential or competitive information. Regardless of your company's policy, it is best to refrain from identifying and/or speaking poorly of the company, employees, vendors, and customers in all social media communications.

A growing number of companies are moving away from e-mail as a primary means of communicating brief electronic business messages and are utilizing wikis, blogs, and instant messaging for both internal and external communications. A wiki is a collaborative website where users have the ability to edit and contribute to the site. Blogs, also called web logs, are online journals where readers are often allowed to comment. Instant messaging (IM) is a form of online communication that occurs between two or more parties in real time. Business etiquette regarding the use of these communication methods is similar to that of e-mail. When at work, use these venues only for business purposes. Proper spelling and grammar and clear and concise communications are necessary. As with all forms of written communication, professionalism and tone matter. View your participation in a wiki as a form of teamwork. When making edits to the wiki, be sensitive to how others are receiving your comments and, in turn, accept the suggestions of others. Your goal is to provide an accurate web page that properly communicates your message. Business blogs are used as both marketing and education tools. The purpose of a blog is to create and enhance relationships, so keep blog posts and comments positive and meaningful. The difference between IM and e-mail is that you are able to identify who is online at the same time you are. Utilize IM only for brief business interactions. While it is tempting to IM individuals when you see they are online at their workstations, remember that

IM at work is not intended as a workplace social tool. You do not want to become disruptive or annoying when utilizing IM. Whatever electronic communication venue you utilize, remember that you are representing your company.

While it is perfectly common and acceptable to utilize social media tools for personal reasons, remember to maintain a positive and professional online image. In chapter 13, we refer to this as an electronic image. An **electronic image** is the image formed when someone is communicating and/or researching you through electronic means. It is becoming common to refer to your electronic image as an **e-dentity.** Routinely conduct an Internet search of yourself to ensure you have a clean online image. If there are negative photos, videos, blogs, or other information that reflect poorly on you, have them removed. Maintain a professional electronic personality by utilizing a professional voice mail message and e-mail address.

Cory's friend Gigi recently got a new job in sales that required her to train and job-shadow her manager for the first few weeks. Cory knew Gigi was addicted to both texting and her social media site, so Cory was glad that she now had something to keep her mind focused. During a sales call, Gigi was not focused and was using a company laptop to play on her social media site instead of reviewing sales figures. Gigi and her client stepped away from the conference table for a minute, and Gigi's boss tried to quickly retrieve a figure from the computer. Unfortunately, all the boss saw was Gigi's social media site. To make matters worse, the site contained a photo of Gigi in a crazy pose outside of her new company headquarters, which included the company's name in the picture.

> **Talk It Out**
>
> If you were Gigi and you knew your new boss saw the social media site open on your computer, how would you respond?

Exercise 10-3   Identify a Professional Personal E-mail Address for Yourself

Create a professional personal e-mail address

_____

Video and Teleconferencing

It is common for meetings to take place through video or teleconference venues such as Skype, WebEx, and Google Talk. A **video conference** is an interactive communication using two-way video and audio technology. It allows individuals in another location to see and hear all meeting participants. A **teleconference** is also an interactive communication; however, it connects participants through the telephone without the opportunity of visually seeing all participants. When participating in a video conference, a computer, a web cam, and a reliable Internet connection are needed. An individual participating in a teleconference requires a reliable phone line and a quiet location. When taking part in a video or teleconference, the participant will receive a designated time and specific instructions on how to establish connection. In addition to following the phone interview tips that will be provided in chapter 15, the meeting participant needs to prepare for and treat the telecommunication meeting as if it were a face-to-face meeting. Follow these basic tips for a successful electronic meeting:

- Plan ahead. Research the venue you will be using to address any unforeseen issue. If possible, arrange a pre-meeting trial to ensure all equipment works properly (including your volume and microphone).
- Dress professionally (if you are visible to other participants). As with face-to-face meetings, visual impressions matter.

- Maintain a professional environment. Conduct your meeting in a quiet and appropriate location. When you are visible to other participants, a bedroom, public place, or outside location is not appropriate.
- Speak to the camera (if you are participating in a video conference). Focus on the web cam as if you were speaking directly to the other participants. Without interrupting or distracting others, feel free to ask questions, take notes, and use hand gestures.
- Avoid distracting noises. Turn off music or any other items that create distracting noises. Do not eat or drink during the meeting.

When teleconferencing, state your name each time you speak. For example, prior to contributing, say, "Hi, this is Ted. I would like to provide a status report on the Phoenix project." Because virtual meetings require a special emphasis on listening, be quiet when others are speaking and do not do anything distracting. Take your turn speaking and do not interrupt. As with face-to-face meetings, which will be discussed in chapter 11, be prepared and actively contribute.

The number of technology-related workplace tools continues to grow, as do their applications. While our means of communicating at work may change, the need for professional communication remains the same. Be respectful and concise in your communication and represent your organization in a professional manner.

Workplace Dos and Don'ts

Do utilize company technology tools only for company business	*Don't* violate your company's technology-use policy
Do practice good computer hygiene by routinely backing up documents	*Don't* forget to routinely scan your computer for viruses and other malicious software
Do recognize the appropriate time and place for workplace technologies	*Don't* allow technology to distract from business matters
Do demonstrate professionalism in business e-mail and texts	*Don't* become addicted to workplace technologies by sharing inappropriate messages
Do practice good meeting habits in video conferencing and teleconferencing	*Don't* let the fact of not being face-to-face in a video or teleconference interfere with practicing professionalism

Concept Review and Application

Summary of Key Concepts

- Send electronic communications in a clear and professional manner.
- Many organizations have technology-use policies that address privacy, liability, and potential misconduct issues.
- Do not forward messages at work that do not involve work-related issues.
- Just as with written communication, when texting for business purposes, the use of proper spelling and grammar is essential.
- When utilizing social media for personal use, refrain from identifying your company and/or speaking poorly of the company and/or its customers.
- Maintain a clean e-dentity.
- Practice good meeting habits in technology-based meetings.

Key Terms

e-dentity	electronic image
teleconference	video conference

If You Were the Boss

1. One of your employees has been sending personal texts during meetings. How should you handle this issue?
2. Many employees are taking photos and/or videos at department meetings and company events. Should you be concerned? Why? As the boss, what should you do?

Video Case Study: E-mail Etiquette

This video presents expert advice on how to communicate professionally utilizing e-mail. To view these videos, visit the Student Resources: Professionalism section in www.mystudentsuccesslab.com. Then answer the following questions:

1. What should be included and what should be avoided in the subject line of an e-mail?
2. In what situations is it acceptable to utilize emoticons?
3. What is the appropriate e-mail use for non-work-related matters?

Video Case Study: Meetings

This video addresses meeting behavior and etiquette. To view these videos, visit the Student Resources: Professionalism section in www.mystudentsuccesslab.com. Then answer the following questions:

1. Out of the four employees, which one demonstrated appropriate meeting behavior? Provide specific examples.

2. How did technology assist the meeting, and how did technology hinder the meeting?
3. What perception of the company may the client have from the conference call? Provide two examples.
4. Name four inappropriate actions of the employees.

Web Links

http://www.forbes.com/2010/07/27/internet-email-workplace-technology-privacy.html

http://www.helium.com/items/436615-what-is-the-impact-of-new-technology-in-the-workplace

http://www.businessweek.com/technology/ceo_guide/

Activities

Activity 10-1

Name two specific technology devices that are used in your job (current or future). How are they used to improve communication?

Device	What Use?

Activity 10-2

Check your e-dentity. Conduct an Internet search on yourself. Is there anything you need to change?

_____

_____

Activity 10-3

What should you say to someone who is inappropriately using his or her mobile device (e.g., during a meeting)?

_____

_____

Activity 10-4

Research at least two different smart phones and explain which is best for a job that requires smart-phone technology for traveling (calls, e-mails, texting, viewing documents).

_____

_____

_____

1. The more the workplace is connected technologically, the greater opportunities for

   _____.

2. Many organizations have _____ that outline expectations including privacy, liability, and potential misconduct issues.

3. Practice _____ to ensure you do not contaminate others' communication tools.

4. When in doubt about the proper use of a technology device, _____.

5. The use of _____ is inappropriate for business messages.

6. Blind copying someone in a business e-mail creates a sense of _____.

7. It is impolite to interrupt a conversation or meeting with _____ electronic communications.

Motivation, Leadership, and Teams

chapter 11

The price of greatness is responsibility.

Sir Winston Churchill (1874–1965)

Objectives

- Describe what motivates people
- Identify the characteristics of effective *leadership*
- Identify leadership styles
- Describe ways to develop leadership skills
- Define a *team* and its function
- Identify the characteristics of a team player
- Describe the elements of successful presentations and meetings

How-Do-You-Rate

	What kind of team member are you?	Yes	No
1.	Co-workers would say that I consistently behave in a professional manner at work.	❑	❑
2.	I normally arrive at least five minutes early to meetings.	❑	❑
3.	When participating in team projects, I always complete my portion of the project on time.	❑	❑
4.	If there is conflict within the team, I work to resolve the team conflict.	❑	❑
5.	I consistently behave as a leader in work-related situations, including knowing when to lead and knowing when to follow.	❑	❑

If you answered "yes" to two or more of these questions, congratulations. You display both leadership and positive team member behaviors.

A Foundation for Performance

The three elements of motivation, leadership, and teamwork create the foundation for productivity and organizational success. This chapter focuses on these important workplace concepts by first addressing the concept of motivation and how an understanding of basic motivation theories will assist you in becoming a more productive employee and leader. You do not have to have a leadership title to exhibit leadership behaviors. Employees should display the characteristics of a leader because they have the opportunity to lead. In addition to motivation and leadership, teamwork will be discussed. These three elements are intertwined, and they also require skill in understanding how to work with others who may or may not be motivated, be a part of your team, or want to lead.

Motivation

Motivation is an internal drive that causes people to behave a certain way to meet a need. Individual workplace behavior is a result of trying to fill a need. If needs are not met, behavior changes. You are most likely taking this course because you believe the information you receive will assist you in achieving your career goal; this will motivate you to succeed. Employees need to be motivated to achieve success and productivity. Several factors can contribute to motivating employees, with the most obvious factor being money. However, monetary payment often may not be the primary motivating factor. In chapter 1, you created a life plan that outlined personal and professional goals. The timelines you attached to each goal help you track your success. Every time you accomplish a goal, you are motivated to achieve more.

Talk It Out

What motivates you at work or at school?

Since motivation comes from within, individuals are motivated by different factors. Some employees are motivated by needs. Abraham Maslow created a hierarchy of needs (see Figure 11-1). This hierarchy of needs essentially states that throughout one's lifetime, as individuals' needs are met, they move up a pyramid (hierarchy) until they self-actualize and have realized their potential. Organizational behaviorists have adapted Maslow's hierarchy to a typical workplace. Maslow's lowest level, **physiological needs,** translates to basic wages in the workplace. People work to receive a paycheck, which is used for food and shelter. These are basic survival needs. The next level in the pyramid is **safety needs.** In the workplace, individuals desire not only a safe working environment, but also job security and benefits. It is only after individuals receive basic wages and experience job security that they invest in workplace relationships, thus reaching the **social needs** level. Employees cannot progress to the next level until positive workplace relationships are realized. This includes being accepted by others. The next level on the pyramid is **self-esteem needs.** An employee's ego/esteem needs are met through public recognition via promotions, degrees, and awards. The final stage of the hierarchy is that of **self-actualization.** In a workplace, this is when employees have achieved meaningful work and now desire to assist others in meeting their needs. They do so by becoming mentors or coaches or by finding other means of helping others achieve their goals. In this stage, they have reached their full potential.

Maslow's theory is still used today to explain what motivates people. Each level of the pyramid addresses different methods to motivate individuals. Recognize that not everyone is motivated by the same factors, nor do others have the same needs as you. Observe other employees' behaviors and words, then try to determine what need requires fulfillment. Once you identify others' needs, you can assist in creating an environment that helps meet these particular needs.

Exercise 11-1 Identify the Need

Evaluate the following comments and determine what need on Maslow's hierarchy is being expressed. Refer to Figure 11-1.

Comment	Need Expressed
I have done a similar project in the past; can I help you?	
I need a raise this year.	
Anyone want to join me for lunch?	
I received a sales award: would you like to see it?	

Other popular motivational theories are David McClelland's Theory of Needs and Victor Vroom's Expectancy Theory. **McClelland's Theory of Needs** holds that people are primarily motivated by one of three factors: achievement, power, and affiliation. Achievement is based on doing something better. The need for

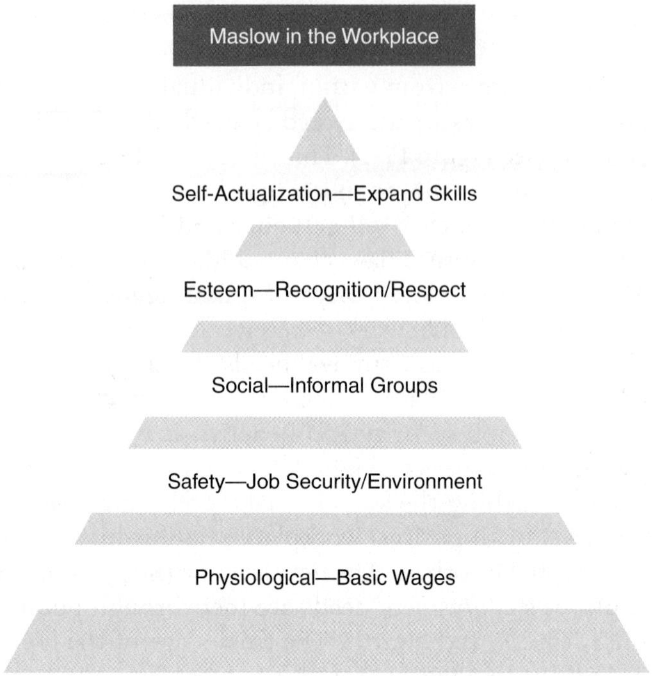

Maslow in the Workplace

Self-Actualization—Expand Skills

Esteem—Recognition/Respect

Social—Informal Groups

Safety—Job Security/Environment

Physiological—Basic Wages

Figure 11-1

Maslow's Hierarchy
of Needs

power is based upon the need to influence others, and the need for affiliation is based upon one's need to maintain positive relationships with others. While many people are motivated by all three needs, some have a tendency to favor one need over the other two. Victor **Vroom's Expectancy Theory** holds that individuals will behave in a certain manner based upon the expected outcome. For example, you may be motivated to study because you expect to perform well on an exam if you study. Your expected outcome is a good score as a result of studying.

While there are other motivational theories, the three presented provide a basic understanding of the concept of motivation. As you assume either a formal or informal leadership position, your understanding of motivation and basic motivation theory will assist in helping you and others achieve peak performance.

Motivation is an internal drive, meaning you motivate yourself. Others can only provide a motivating environment. It is common to have an off day in which you are not motivated to perform. If you find yourself having an non-productive day, take time out and ask yourself what situation put you in that frame of mind. Use positive self-talk and review your goals to get back on track and be productive. In some situations, like a work layoff or workplace safety issue, you may not be able to control the situation that affected your performance. In one of these instances, try to identify what element of the situation you can control and work from there. You are the only one who can control your attitude and your desire to perform well.

Leadership

When reference is made to leaders, people think of managers. But the reality is that each employee should display leadership. **Leadership** is a process of a person guiding one or more individuals toward a specific goal. A leader does not need a title to be a leader. Leaders motivate others through relationships. At work, these relationships are based on trust, professionalism, and mutual respect. A leader is one who will help guide and motivate others. In other words, a leader will help others want to accomplish a job successfully. In comparison, a boss who is not a leader will tell others what job to complete without guiding and motivating.

There are three primary leadership styles: autocratic, democratic, and laissez-faire leadership. **Autocratic leaders** are authoritarian, meaning they make decisions on their own. **Democratic leaders** make decisions based upon input from others. People are encouraged to share their ideas. The democratic leader will evaluate the ideas and come to a decision that reflects the ideas.

Laissez-faire leaders allow team members to make their own decisions without input from the leader. Employees have complete freedom in making decisions concerning their work. There is no best leadership style and the appropriate leadership style is dependent on the situation.

Effective leaders display characteristics that make them stand out from others. These characteristics include working well with others, trustworthiness, consistent ethical behavior, and being focused with a vision. Leaders are also excellent communicators. Although these characteristics are not developed overnight, they provide you the ability to become a successful leader not only in your workplace, but also in every other area of your life. At work, make an effort to assume a leadership role. Know your work and its purpose, and be someone others can trust. Problem-solve, form and communicate a plan, then follow up on projects. Perform your job to the best of your ability. A leader encourages others to succeed. Therefore, groom others and provide them the opportunity to lead.

Leaders understand the importance of accountability and maintaining positive workplace relationships. Effective leaders do not do all the work themselves—they **delegate.** Delegating is when a manager or leader assigns part or all of a project to someone else. As a leader, empower others, teach others, and mentor others. Ultimately, leaders take responsibility. Become a model for others by taking your responsibilities seriously by consistently performing in a quality manner.

Talk It Out

If the room were on fire, how would each type of leader direct his or her employees?

Web Quiz

What is your leadership style? Use the following website or find another to determine more about your leadership skills.

http://psychology.about.com/library/quiz/bl-leadershipquiz.htm

---

Exercise 11-2 Leadership Characteristics

Identify three people whom you consider leaders and name the leadership characteristics.

Leader	Leadership Characteristic
1.	
2.	
3.	

Becoming A Leader

At work you may be assigned a leadership position by your boss, by a team, or simply because no one else wants to lead. No matter how a leadership position is obtained, be willing and prepared to lead. Begin preparing today by learning new skills, joining committees, training, and attending workshops. Volunteer to serve on a team and learn what skills are necessary to be a successful team leader. Observe successful leaders and/or find a mentor to help you develop good leadership skills. Learning new skills will enable you to think and behave like a leader. You will also improve your communication skills, which are necessary for effective leadership.

An important element of professional success includes getting involved in your community. One excellent method of increasing your leadership skills away from work is to share your expertise with a local nonprofit organization. Find a creative way to share your time and talent with those less fortunate or with those who are just learning a skill you have already mastered. Many nonprofit organizations are in need of individuals to serve on their Board of Directors, to head projects, or to perform specific activities. Volunteer experiences provide excellent opportunities to develop both leadership and team-building skills. Additionally, assisting others stimulates creativity, relieves stress, and is also an excellent way to meet and network with others.

Teams and Performance

Most individuals have experienced being part of a successful team. Perhaps it was a sports team, or maybe it was in school when a group of students successfully completed a big project. Whatever the task, individuals were part of a unit whose members shared a goal and respected one another. These important factors resulted in success. Learning to get along with others is a skill that is necessary in the workplace. You will most likely be working with others in a group or as part of a team. Each team should strive toward creating synergy. **Synergy** is defined as two or more individuals working together and producing more than the sum of their individual efforts. When people are truly working together as a team, performance is at a premium and the result exceeds what each individual could do alone. This section discusses teamwork, factors vital for team success, and the impact teams have on an organization's overall performance.

It is becoming increasingly common for companies to rely on teams to accomplish goals. A **team** is a group of people linked to a common purpose. In today's workplace, you will most likely work in a team. The team will be assigned the task of reaching a goal. In a team setting, each member shares a common goal, and members are accountable to one another and to the organization as a whole. Because members share accountability, teams provide opportunities for members to take a leadership role in helping the team successfully reach its goal. In a team setting, each team member has a sense of ownership for the team's performance. This can occur only when team members are active participants and are accountable to fellow team members.

Several types of teams exist at work. Teams that occur within the organizational structure are formal teams. **Formal teams** are developed within the formal organizational structure and include functional teams (e.g., individuals from the same department) or cross-functional teams (individuals from different departments). **Informal teams** are composed of individuals who get together outside of the formal organizational structure to accomplish a goal. Examples of informal teams include a company softball team and a group of coworkers collecting food for a local charity. Another type of team that is common in today's workplace is the virtual team. **Virtual teams** are teams that function through electronic communications because they are geographically dispersed. It is quite common for virtual teams to operate in various time zones and across national borders. Effective communication and pre-meeting planning is essential when working in a virtual team. Refer to chapters 9 and 10 for additional information on effective communication and appropriate use of communication technologies.

No matter what type of team situation you are involved with, you need to get along with your team members and behave professionally. Your performance for getting the job done depends on this team effort. A team composed of individuals who behave professionally performs better.

Teams go through five stages of team development: forming, storming, norming, performing, and adjournment. In the **forming stage,** you are getting to know and form initial opinions about team members. Assumptions are based on first impressions. Sometimes these impressions are right; other times, they are wrong. In stage two, the **storming stage,** some team members begin to have conflict with each other. When team members accept other members for who they are (i.e., overcome the conflict), the team has moved into the **norming stage.** It is only then that the team is able to enter the **performing stage,** where they begin working on the task. Once the team has completed its task, it is in the **adjourning stage,** which brings closure to the project. Note that it is normal for a team to go through these phases. As a team member, expect and accept when your team is moving through each phase. Some teams successfully and rapidly move through the forming, storming, and norming phases and get right to work (performing), while other teams cannot get beyond the initial phases of forming or storming. Make every effort to move your team along to the performing stage, and recognize that minor conflicts are a part of team development. Successful teams move beyond the conflict and accept each member for his or her unique talents and skills.

You may work with team members you know and see every day in the workplace. However, you may have to work with a team of people you have never met before. Some team members may be from your immediate department (functional teams), some may be from outside of your department (cross-functional teams), and some may be from outside of the company. Good people skills and a willingness to lead are what make individuals valuable team members.

In a team situation, you will usually have your own job to perform, but you are also accountable to your fellow team members. The success of others within the company depends on how you do your job. Although you may be working independently from your team members, it is still important that you complete your job done on time and correctly. An effective team member is able to work with everyone on the team. You may have to work with a person with whom you do not care to work. No matter what disagreements you may have, get along with this person and be professional at all times. This is a skill needed for any job.

Characteristics of a Team Member

Common team projects include improving product quality, providing excellent customer service, and creating and/or maintaining company records. A good team member is one who does his or her job in a manner that is contributing to the project's goal. This means good team members are trustworthy, are efficient, and communicate at all times.

As a team member, know the objectives and goal of the team. The activity performed for your team should support the team's objectives and goal. In chapter 1, you learned how to create personal goals. In chapter 7, you learned that organizations create goals. When there is a team working on a specific project, there is a goal, so the first step for effective teams is to set objectives to reach that goal. Do not just jump into a project without a clear understanding of the expected outcome. It is also important to not reinvent the wheel or waste time and money. The best way to avoid these common mistakes is to solicit ideas and input from all team members.

Once the team has identified its goal and objectives, the team can identify various alternatives for how best to successfully achieve the goal. One popular way of doing this is through brainstorming. **Brainstorming** is a problem-solving method that involves identifying alternatives that allow members to freely add ideas while other members withhold comments on the alternatives. Brainstorming is successful because it is fast and provides members the opportunity to contribute different and creative ideas. Brainstorming starts with the presentation of a problem, such as how to improve office communication. Members then have a set time to make any suggestion for improving office communication. The suggestions can be obvious (e.g., a newsletter) or fun and creative (have a daily off-site office party). No matter the suggestion, members are to withhold comment and judgment on the idea until the brainstorming session is over. In effective brainstorming sessions, even an off-the-wall comment such as the suggestion to have a daily off-site office party may spark a more practical idea that contributes to solving the problem (e.g., have a company-wide gathering).

Although conflict is a natural part of team development, occasionally there are teams that are filled with hard-to-resolve conflict. In chapter 12, you will learn various ways to overcome conflict. Do not let one member ruin the synergy of a team. If possible, confidentially pull the member aside and ask that person what it is about the team or project that he or she finds objectionable. Also ask the team member how he or she feels the issue can best be resolved. Calmly and logically help the individual work through the issues. Accept the fact that he or she may not (1) recognize there is a problem, (2) openly share the reason for the conflict, or (3) want to come to a solution. If you or others on the team attempt to solve the problem with the difficult team member and he or she rejects the effort, your team needs to move forward without that person. One team member should not have so much power that he or she negatively affects the efforts of the entire team. Although team conflict is a natural stage of team development, it should not cripple a team. When the problem team member is not around, do not allow other team members to talk negatively about the individual. Your job is to be a productive, positive team member who assists in successfully accomplishing the team's goal.

Exercise 11-3   Brainstorm for Saving

Brainstorm as many ideas as possible to help you and/or your classmates save money while going to college.

In addition to knowing the goals of the project and what your specific roles and responsibilities are in the team effort, know the responsibilities of all the other team members. Whenever possible, identify ways to support other team members and assist them in accomplishing the team's objectives. Take responsibility to attend all team meetings and be on time. Participation, sharing, support, understanding, and concern are all part of serving on a team. During team meetings, be involved in discussions and determine what work is needed for accomplishing the goal. Do not be afraid to speak up during team meetings. Some of your ideas may not be considered, but that does not mean they are not important. Be responsible, and finish assignments in a timely manner. As a team, review all aspects of the project together before completing the project. Remember, team members are accountable to one another.

Cory's department was having problems meeting its production goal. The manager asked selected members of the department to form a team and create a plan for increasing production. Cory volunteered to serve on this team. It was the first team project Cory had been involved in, and did not know what to expect. Fortunately, Cory had a good team leader. The team leader sat down with the team and helped identify a team goal and objectives so that members knew exactly what needed to be done and who would be responsible for each activity. At the next meeting, the team leader led a brainstorming session. Some good ideas were shared. Cory had an idea but was afraid to speak up, thinking the idea might not be as good as the others. Remembering that members need to freely add ideas during brainstorming, Cory decided to share an idea. It turned out the team liked the idea, and it became an important part of the project plan.

Communication is a key element of effective teamwork. Do not make assumptions about others or a team project. If you have questions regarding any aspect of a project, respectfully speak up. Earlier in this chapter, you learned that it is normal for teams to experience conflict. If others do not agree with your ideas, keep a positive attitude. If your team takes a wrong turn, do not waste time on blame; take corrective action and learn from any mistakes that are made. Each team member should be able to state his or her position and ideas, and it should then be a team effort to decide which ideas to use. Do not assume that any team member's idea will not be worth hearing. The whole point of a team project is to get as many ideas as possible in order to come up with the best solution for reaching the goal. If the team makes a decision with which you did not agree, you have expressed and explained your objection, and the team still decides to continue, support the team's decision and keep assisting the team in achieving its goal. Conflict is a normal part of teamwork. Learn to work through conflict. This is where open, honest, and timely communication with all team members is important.

Be an active participant on your team. Do not allow team members to do your work because you know they will do it for you. Sometimes in a team situation, one member contributes nothing because that member knows others will do the work. If you have a lazy team member, continue to do your best and try to work around that person. Try talking to the poorly performing team member and identify why he or she is not doing his or her share. If the team member provides a good reason, suggest that he or she excuse himself or herself from the team. If the team member simply refuses to perform, you may need to decide as a team to have the unproductive team member dismissed or replaced.

Exercise 11-4   Good Team Member Characteristics

Name the two most important characteristics you would want to see in your team members and explain why.

Characteristics	How Does this Help the Team Achieve Success?
1.	
2.	
3.	

Meetings

A common form of team interaction and workplace communication is a meeting. Meetings are either informational, discussion driven, decisional, or some combination of the three. Meetings can be formal or informal. The most common form of meetings in the workplace is a department meeting, which is when a boss formally meets with his or her employees.

Prior to meetings, a **meeting agenda** is normally distributed to all attendees. A meeting agenda is an outline of major topics and activities that are scheduled to be addressed during the meeting. Some agendas have time limits attached to each item. If you receive an agenda prior to a meeting, take time to read the agenda and become familiar with the topics of discussion. If there is an item you would like placed on the agenda, notify the person in charge of the meeting. If you are responsible for an agenda item, plan what you are going to share and/ or request prior to the meeting. Prepare handouts for each attendee if necessary.

The most common type of meeting is a face-to-face meeting where all parties are physically present in one location. When you arrive at a face-to-face meeting, arrive early. Depending on the size of the meeting, there can be one table, or many tables filled with meeting attendees. If there is a head table, do not sit at the head table unless you are invited to do so. If there are no assigned seats and you are speaking, sit toward the front of the room. The **meeting chair** is the individual who is in charge of the meeting and has prepared the agenda. This person normally sits at the head of the table. If the chair has an assistant, the assistant will usually sit at the right side of the meeting chair. Other individuals in authority may sit toward the front of the table, or they will sit at the opposite end of the table. If you are unsure of where to sit at a conference table, wait to see where others sit, and then fill in an empty seat.

It is not only important, but respectful for employees to show up on time and be prepared for meetings. Most formal business meetings will follow some form of **Robert's Rules of Order,** a guide to running meetings. Robert's Rules of Order is oftentimes referred to as parliamentary procedure. At the start of a meeting, the meeting chair will call the meeting to order and, if appropriate, review the minutes from the last meeting. After the review of minutes, the meeting chair will ask that the minutes be approved. Once the minutes are approved, the agenda issues will be addressed in the agenda order. At the close of the meeting, the meeting chair will adjourn the meeting.

As a meeting participant, take your turn speaking by contributing thoughtful and relevant information when appropriate. Keep your discussion to the topic at hand and assist the meeting chair by keeping the discussion moving, with all contributions being professional, respectful, and focused on the goals of the company.

When distance separates meeting participants, virtual meetings take place. These meetings occur through the use of technology such as videoconferencing, telephone, or the Internet. A more in-depth discussion on professional behavior related to these electronic communication venues is presented in chapter 10.

Team Presentations

Some work situations require employees to create and provide a presentation as a team. The presentation material provided in chapter 9 also applies to team presentations. When working with others, the first step is for all team members to agree upon the presentation goal. The team should then create the presentation outline. Using the outline as a foundation, discuss and agree upon the verbal, visual, and support content. Just as with other team situations, each member needs to take responsibility and be accountable to one another. Do not just split up sections and piece a presentation together at the last minute. Team presentations must be completed and reviewed by the entire team before presenting. Demonstrating positive human relation skills is a key to the success of a team. Each member must communicate, share duties, and behave in a respectful and professional manner.

Workplace Dos and Don'ts

Do be an active participant by being accountable to fellow team members	*Don't* ignore the needs of others in the workplace
Do be a good team member by being trustworthy and efficient and by communicating at all times	*Don't* leave the leadership process up to others
Do express yourself during team meetings	*Don't* think your ideas are not of value
Do recognize that people are motivated by different factors	*Don't* ignore team meetings and deadlines
Do make every effort to increase your leadership skills	*Don't* allow negative team members to disrupt the team's performance

Concept Review and Application

Summary of Key Concepts

- Motivation is an internal drive that causes you to behave a certain way to meet a need
- Everyone has the ability to become a successful leader
- Most companies use teams to accomplish goals
- An effective team comprises individuals who share a goal and respect for one another
- A good team member is one who does his or her job in a manner that is productive toward the end project
- Although team conflict is a natural stage of team development, do not allow conflict to cripple a team
- Communication is a key element of effective teamwork

Key Terms

adjourning stage	autocratic leaders	brainstorming
delegate	democratic leaders	formal teams
forming stage	informal teams	laissez-faire leaders
leadership	McClelland's Theory	meeting agenda
meeting chair	of Needs	motivation
norming stage	performing stage	physiological needs
Robert's Rules of Order	safety needs	self-actualization
self-esteem needs	social needs	storming stage
synergy	Vroom's Expectancy	Virtual teams
teams	Theory	

If You Were the Boss

1. You have assembled a group of employees into a team to reach the goal of improving customer service in your department, but all they do is argue when they meet. What should you do?
2. Your employees have successfully met their production goals this week. Based on Maslow's hierarchy of needs, how can you motivate them to meet next week's goals?

Web Links

http://www.nwlink.com/~donclark/leader/leadhb.html
http://www.associatedcontent.com/article/317564/theimportance_of_teamwork_in_the_workplace.html
http://www.accel-team.com/human_relations/hrels_02_maslow.html
http://www.deepermind.com/20maslow.htm

Activities

Activity 11-1

If you were teaching this class, what specific topics or activities could you include in the course to help students better meet each level of Maslow's hierarchy?

Level	Motivation Factor
Self-Actualization	
Esteem	
Social	
Safety	
Physiological	

Activity 11-2

Research President Abraham Lincoln and answer the following questions.

What key leadership qualities made him unique?

_____

_____

What challenges did he face?

_____

_____

How can you apply lessons learned from your President Lincoln research to your leadership development?

_____

_____

Activity 11-3

Write about a time when you belonged to a successful team. Identify at least three specific factors that made the team successful.

Team Success Factors
1.
2.
3.

Activity 11-4

Look up any two rules of Robert's Rules of Order online. Explain what you learned.

Rule	What you learned
1.	
2.	

1. _____ hierarchy of needs is used to explain _____.

2. Every team goes through _____: forming, _____, norming, _____, and _____.

3. _____ is a way for teams to identify various alternatives or solutions for how best to successfully achieve the goal.

4. A/An _____ is one who will work with others to help guide and motivate.

5. Communication with all team members must be _____, _____, and _____.

6. _____ is an internal drive; therefore, no one can motivate you. Others can provide only a _____ environment.

7. At work, _____ are based on trust, professionalism, and mutual respect.

Conflict and Negotiation

Whenever you're in conflict with someone, there is one factor that can make the difference between damaging your relationship and deepening it. The factor is attitude.

William James (1842–1910)

MyStudentSuccessLab Visit www.mystudentsuccesslab.com for added practice, activities, assessment, and videos.

How-Do-You-Rate

	How do you handle conflict at work?	True	False
1.	If I have a conflict with my boss, it is best to immediately go to the human resource department and file a grievance.	❑	❑
2.	A successful negotiation results in always getting my way.	❑	❑
3.	A successful strategy for combating workplace bullies is to openly bully them in return.	❑	❑
4.	Names such as "honey," "babe," and "darling" are acceptable at work if the coworker knows I'm kidding.	❑	❑
5.	If I disagree with someone, I should keep my disagreement to myself and not cause conflict.	❑	❑

Objectives

- Define *conflict* and its impact on performance
- Name and describe the various conflict management styles and the appropriate time to utilize each one
- Describe the process and purpose of *negotiation*
- Define the various forms of workplace *harassment*
- Identify resources available to employees who are confronted with workplace harassment
- Describe how to deal with a hostile work environment or *workplace bully*
- Name warning signs of workplace violence

If you answered "false" to two or more of these questions, you have a tremendous opportunity to learn more about conflict management. Employees have a right to stand up for themselves without violating the rights of others. Handle conflict at the lowest level possible, and attempt to resolve conflict as soon as you realize there is a problem.

Conflict

There is no workplace that is without conflict. The key to successful conflict management is knowing how to appropriately handle the conflict in a manner that reflects well on both you and your organization. Although most individuals regard conflict as a negative experience, it does not have to be negative. Conflict can result in a positive outcome if you approach it with the right attitude. This chapter addresses the issue of conflict and its impact on performance. Various methods of dealing with conflict, in addition to tips on how to deal with difficult people, are also presented. Finally, the issues of harassment, workplace violence, and negotiation are discussed.

Conflict occurs when there is a disagreement or tension between two or more parties (individuals or groups). This disagreement or tension is the result of a perceived threat to one's needs, interests, or concerns. The perceived threat is often based on an individual jumping to conclusions or making assumptions. We generally do not experience major conflict with those of whom we have positive relationships because we are not threatened by these individuals. When we are working with individuals we either do not know or do not have favorable relationships with, we may feel threatened and become defensive when they have different perspectives than ours. Although conflict at work cannot be avoided, you can control your reaction to the conflict.

Resolving Conflict

Conflict means that individuals are looking at a situation from different perspectives. Different perspectives mean diversity of thought. If you view conflict as a breakdown in communication, work on overcoming the problem instead of finding fault or blaming. Do not make conflict personal. Frame the conflict around an issue or situation, not a person. How an individual deals with conflict reflects his or her attitude, maturity level, and self-confidence.

If you find yourself coming into conflict with someone, take a moment and ask yourself if you are making assumptions about the individual and/or situation. Avoid making assumptions by clarifying both facts and your understanding of the situation. Be honest with yourself and recognize your feelings. If you feel the party with which you are in conflict poses a threat to you, identify why. You may find the source of the conflict is your own insecurity. Conflict resolution begins with you, your attitude toward the other party, and your willingness to resolve the issue.

When someone disagrees with you or hurts you, a natural tendency is to become angry. A common reaction to anger is to retaliate or get even. Unfortunately, this behavior does not reflect that of an individual who is striving to become a logical, mature professional. Follow these basic rules when dealing with conflict:

- Whenever possible, resolve the conflict in person
- Remain calm and unemotional
- Be silent and listen
- Try to view the disagreement from the other person's perspective
- Explain your position and offer a solution
- Come to a solution

Today's technologically connected workplace is resulting in increased reliance on brief, written communications. The digital communication medium opens the door to misinterpretation of messages, which creates conflict. As soon as you recognize a potential electronic miscommunication with another party, try to resolve the conflict face-to-face. Doing so allows you the opportunity to more quickly clarify understanding through both verbal and nonverbal communication. As presented in chapter 10, it is unprofessional to create and support a negative string of written messages. These types of messages leave a permanent record of negative behavior for all involved parties.

Rarely, if ever, does anyone win when people respond to conflict in anger. An individual who becomes emotional has difficulty managing his or her logic in resolving the issue. When confronted with conflict, remain calm and unemotional. Acknowledge your hurt feelings or anger, but do not let these dominate your response. With a clear mind, it is easier to view the disagreement from another perspective. Try to identify why the other person behaved the way he or she did. Before responding, look for facts and feelings in the message being sent. This will help you identify if the message was misinterpreted because of an emotional response or a miscommunication of a fact.

After thinking about the disagreement from the other person's perspective, calmly and rationally explain your position along with a solution. This is the step that could easily lead to an argument if you become emotional. While you are explaining your position, the other party may interrupt and state his or her position. Do not argue. Allow the other party to speak while you remain quiet and listen. This is tough, because we want to defend our opinions. Respond in a mature, professional manner. When the other party is finished speaking, take your turn. If he or she again interrupts, ask if you can take your turn responding. In your conversation, look for common ground. Identify the true source of the disagreement. Try to provide several alternatives to solving the problem, and then agree on a solution. In the workplace there may be situations where both parties may need to agree to disagree.

The following list offers several basic concepts to deal with conflict in the workplace:

- Only you can control how you respond to a situation.
- Do not let feelings dictate actions. Remain calm and unemotional.
- Attempt to resolve a conflict immediately; work with the other party.
- Accept responsibility for your actions and apologize if necessary.
- Retaliation (getting even) is not the answer.
- Keep your conflict issues confidential.

If the conflict is negatively affecting your job performance:

- Document the offensive or inappropriate behavior regarding the conflict.
- Seek assistance within the company to resolve the conflict. If possible, begin with the supervisor.
- If an internal remedy cannot be reached, seek outside assistance.

Exercise 12-1   Handling Interruptions

Engage in a conversation with a classmate about the best way to take notes in class. Have the other classmate interrupt you several times. Practice handling the interruption in an adult, mature manner. What did you say to that person?

_____

_____

_____

_____

Conflict Management and Negotiation

Depending on the offense and workplace situation, there are several conflict management styles. These include forcing, avoiding, accommodating, compromising, or collaborating.

If a behavior is offensive or unacceptable, use the **forcing conflict management style.** This style deals with the issue directly. Remain calm and unemotional. Do not turn the discussion into an argument. Your goal is to communicate that the inappropriate behavior is unacceptable and provide your solution to the problem. Forcing behavior means you are trying to make someone do things your way. The other party has no say whatsoever.

The **avoiding conflict management style** is used when you do not want to deal with the conflict so you ignore the offense. Sometimes we avoid a conflict because the offense is not a big enough deal to upset others. Other times, we avoid the conflict because we are not strong or confident enough to stand up for our rights.

If preserving a relationship is a priority, you may use the **accommodating conflict management style.** The accommodating style allows the other party to have his or her way without knowing there was a conflict.

A **compromising conflict management style** occurs when both parties give up something of importance to arrive at a mutually agreeable solution to the conflict. This differs from the **collaborating conflict management style,** in which both parties work together to arrive at a solution without having to give up something of value.

When faced with conflict, your goal is to create a solution that is fair to all involved parties. This is called **negotiation.** Both sides can come to an agreement if both parties:

- Want to resolve an issue
- Agree on an objective
- Honestly communicate their case/situation
- Listen to the other side
- Work toward a common solution that is mutually beneficial

In working toward a successful negotiation, practice good communication skills. As stated in the preceding list, listen. Do not interrupt or pass judgment until the other party has stated its case. As you learned in chapter 9, observe the other party's body language through hand and arm gestures and body positioning. Attempt to identify whether the other party is willing to resolve the issue. Also evaluate the party's ability to make eye contact. Put aside personal feelings and focus on coming to a mutually agreeable solution.

If two parties are not able to resolve an issue themselves, or if the issue affects workplace performance, it is common for a neutral third party to serve as a **mediator.** The mediator's primary objective is to assist the two feuding parties in coming to a mutually agreeable solution.

If you consistently allow others to have their way, you are displaying **passive behavior.** While it is acceptable to use passive behavior at times, there are appropriate times to use **assertive behavior.** Assertive behavior is when you stand up for your rights without violating the rights of others. Professionals should behave in an assertive manner. This is done by displaying confidence and not being ashamed to defend your position by sharing your concerns in an inoffensive manner. Individuals exhibiting **aggressive behavior** stand up for their rights in a way that violates others' rights, in an offensive manner. Others do not have to be harmed or put down for you to be heard or for you to have your way. Someone loses when aggressive behavior is exhibited. Treat others in a respectful, professional manner. If you are offended or see that someone else's rights are being violated, speak up. You can stand up for your rights (or those of another) without harming others. Do not demean others as a form of retaliation when someone displays aggressive behavior toward you.

Talk It Out

How can you become more assertive?

Harassment

Offensive, humiliating, or intimating behavior is called **harassment.** As discussed in chapter 8, the human resource department is your advocate in cases of workplace harassment. There are various anti-discrimination laws that protect individuals from harassing behavior. One of the most common forms of workplace harassment is sexual harassment. The Equal Employment Opportunity

Commission (EEOC) defines **sexual harassment** as unwanted advances of a sexual nature. The two types of sexual harassment are quid pro quo and hostile behavior. **Quid pro quo harassment** is behavior that is construed as payback for a sexual favor (e.g., you sleep with your boss, and the boss gives you a raise in return for the sexual favor). The EEOC states that quid pro quo harassment can include "verbal, visual or physical conduct of a sexual nature." **Hostile behavior harassment** includes any behavior of a sexual nature by another employee that you find offensive. The EEOC states this behavior can include "verbal slurs, physical contact, offensive photos, jokes, or any other offensive behavior of a sexual nature." Sexual harassment can occur between a man and a woman, a man and another man, or a woman and another woman. It does not limit itself to a boss and employee relationship.

In addition to a sexual harassment policy, companies should also have a policy regarding professional behavior. Each employee is entitled to be treated in a respectful and professional manner by coworkers. A policy regarding workplace behavior prevents workplace incivility and communicates to all employees that unprofessional behavior will not be tolerated. In the workplace, there will be individuals whom you may not care to befriend. You do not have to be friends with all of your coworkers, but you are required to respect colleagues and treat them in a professional manner. There is no place for rudeness in the workplace. Choose to be courteous. You also do not have to like your coworkers, but they should not be aware of your negative feelings toward them. Mature adults treat coworkers with courtesy and respect.

Exercise 12-2   Identify Harassment

What kind of behavior have you exhibited that could be construed as harassing?

_____

_____

How can you change your behavior or attitude to ensure that no one is offended by or could misinterpret your behavior as inappropriate?

_____

_____

All companies should have an anti-harassment policy. Employers need to provide training and a protocol for filing and investigating a complaint. If you are a victim of harassment, take the following steps:

1. If the behavior is offensive but relatively minor, tell the individual that his or her behavior is offensive and ask him or her to stop. Document the conversation in your personal notes. Include the date, the time, and any witnesses to the incident.
2. If the behavior continues or if the behavior is extremely inappropriate and/or outrageously offensive, immediately contact your supervisor or human resource department. Tell the person you contact what happened, that you are offended by the harassing behavior, and that you want to file harassment charges. Provide facts and names of anyone who witnessed the offensive behavior.

Once you have filed a complaint with your employer, he or she has a legal obligation to conduct a confidential investigation. Everyone is innocent until proven guilty. Do not feed the rumor mill with information regarding your complaint. Keep the issue confidential. Remain professional and reserve comments for the investigative interview. Document the dates and times of whom you speak with regarding the complaint, interviews, and comments made. When the investigation is complete, the supervisor or human resource department will render a decision. If you are not satisfied with the outcome, you have the right to file a complaint with your state's Department of Labor or Department of Fair Employment and Housing or the Federal Equal Employment Opportunity Commission. It is unlawful for an employer to retaliate against or punish anyone who files a sexual harassment claim, even if the claim is found to be without merit. No one should be punished for filing a claim. However, employees should file only legitimate complaints.

Many companies have "zero tolerance policies," which means the company strictly enforces its anti-harassment policies. Harassment policies are extremely important policies. Behave appropriately, and do not exhibit behavior that could be offensive to others. This includes off-color jokes, inappropriate touching, inappropriate conversations, and suggestive attire. Many times, individuals think they are joking when in fact their behavior is offensive to others.

Katie, the mailroom clerk who works in Cory's office, returned from a vacation at the beach. When Cory asked Katie about her vacation, she told Cory and other coworkers all about her new tattoo. One of Cory's coworkers, John, asked where on her body she got her tattoo. Katie grinned at John and patted her chest. The next day, when Katie delivered the mail, John asked Katie when he would get to see her tattoo. Katie grinned and went on her way. For the next few days, John kept asking about the tattoo and Katie kept grinning and walking away. The following week, John was called into the boss's office. Cory later found out that Katie filed sexual harassment charges against John based on John's curiosity regarding Katie's new tattoo.

Web Quiz

Take the following online quiz or find a similar one that identifies how well you understand appropriate workplace behavior.

www.workrelationships.com/quiz/

Exercise 12-3   Identify Violations

Whose rights were violated in the previous story regarding Katie, John, and the tattoo? Justify your answer.

_____

_____

_____

If you were Katie, should you have handled the situation differently? Why or why not?

_____

_____

_____

If you were John, what would you have done differently?

_____

_____

_____

Workplace Bullies

A form of workplace harassment is that of workplace bullying. Even if you are treating everyone with respect, you may have a coworker who is not reciprocating with the same respectful and professional behavior. This coworker may be behaving in an offensive, humiliating, or intimating manner. This type of employee is called a **workplace bully.** Workplace bullies are employees who are intentionally rude and unprofessional to coworkers. They seek ways to intimidate or belittle coworkers. Workplace bullying generally occurs among peers (the bully is on the same level as his or her target). Sometimes bullies publicly harass coworkers. Other times, they are discreet in their harassing tactics. Employees who are consistently rude and who bad-mouth other employees or demonstrate intimidating behavior are displaying workplace incivility. Both bullying and incivility can result in a hostile work environment, which contributes to both an increase in stress-related performance issues and, worse yet, workplace violence. Workplace bullying and incivility are not only immature behavior; they are unacceptable at work. If you experience workplace bullying:

- Do not retaliate with the same bad behavior. Remain calm and unemotional. Remember that the bully enjoys seeing that he or she has upset you. This was the goal of his or her behavior. While it is tempting to seek sympathy from coworkers, keep the issue confidential.
- Document dates, words, and witnesses of inappropriate behavior.
- Share your factual and documented information with your boss or human resource department, and file a formal complaint.
- If you think your company has not appropriately resolved the issue in a reasonable time and manner, seek outside assistance. This assistance can come from a union, a counselor or mental health professional, a state or federal agency, or a private attorney.

Know Your Rights

Each employee has a right to work in an environment free from harassment, discrimination, and hostility. Your boss and human resource department cannot assist you in resolving conflict if they are not aware of the issue. Share your concerns regarding harassment, discrimination, and workplace incivility immediately with your superiors. Prior to seeking outside assistance, exhaust all internal remedies (company resources that exist to take care of these issues). If you think you need outside assistance to preserve your rights, several state and federal resources are available to assist you. These include your state's Department of Fair Employment and Housing, the Federal Equal Employment Opportunity Commission, your State Personnel Board, the Department of Labor/Labor Commission, and the Department of Justice. These resources are available to act on your behalf and ensure you are being treated in a fair and nondiscriminatory manner.

Resolving Conflict at Work

Several steps should be taken when attempting to resolve a conflict at work. They are presented in Figure 12-1. Whenever you are faced with a conflict, attempt to resolve the issue confidentially and as quickly as possible. Too often,

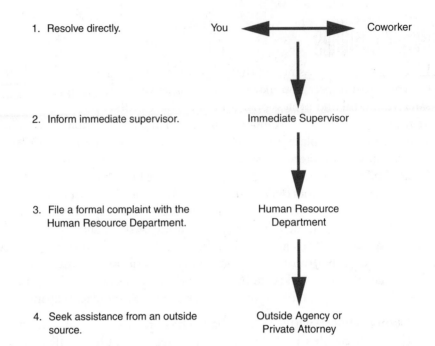

1. Resolve directly.   You ◄──────────► Coworker

2. Inform immediate supervisor.   Immediate Supervisor

3. File a formal complaint with the   Human Resource
   Human Resource Department.   Department

4. Seek assistance from an outside   Outside Agency or
   source.   Private Attorney

Figure 12-1

Resolving Conflict

individuals ignore a problem and hope it will go away. Unfortunately, these unresolved molehills frequently grow into giant, unresolved mountains. If you choose to utilize an accommodating or avoiding conflict resolution style, accept your decision to not bring the conflict to the attention of the offender and move on without holding a grudge.

If the conflict is negatively affecting either your or someone else's performance, inform your immediate supervisor. During this step, think like a boss and ask yourself if the matter is appropriate to be brought to the attention of a superior. You do not want to appear as a complainer. Document relevant information and conversations. If the problem continues and you are not satisfied with the way your immediate supervisor is handling the situation, contact your human resource manager. The human resource manager will review existing policies and, if the situation warrants, will conduct an investigation. If you are not fully satisfied with the decision or handling of the situation, you have the right to seek assistance from a private attorney or an outside government agency identified earlier in this chapter. Prior to seeking assistance from any outside agency, attempt to resolve the problem within your organization's structure. If you have representation from a union, involve the union as early in the process as possible.

Resolving a Conflict Under a Union Agreement

If you belong to a union and you have a conflict with your supervisor or any other member of management, refer to your union contract to identify what steps and rights are afforded to you as a union member. Each workplace represented by a union has a shop steward. The **shop steward** is a coworker who is very familiar with the union contract and procedures available to assist you in resolving a workplace conflict. A problem or conflict that occurs in a union setting is called a **grievance.** Go to your shop steward and share your concern, along with any documentation or evidence you may have. If the conflict is valid and covered in your union agreement, the shop steward will meet with you and your supervisor in an attempt to resolve the issue. If the issue cannot be resolved at this level, a union representative will meet with the human resource management department. The issue will continue to work up the chain of command until it is resolved. The formal steps taken in resolving a conflict between the union and an employer is called a **grievance procedure.** If you are represented by a union and your conflict is valid, your union representatives will assist you in protecting your rights through the grievance process. However, the union's purpose is not to shield you from punishment if you are guilty of wrongdoing. The purpose of the union is to enforce the union contract.

Workplace Violence

Unresolved conflict has the potential to escalate into workplace violence. According to the U.S. Department of Labor, workplace violence is the third leading cause of workplace fatal injuries. Workplace violence includes any type of harassing or harming behavior (verbal or physical) that occurs in the workplace. This violence can come from coworkers, a boss, a customer, or a family member. It is vitally important that you recognize the warning signs and take appropriate precautions to decrease the probability that you become a victim.

If you are a victim of harassment, seek assistance and report unprofessional behavior to your boss or to the human resource department before the behavior escalates to violence. Personal issues can impact workplace performance, as well. If you have a personal issue that you feel may negatively impact the workplace, share your concerns and seek confidential assistance from a coworker, your boss, or the human resource department as soon as possible. Some companies offer **employee assistance programs (EAPs).** An EAP typically provides free and confidential psychological, financial, and legal advice. This benefit is generally extended to everyone who lives in your household. If you are experiencing a stressful situation at work or home, take advantage of this benefit. Even if your company does not offer an EAP, seek assistance from your human resource department as they may be able to help you identify an appropriate community resource.

Cory shares a cubicle with a woman who is newly married. She appeared to be happily married and had told Cory about the romantic dinners and gifts her new husband provided. One day, the woman showed up to work and kept to herself. Throughout the morning, Cory found it strange that she kept covering her face. Finally, as the lunch hour neared, Cory asked the woman if everything was okay. The woman looked up at Cory with a black eye and a bruised face and told Cory that she was leaving her husband. She went on to tell Cory that the husband had become increasingly jealous of any friendship the woman had with other men and had hit her the night before. Cory asked her if she felt safe. The woman responded, "No." Cory reminded the woman about the confidential and free EAP benefit their company offered. Cory then assisted her in ensuring her safety and getting immediate help.

As exemplified in Cory's experience, stress at home can impact performance at work. Many times, victims of domestic violence fail to seek assistance out of embarrassment or fear. Your employer will want to assist you. If you feel your conflict (either at work or at home) does not warrant professional assistance, find a friend with whom you can confidentially and neutrally discuss the issue. Take responsibility at work to ensure a safe working environment. Do not be afraid to ask for an escort to and from your car if you are working nontraditional work hours or if your car is parked in a remote location. Keep emergency phone numbers posted in a visible area next to your phone, and know where all the emergency exits are located. Report suspicious behaviors or situations that have the potential to become violent. It is much better to be safe than sorry.

Agree to Disagree

As we learned in this chapter, sometimes conflict cannot be avoided. In your efforts to work in harmony with coworkers, you will find that others may hurt you. As important as it is to apologize when we have harmed others, it is equally as important to forgive. Too often, coworkers have apologized and the harmed individual has failed to forgive. Forgiving does not mean that you have forgotten the hurt. It does mean that you will give the individual another opportunity to prove his or her apology was sincere by a change in behavior.

A mature coworker is always willing to forgive and not hold grudges. Those who hold grudges never forgave in the first place and may be seeking a means of retaliation. Doing so demonstrates immaturity. You do not have to like all of your colleagues, but you need to demonstrate professionalism and respect toward them. Conflict at work is inevitable. How you allow the conflict to affect your performance is your choice.

Exercise 12-4   Resolving Issues

Identify grudges you have held or people you need to forgive. Make a point of resolving one of those issues within the next week.

_____

_____

Workplace Dos and Don'ts

Do resolve a conflict as quickly as possible and at the lowest organizational level	*Don't* allow a small conflict to grow over time
Do utilize the appropriate conflict-management style	*Don't* demonstrate aggressive behavior when standing up for your rights
Do know your rights regarding sexual harassment and discrimination issues	*Don't* utilize offensive language or hostile behavior
Do document any activity that you feel may escalate into potential problems	*Don't* retaliate when a workplace bully behaves inappropriately
Do agree to disagree when a conflict cannot be resolved	*Don't* hold grudges or behave in an immature manner

Concept Review and Application

Summary of Key Concepts

- A natural element of working with others is conflict
- How you deal with conflict determines your maturity level and professionalism
- Depending on the offense and workplace situation, there are several methods of dealing with conflict
- Employees have a right to work in an environment free from harassment
- Immediately report any harassing behavior
- Attempt to resolve conflict at the lowest level, as soon as possible
- Recognize the warning signs and take appropriate precautions to decrease the probability that you become a victim of workplace violence
- It is considered immature to hold grudges. If you cannot resolve a conflict, sometimes it may be best to agree to disagree

Key Terms

accommodating conflict
    management style
avoiding conflict
    management style
forcing conflict
    management style
hostile behavior
    harassment
sexual harassment
workplace bullies

aggressive behavior
collaborating conflict
    management style
conflict
grievance
grievance procedure
mediator
passive behavior
shop steward

assertive behavior
compromising conflict
    management style
employee assistance
    program (EAP)
harassment
negotiation
quid pro quo
    harassment

If You Were the Boss

1. A fellow supervisor usually argues about an issue before arriving at a decision. Knowing this is typical of this person's behavior, how should you handle your next confrontation?
2. One of your employees tells you that another employee has been harassing him. What should you do?

Video Case Study: Conflict

This video addresses workplace conflict during a brainstorming session. To view these videos, visit the Student Resources: Professionalism section in www.mystudentsuccesslab.com. Then answer the following questions:

1. If you were leading this meeting, how would you have handled Jane's behavior?
2. If you were a member of this team, would you have intervened in the conflict between Rachel and Jane? Why or why not?
3. What were the conflict management styles exhibited by each team member? What conflict style should have been exhibited by each team member?

Video Case Study: Sexual Harassment

This video addresses the topic of sexual harassment. To view these videos, visit the Student Resources: Professionalism section in www.mystudentsuccesslab.com. Then answer the following questions:

1. Was there anything inappropriate about Kenneth's comments to Rachel? If so, please be specific concerning which comments were inappropriate and explain why.
2. Did Rachel make any workplace-related mistakes to contribute to Kenneth's perception of her? If yes, please explain.
3. Did Rachel handle the conversation appropriately? Why or why not?
4. Based upon the conversation between Kenneth and Rachel, what should be Rachel's next steps? Be specific.

Web Links

http://www.cdc.gov/niosh/violcont.html
http://www.boston.com/jobs/galleries/workplaceconflict/

Activities

Activity 12-1

Based on what you learned in this chapter, identify the proper way to deal with these poor behaviors.

Poor Management Quality	How to Deal With
1. Uses foul language	
2. Steals company property	
3. Tells you to lie	
4. Allows employees to harass other employees	
5. Takes all the credit for everyone else's work	

Activity 12-2

You have a coworker who believes his ideas are always the best and will not compromise. Applying each conflict management style, how would you respond?

Conflict Management Style	Your Response
Forcing	
Avoiding	
Accommodating	
Compromising	
Collaborating	

Activity 12-3

What steps would you take if you disagreed with a coworker when working on a team project?

_____

_____

_____

_____

Activity 12-4

Identify a time you felt you were harassed or had your rights violated.

Based on the information you learned in this chapter, what should you have done differently?

_____

_____

What outside resource could/should you have contacted?

_____

_____

1. _____ occurs when there is a disagreement or tension between two or more parties (individuals or groups).

2. Your goal when _____ is to create a win-win situation for all involved parties.

3. There are two types of sexual harassment:

   _____ and

   _____.

4. _____ harassment is when payback is expected for a sexual favor. It can also be construed as verbal, visual, or physical conduct of a sexual nature.

5. A/An _____ includes any behavior of a sexual nature by another employee that you find offensive. This may include verbal slurs, offensive photos, jokes, or any other offensive behavior of a sexual nature.

6. _____ seek ways to intimidate or belittle coworkers.

7. If you belong to a/an _____ and you have a conflict with _____, refer to your _____ to identify what steps and rights are afforded you by being a union member.

8. _____ when you have harmed others.

Job Search Skills

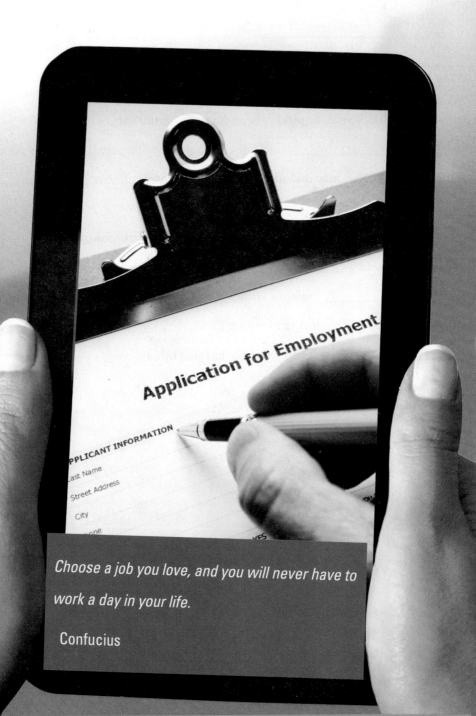

chapter 13

Choose a job you love, and you will never have to work a day in your life.

Confucius

MyStudentSuccessLab   Visit www.mystudentsuccesslab.com for added practice, activities, assessment, and videos.

How-Do-You-Rate

	Are you job search savvy?	True	False
1.	It is best to attend a job fair alone.	❑	❑
2.	It is acceptable to distribute personal business cards at social functions.	❑	❑
3.	It is not necessary to share personal information such as a birthdate and Social Security number during a job search.	❑	❑
4.	A job search portfolio is a foundation for the interview portfolio.	❑	❑
5.	Most realistic job leads are found through informal networks.	❑	❑

Objectives

- Utilize the *self-discovery* process to identify the right career
- Conduct a *targeted job search,* including a realistic job preview
- Determine the *cost of living* in your desired work location
- Ensure a professional *electronic image*
- Create a *job search portfolio*
- Identify references to be used in your job search
- Identify sources for job leads
- Demonstrate appropriate behaviors for the application process
- Define *networking* and create a professional *network*

If you answered "true" to three or more of these questions, congratulations—you are well on your way to finding the job of your dreams. Knowing how the job search process works, creating a job search plan, and properly utilizing job search tools pave the way to job search success.

The Job Search

An effective job search is the key to finding a great job. A successful job search involves creating a plan, conducting research, and taking action. Doing so takes time, organization, communication, and professionalism (all key skills you have developed throughout this text). This chapter is designed to help you create a job search strategy. A successful job search strategy identifies what type of job you will be looking for, what tools and resources you will need, and how these tools and resources are best used. The ultimate goal of a job search is to secure an interview that paves the way toward obtaining the job of your dreams.

Choosing the Right Career

Creating a job search plan begins with choosing the right career. This involves **self-discovery.** Self-discovery is the process of identifying key interests and skills built upon the career goals you set in chapter 1. Knowing your key selling points and linking these with your career goals will assist you in landing a job you will enjoy. The process of a career self-discovery includes identifying key interests and accomplishments from your work, educational, and personal experiences. A method for identifying key interests is creating an accomplishments worksheet. This is done by inventorying skills you have acquired from either your work or nonwork experience. Education and nonwork experience such as volunteerism are career-building experiences. The following trigger words assist you in identifying accomplishments:

Trigger Words

Adapted	Developed	Organized
Addressed	Earned	Planned
Analyzed	Established	Projected
Arranged	Financed	Recommended
Assisted	Implemented	Risked
Built	Increased	Saved
Calculated	Instructed	Staffed
Chaired	Installed	Taught
Cleaned	Introduced	Typed
Coached	Investigated	Updated
Communicated	Learned	Won
Coordinated	Located	Wrote
Created	Managed	
Determined	Motivated	

Exercise 13-1 Complete the Following Accomplishments Worksheet

Prior to answering each question, review the trigger words. Whenever possible, quantify your answers by documenting how many, how often, and how much. Do not worry if you cannot answer every question. The purpose of this exercise is to begin identifying accomplishments.

Question	Your Response (Quantify Your Answers)
1. What have you done in your career or career-building activities that you are most proud of?	
2. List something that you have achieved at work or school.	
3. What tasks have you performed at work and in career-building activities?	
4. What results have you produced from the tasks performed?	
5. List three things that demonstrate your ability to produce results.	
6. What have you done that shows an ability to successfully work with people?	
7. What else have you accomplished professionally or educationally that makes you proud?	
8. What extracurricular activities have you been involved with?	
9. List special skills or foreign languages you speak or write.	
10. What areas of interest do you have?	

Your accomplishments will be used to identify the right career, and they will also provide an excellent foundation when you begin to build your résumé.

After you have completed your accomplishments worksheet, reread your responses. They will most likely reveal a targeted career of interest to you.

A second means of identifying key skills and jobs of interest is to take a career assessment. Common career assessment tools include the Golden Personality Type Indicator, the Myers-Briggs Type Indicator, and the Strong Interest Inventory. Many college career centers offer these assessments, as do various online sources.

Conducting a realistic job preview identifies day-to-day and common tasks that are performed and required for a specific job. This common human resource management practice is used on job finalists prior to a job offer to ensure the candidate is fully aware of both the positive and negative aspects of a specific job. Be proactive and conduct your own realistic job preview. Identify any additional education or other requirements. For example, if you are a felon, you may not work in some areas of health care and education. There are other careers that require a clean DMV or credit history. Thoughtfully researching and understanding what is required to secure and succeed in a desired job early in the career exploration process will save time and money if the wrong career is selected.

Talk It Out

Review your completed accomplishments worksheet. What career area do you believe suits your skills and previous experiences?

Career Objective and Personal Profile

A foundation for both your job search strategy and building a winning résumé is to write a career objective or personal profile. A **career objective** is an introductory written statement for individuals with little or no work experience. A **personal profile** is an introductory written statement for individuals with professional experience related to their target career. These statements are used on a résumé to relate to the target career and/or employer, briefly introduce key skills, and express interest in a position. The responses from your completed accomplishments worksheet and career assessment provide a good summary of your current career goal based upon the knowledge, skills, and abilities you possess. Use this information as a foundation to create a statement that briefly and professionally describes you and your career goals. Depending on the layout of your résumé, this information will either have the heading "Career Objective" or "Personal Profile." This statement will be the first item listed on your résumé.

As mentioned earlier, a career objective is an introductory written statement for individuals with little or no work experience. This is a brief statement that will include your interest in a specific position, a brief one-line description of your skills related to the position, and how your skills can benefit your target employer. The career objective is the only place on a résumé where it is acceptable to use the words "I" and "my."

Web Quiz

Take the Career Planner Quiz to get a snapshot of your target job or find another career website.

http://careerpath.com/career-tests/?lr=cbmsn&siteid=cbmsnchcpath

Examples of Career Objectives

Objective: Seeking a position with an established accounting firm where I can utilize and apply my current accounting and computerized skills toward the excellence of Bell Company.

Objective: To obtain an Account Clerk position at Bell Company, where I can demonstrate and increase my general accounting skills to contribute to the success of the company.

Those with extensive work experience will utilize a personal profile. In creating a personal profile, review your key skills and accomplishments and group these items into general categories. Also identify key qualities you possess that are required for your target job. Take this information and turn it into a two- to three-sentence statement that provides a snapshot of your professional qualifications in a manner that sells your knowledge, skills, and abilities.

An Example of a Personal Profile

Personal Profile: Highly professional and detail-oriented accounting professional with demonstrated leadership and success in the areas of payroll, collections, and project management. Excellent analytical, communication, computer, and organizational skills. Bilingual (English/Spanish).

Industry Research

One step toward a successful job search is research. When a job fits your personality and skills, you will more likely succeed. A satisfying career comes from working at a company that reflects your values and performing a job you enjoy. In chapter 1 you created goals for your career and personal life. Conducting industry research will reinforce that you have made the right career decision to support your life plan. In order to determine what type of industry you will research, identify industries that require your key skills. You may realize there is more potential for jobs that require your key skills than you thought.

Once you have identified industries requiring your skills, begin identifying specific jobs in these industries. Note the different job opportunities that exist within each industry. In addition, look at various job titles. Being aware of the various job titles you qualify for allows you more flexibility when job searching. After determining industries and job titles that fit your skills, identify the environments available, including where the jobs are located and specifically what type of work environment you desire.

For example, if you finished college with a business degree, you begin by conducting industry research on the skills you have acquired. Many different industries need employees with a business background, such as health care, educational institutions, and manufacturing. Once you have determined which industry or industries you would like to work for, you can begin reviewing job titles that fit the skills you have acquired in college, such as financial analyst, general accountant, marketing assistant, or human resource generalist. After identifying specific job titles that match your skill sets, decide what type of work environment you desire. If you select health care, you may have the choice of working in a hospital, a clinic, or a private physician's office.

Conducting industry and work environment research will provide you information that will make your job search easier and more successful. Instead of sending out hundreds of résumés in hopes of securing just any job, target companies that are a good match with your life plan, your skills, and your desired work environment.

The Targeted Job Search

After you have a clearly defined career objective and have identified jobs that suit your personal and career goals, it is time to begin a targeted job search. A **targeted job search** leads you through the process of discovering open positions for which you are qualified, in addition to identifying specific companies for which you would like to work.

Part of a job search is to determine in what city you want to work. If your job search is limited to your local area, you will be restricted to local employers. If you are willing to commute outside of your area, determine how far you are willing to commute (both directions) on a daily basis. If you wish to move out of the area, identify what locations are most appealing. Should you desire to move to a new location, do not forget to consider the cost of living in your desired location. The **cost of living** is the average cost of basic necessities such as housing, food, and clothing. For example, it is much more expensive to live in Manhattan, New York, than it is to live in Cheyenne, Wyoming. While a job in Manhattan may pay a lot more than a job in Cheyenne, living expenses typically justify the higher salary.

Exercise 13-2   Identify Target Employers

Identify your target work location and three companies/employers in your target location that may be of interest to you.

1.

2.

3.

Preparation

With the popularity of social networking sites, your personal life has a greater chance of being exposed in the job search process. Ensure you have a favorable **electronic image.** An electronic image is the image formed when someone is communicating with you and/or researching you through electronic means. This involves conducting an Internet search on you through personal pages and search engines. Since the majority of information on the Internet is public information, an increasing number of employers are conducting web searches on potential employees to gain a better perspective of the applicant's values and lifestyle. With today's overabundance of electronic social networking and information sites, personal blogs, and other file-sharing services, ensure that defamatory photos, writings, or other material will not be a barrier in your job search. When conducting an Internet search on yourself, remove any information that portrays you in a negative light. If you are actively involved in social networking sites, carefully evaluate any personal information that is contained on the sites of your friends. If negative information is contained on sites of your friends, explain your job search plans and politely ask them to remove the potentially harmful information.

An additional step toward ensuring a clean electronic image is to maintain a professional e-mail address. Sending a potential employer an e-mail from the address "prty2nite" is not the image you want to project. If necessary, establish a new e-mail address that utilizes some form of your name or initials to maintain a clean and professional electronic image. Two final considerations in maintaining a professional electronic image are, as mentioned in chapters 9 and 10, the maintenance of a professional voice mail message and the avoidance of text slang in all written communication. Your job search strategy will involve extensive communication with employers and other individuals who will assist you with your job search. Interaction with these parties needs to be professional.

Talk It Out

What type of photos, writings, or materials do you think are inappropriate for a potential employer to see?

Job Search Portfolio

A **job search portfolio** is a collection of paperwork used for job searches. Some items from your job search portfolio will become a part of your interview portfolio, which you will create in chapter 15. You will use the items you collect for your job search portfolio to keep you organized and prepared while searching for a job.

It is best to have a three-ring binder with tabs to keep all paperwork organized and protected. Do not punch holes in original documents. Place original documents in plastic notebook protectors. When you begin collecting items for your portfolio, keep the original and at least two copies of each item available at all times. These copies will be transferred to your interview portfolio when needed.

Because many of today's job searches occur over the Internet, it is also recommended you create an electronic job search portfolio. An **electronic job search portfolio** is a computerized folder that contains electronic copies of all job search documents. For your electronic job search file, scan copies of all documents you will be keeping in your hard-copy portfolio. When you share documents with potential employers and others over the Internet, these electronic documents will be sent as attachments.

A useful networking and introduction tool is a personal business card. A personal business card is a small card that contains contact information including your name, mailing and e-mail addresses, and phone number. It is a good practice to share your personal business card with anyone you meet, especially in networking, informational interview, and mentoring encounters. Doing so makes it easier for your new acquaintance to remember you and contact you in the future. Personal business cards are inexpensive and valuable networking tools and need not be professionally printed. Templates are available on the web and can easily be printed on cardstock paper, or you can purchase special business card packages online or at an office supply store. When designing a personal business card, ensure it contains all relevant contact information and reflects a professional image. Use an easy-to-read font style. Do not include fancy graphics, pictures, or too many words. Simple is better.

The following is a list of items to keep in your job search portfolio. These items and their purpose will be discussed in this and the next two chapters.

Item	Description
Network list	A list of professional relationships used for job contacts
Personal business cards	Cards with personal contact information used to share for job leads
Résumé	A formal profile that is presented to potential employers
Cover letter	Introduces a résumé
Reference list	A list of individuals who will provide a professional reference
Letters of recommendation	A written professional reference to verify work experience and character
Transcripts	Documents that verify education. Have both official (sealed) and copies available. Sealed transcripts may be required
Current state licenses	Documents that verify the ability to practice certain professions
Awards, certificates, work samples	Documents that demonstrate proficiency in specific skills
Completed generic application	Generic job application that makes information readily available
Copy of ID and/or driver's license	A valid ID and proof of ability to drive (if driving is a job requirement)
Copy of recent DMV record (if relevant to your career)	Used to ensure a safe driving record
Personal commercial	Statement that assists with interview
Small calendar, note pad, pen	To track important dates and make notes
Performance appraisals from previous jobs	Proof of positive work performance

Many careers that involve driving require a copy of your driving history. This information is secured by contacting your local Department of Motor Vehicles (DMV). If you have a poor driving record, check with your local DMV to identify how long this history stays on your record. Those with a blemished driving history may have a tougher time securing a job in a field that involves driving. When sharing your DMV record, as with all other portfolio items, provide only a copy (unless otherwise required) and maintain the original in your job search portfolio.

Employment Applications

Keep a completed generic employment application in your job search portfolio so you have required information readily available. If you have a smart phone, store this information on your device for quick and easy retrieval. When completing the application in its entirety, do not list your Social Security number or birth date. This information is not given to a prospective employer until you are a finalist for a job to protect against the potential of age discrimination and/or identity theft. Let the employer know you will supply this information upon hire.

An employment application is a legal document. When completing the application, read the fine print prior to signing the document. Commonly, at the end of the application, there will be a statement that grants the potential employer permission to conduct reference and various background checks, including a credit check if the information is relevant to the job for which you are applying. Fully understand why this background information is necessary and how it will be used in the hiring process. If you do not fully understand the statements on the application, clarify these statements prior to signing the application.

It is common for employers to request that the applicant complete an employment application and submit this document along with the résumé package. If you submitted only a cover letter and résumé, you may be asked to complete an application after you have been interviewed. Some employment applications can now be completed through a kiosk located at a worksite. Applications may also be downloaded, completed, and submitted directly from a target company's website. A keyboarded employment application is best. If keyboarding the application is not possible, complete the application by printing neatly in black ink. In some instances, after you have completed an online application, you may be asked to take a pre-employment test as part of the application process. An additional discussion on pre-employment tests is presented in chapter 15.

Personal References and Recommendations

Create a list of professional references that a potential employer can contact to verify your work experience and personal character. References are not to be included on your résumé. References are listed on a separate page. Do not send your reference list with your résumé unless it is requested by the employer. However, have a copy available to share if the employer requests references during the interview. Prior to including individuals on your reference list, ask each person if he or she is willing to serve as a reference. Be sure each person on this list will provide a positive reference. Have at least three names to submit as references. Include each reference's name, contact phone number, business mailing address, relationship, and e-mail address. References can be past or present employers and supervisors, coworkers, instructors, or someone with whom you have volunteered. Do not use relatives, friends, or religious leaders unless you have worked or volunteered with or for them.

In addition to reputable references, it is wise to have at least three **letters of recommendation.** A letter of recommendation is a written testimony from another person that states that you are credible. Letters of recommendation need to reflect current job skills, accomplishments, and positive human relations skills and should be no older than one year. Letters of recommendation can be from past or present employers, coworkers, instructors, or someone you worked for as a volunteer. It is common and acceptable to have someone write a formal letter of recommendation and serve as a personal reference.

In addition to routinely updating your résumé, keep your references list updated. Provide references relevant to your career. Occasionally check with your references and verify if they are still willing to serve as references. Keep these individuals current on your job search status and career goals.

Exercise 13-3 List Your References

List three people you can use as references. Then list three people you can ask to write you a letter of recommendation. Include their relationship to you.

Reference	Relationship
1.	
2.	
3.	

Letter of Recommendation	Relationship
1.	
2.	
3.	

Sources of Job Leads

There are many sources for job leads. Do not wait for potential employers to find you. Actively search association and employer sites of targeted industries. The most obvious job lead is directly from a targeted company. It is also acceptable to personally visit the target company's human resource department for current job announcements. If you do not have a targeted company but have a location where you would like to work, conduct an Internet search using the target city and target position as key search words. Search for associations in your targeted industry. They may offer online job banks. Many employers now post job announcements on social networking and corporate websites. Check online message boards and popular job search sites. Also, conduct key-word searches on community message boards. Keep track of the sites you are utilizing for your job search and monitor activity. Many larger cities and counties offer one-stop centers for job seekers. These government-funded agencies provide job-seeker assistance and serve as a link between job seekers and local employers. Other job sources include job fairs, newspaper advertisements, industry journals, and current employees who work in your targeted industry and/or company. Most individuals rely on posted job positions. However, many jobs are unsolicited (not advertised to the general public). The way to become aware of these unsolicited jobs is to use your professional network. The larger your professional network, the more you will become aware of unannounced job leads. A discussion on how to create and utilize a professional network is presented later in this chapter. Once you have established a network, inform network members of your desire for a job and ask for potential job leads.

Treat all face-to-face job search situations, including distributing your résumé, meeting a potential network contact, or visiting a company to identify open positions, as if you are going to an interview. Dress professionally, go alone, have extra copies of your résumé, display confidence, and bring your interview portfolio. The interview portfolio will be discussed in detail in chapter 15. In networking situations where there are many job seekers, such as a job fair, be polite and professional in your interactions with everyone. Do not interrupt or be rude to other job seekers. Take the lead in introducing yourself to company representatives. Sell your skills and confidently ask the company representative if he or she has an open position requiring your skills. Your goal in such a situation is to favorably stand out from the crowd, share your résumé, and arrange an interview. There are situations where applicants are invited to "on the spot" interviews. Your professional appearance and interview portfolio will show that you are prepared. Dressing casually and/or having a child or friend in tow will communicate unprofessionalism to a potential employer.

If you are unable to find a job lead, send an unsolicited cover letter and résumé to your target company either electronically or through traditional mail. When sending an unsolicited résumé, send two copies: one to the human resource manager, and the other to the manager of your target job. Prior to sending your résumé, call the company to secure the names of both individuals. Ensure you have identified the correct spelling and gender for the individuals to whom you will be sending your résumé. Sending two résumés to the same company increases the opportunity of securing an interview. The targeted department manager will most likely read and file your résumé for future reference. The human resource manager will also review your résumé and may identify other jobs for which you are qualified.

Networking

During the time you will be looking for a job or advanced position, establishing a professional network is important—as is maintaining this network throughout your career. **Networking** is the act of creating professional relationships. Think of networking as a connection device. The purpose of creating a professional network is to have a resource of individuals whom you can call upon for professional assistance and/or advice. While the intent of this discussion is to utilize a professional network for job search purposes, as presented in chapter 4, a professional network is also a useful tool for collaborating and assisting others.

Professional networking is necessary throughout a job search. There are two primary forms of networking. The first form is the traditional method, which involves face-to-face interaction. The second method utilizes social media. Traditional networking involves interacting with and meeting as many people as possible who work or know someone who works in your targeted industry. There are many formal networking opportunities for job seekers, including attending association meetings, service clubs, and conferences or trade shows. Additionally, many college career centers provide networking events for students to interact with local employers. Job fairs, volunteer fairs, and trade shows are excellent venues for professional networking. The key to successful networking is to begin creating a network before you need one. This provides you time to develop your networking skills, increase your confidence, and identify which venues work best. Many college recruiters enjoy meeting students a year prior to graduation. Students who are networking early in their job search convey organization, planning, and strategic skills, which are skills highly desired by employers.

Developing a professional network is easy. You inform one person that you are looking for a job. That person informs others, then those people inform

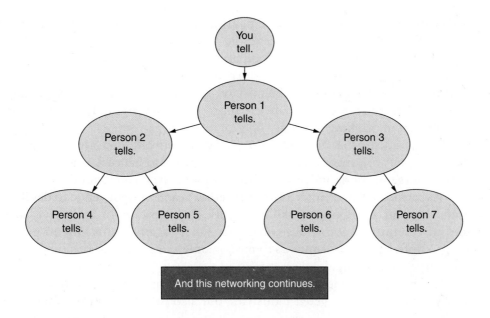

Figure 13-1

Networking

others, and soon you have many people who know that you are searching for a job. View Figure 13-1 to see how a network grows.

Almost every person you know may be a part of your network, including coworkers, supervisors, instructors, family, and friends.

Cory has been working as an account clerk for a year. During this year, Cory has acquired new accounting skills, has learned new software packages, and has graduated with an accounting degree. Cory begins by telling supervisors and coworkers what skills and education have been acquired. In addition, Cory mentions the new skills and software packages learned over the last year and shares future goals. Cory then tells family members and friends the same information. This is the beginning of Cory's professional network. Cory creates a network list and begins tracking and updating these people. Cory will continue to update the people on the network list about new skills acquired and job search progress.

When engaging in traditional networking, remember that the success of one's networking attempts begin with a positive attitude. Review what you have learned in previous chapters of this text regarding professional behavior. First and foremost, believe in yourself and your abilities. Be confident and willing to approach and initiate an introduction with strangers. People are drawn to positive people. When actively networking, dress professionally, because first impressions matter. Have both your personal business card and a brief statement of your key skills to informally share with anyone you meet. When you share a business card, ask for one in return. Obtaining the card provides you the opportunity to follow up. Also use the information from your new contact's business card to update your network list. Practice the art of introducing yourself in a positive and professional manner, beginning with a professional handshake. Listen carefully to the name of the individual you are meeting. After the handshake, exchange business cards. Prior to telling your new contact about you and your job search, ask about him or her. Get the individual to talk about where he or she works, what he or she does, and what he or she enjoys about the job. Use this time to build rapport. At the appropriate time, tell the individual about you and your job search. As your conversation continues, watch for body-language cues. If the person is engaged, he or she will make direct eye contact and turn his or her body toward you. If the person does not want to visit too long, he or she will look away and/or turn his or her body away from you. Utilize these cues to either continue the visit or politely thank him or her for the visit and end the conversation.

While it is common to have food and beverages available at formal networking events, it is best to refrain from eating and drinking until you have met your desired network contacts. Practice proper etiquette by not overindulging in food items. You are in attendance to meet people, not to eat. It is always best to refrain from drinking alcohol.

There are also other methods to expand your network, such as volunteering for community organizations. Volunteering provides a chance to meet people in different organizations and learn about new positions throughout the community. As mentioned in chapter 11, volunteering is an excellent venue to develop leadership and team-building skills, network, and, most importantly, give back to your community. Join clubs and professional organizations. Attend workshops, conferences, and seminars to meet people from corporations that are in your targeted career field.

Current technologies now provide ample social media outlets to not only post your résumé to targeted industries, but also to create an electronic network. Some popular online professional networking venues are LinkedIn and Facebook. Both of these venues have special support services for job seekers, but there are many industry-specific networking venues online. When utilizing a social networking site for your job search, ensure that your career information is current and consistent with your résumé. However, be cautious when sharing personal information over these venues.

Within twenty-four hours of a networking experience, follow up with a brief message telling the individual that it was a pleasure meeting him or her. Attach your résumé to your message, and tell your new contact to feel free to pass your résumé along to others. If you are interested in conducting an informational interview with your new contact, do not attach your résumé. The purpose of your message will be to not only thank the individual for his or her time, but also to ask for and arrange an informational interview. An **informational interview** is when a job seeker meets with a business professional to learn about a specific career, company, or industry. You are not asking for a job during an informational interview. You are only expanding your professional network. During an informational interview, ask the business professional questions about targeted careers, hiring, and the culture of the company. By meeting and talking with business professionals, you have increased your professional network. When you network, do not be afraid to ask those with whom you network for additional contacts who may be able to assist you. Networking involves giving and taking. If you read an industry-related article, attend a conference, or are working on a project that may interest someone in your network, share the information and demonstrate how you can be of value to them.

Talk It Out

What is appropriate and inappropriate information to share when creating an online network?

Exercise 13-4   Identify Your Current Network

Where have you met people who you can include in your professional network?

1. _____

2. _____

3. _____

Create and maintain a network list. A **network list** is an easily accessible list of all network contacts' names, industries, addresses, and phone numbers so you can contact each person for quick reference. Provide each contact who is actively assisting with your job search a copy of your most current résumé. Keep all contacts on your network list updated throughout your job search. When keeping in contact with members of your network, be sensitive to their time. Do not annoy them or be inconsiderate in your interactions. Ensure that your network contact list is up-to-date. Find and consistently utilize a database system that is convenient for you. Most individuals use an electronic database, while some still prefer a traditional address book. Whatever you use, keep it current. If you find a job, immediately remove job search postings and inform members of your network who were actively assisting you with your search for a job.

Networking for both business and job search purposes is work, but the effort reaps tremendous benefits if done appropriately. Every few months, review your professional network list. If there is someone with whom you have not recently connected, contact him or her to say hello and keep him or her updated on your career and growth plans.

Protecting Your Privacy

The job search process involves sharing personal information. Be cautious and share only personal information with reputable sources or you may become a target for identity theft. If you are applying for a job and have never heard of the employer, conduct research to verify that the employer is legitimate. As stated earlier, do not share your birth date or Social Security number with any employer until after you are a finalist for the job.

Cory's friend Terry was looking for a job. Terry found a job on an online classified job site that sounded legitimate. The employer asked that Terry submit a résumé online. Within a few days after sharing his résumé, Terry received an e-mail telling him that he was a finalist for the job. The only step left in the process was for Terry to forward a copy of his credit report. Although Terry was desperate for a job, he thought this was a little strange, so he asked Cory what Cory thought of the situation. Cory conducted an Internet search for Terry and could not find any evidence that the company Terry was applying to even existed. Cory asked Terry if he completed an application that gave the potential employer permission to view Terry's credit information, and Terry said no. Cory and Terry agreed that sharing personal information with an unknown company was not a good idea.

Keeping the Right Attitude

Throughout this text, you have learned how to be successful in the workplace. The importance of maintaining a positive attitude throughout your career cannot be stressed enough. This holds true during your job search. The job search process is a lot of work and can sometimes be frustrating. Do not get discouraged if you do not get an interview or job offer on your first try. In tight job markets, it may take many interviews before receiving a job offer.

To maintain a healthy attitude during this time of transition, follow these tips when looking for a job:

1. *Stay positive:* Start each day with a positive affirmation. Speaking aloud, tell yourself that you are a talented and great person who deserves a good job (and believe what you say). Your attitude is reflected in your actions. If you allow negative elements to influence your job search, you will be at a disadvantage.

2. *Stay active:* Create a daily and weekly "to do" list. Every day, check the websites of your targeted industries, associations, and companies in addition to checking relevant job sites. Schedule time for industry and company research, as well as time for networking. A job search is a job in itself. You do not want to be an unproductive employee in the workplace, so begin creating good work habits now by making the most of your time in a job search.

3. *Keep learning:* Use job search down time to learn or develop a skill. As with your routine industry and company research and daily review of targeted job postings, schedule learning time. Identify a skill that will assist you when you are offered a job. Finances do not have to be a barrier to learning new skills. There are many free tutorials available on the Internet. Topics to consider include computer skills, writing skills, or any skill specific to your chosen industry.

4. *Stay connected:* Although it is natural to not want to socialize with others when discouraged, the job search period is the time when you most need to be in the presence of others. In addition to keeping your current network updated on your job search, identify further reasons to communicate with your network. Consistently work on expanding your network by attending association meetings and events, volunteering, and scheduling informational interviews. Plan at least one meeting and/or activity each day. As opposed to sitting around the house waiting for the phone to ring, dressing professionally and networking every day will contribute to your maintaining a positive outlook.

5. *Stay focused:* During this time of transition, manage your professional job search, your personal health, and your environment. Manage your professional job search by maintaining an up-to-date calendar with scheduled follow-up activities relating to your job search. Because a job search is a stressful experience, practice healthy stress management techniques, including a proper diet, regular exercise, and positive self-talk. Invest a portion of your time in something of interest other than your job search. Consider volunteering for an organization of special interest to you. Doing so will provide a mental break, provide possible new network contacts, and provide you the satisfaction of helping others. Managing your personal environment involves making wise choices regarding personal finances. Be cautious and conservative with your money. Make thoughtful purchases and avoid emotional spending. Finally, surround yourself with individuals who are positive and supportive of you and your efforts.

If you are currently working and you begin looking for a new job, keep your job search confidential. If you are listing your supervisor as a reference, let him or her know you are looking for a new job and briefly explain why. Do not quit your current job before accepting a new job. Also, do not bad-mouth your company or anyone who works for your current or former employer(s).

Workplace Dos and Don'ts

Do keep your original job search documents in a portfolio	*Don't* give employers your original documents and expect them to be returned to you
Do keep a network list and keep the people on your list updated	*Don't* be annoying or inconsiderate of your network contacts' time
Do realize that a targeted job search takes time	*Don't* get discouraged if you do not get an interview or job offer on your first try
Do explore various sources of job leads, including your personal network, the Internet, and industry journals	*Don't* limit your job leads to one source

Concept Review and Application

Summary of Key Concepts

- The career objective or personal profile is a brief statement that sells your key skills and relates to your self-discovery
- A targeted job search leads you through the process of identifying open positions for which you are qualified, in addition to identifying companies for which you would like to work
- Ensure you have a professional electronic image while job searching
- Professional networking is the act of creating professional relationships
- In addition to people you already know, develop additional network contacts through various sources of job leads
- Creating and maintaining a job search portfolio will keep you organized and prepared during the job search process
- Create a list of professional references for employers

Key Terms

career objective

electronic job
  search portfolio

networking

self-discovery

cost of living

informational interviews

letters of
  recommendation

targeted job search

electronic image

job search portfolio

network list

personal profile

If You Were the Boss

1. What information would you supply to a job seeker during an informational interview with you?
2. If you discovered that one of your top interview candidates had an unprofessional website, what would you do?

Video Case Study: Job Fair

This video addresses inappropriate and appropriate behavior when participating in a job fair. To view these videos, visit the Student Resources: Professionalism section in www.mystudentsuccesslab.com. Then answer the following questions:

1. What inappropriate behaviors did Kevin exhibit at the job fair? Be specific in your answer.
2. What inappropriate behaviors did Sean exhibit at the job fair? Be specific in your answer.
3. What appropriate behaviors did Rachel exhibit at the job fair? Be specific in your answer.
4. Did Rachel close her interview appropriately? Why or why not?

Video Case Study: Job Search Strategies

This video presents expert advice on how to conduct a professional job search. To view these videos, visit the Student Resources: Professionalism section in www.mystudentsuccesslab.com. Then answer the following questions:

1. What are important considerations and activities that should take place during the research phase of a job search?
2. What is a network, and how do you create it?
3. What specific advice does the expert provide regarding cold-call applications?

Web Links

http://www.rileyguide.com/network.html#netprep
http://jobsearch.about.com/od/networking
http://www.truecareers.com
http://www.weddles.com/associations/index.cfm
http://money.cnn.com/magazines/fortune/rankings/
http://www.glassdoor.com/index.htm

Activity 13-1

Create a reference list with at least three names; include the following information.

Reference 1
Name
Job title
Place of employment
Address
Telephone number
E-mail address
Relationship (why is he or she a reference?)
Reference 2
Name
Job title
Place of employment
Address
Telephone number
E-mail address
Relationship (why is he or she a reference?)
Reference 3
Name
Job title
Place of employment
Address
Telephone number
E-mail address
Relationship (why is he or she a reference?)

Activity 13-2

Using the following network table to create a networking list.

NETWORK TABLE				
Network List				
Name	**Address**	**Phone No.**	**E-Mail Address**	**Last Date of Contact**

Activity 13-3

Using an Internet job site or other job sources, identify three specific job titles that match your career goals and current qualifications.

Job Titles
1.
2.
3.

Activity 13-4

Design a personal business card.

Activity 13-5

Secure a job application online or from a local employer. With the exception of your signature, complete the application. Include this document in your job search portfolio.

1. The act of creating professional relationships is referred to as _____.

2. The following people could be included in a professional network:

   _____,

   _____,

   _____,

   _____, and

   _____.

3. One of the most obvious job sources is utilizing your _____.

4. Keep your phone message _____.

5. The process of identifying your key interests and skills built upon career goals is known as _____.

6. The _____ or _____ is an introductory written statement at the beginning of a résumé.

7. A _____ is an image formed when someone is researching you through a computer search.

8. An employment application is a _____.

Résumé Package

Whenever you are asked if you can do a job, tell 'em, "Certainly I can!" Then get busy and find out how to do it.

Theodore Roosevelt (1858–1919)

MyStudentSuccessLab Visit www.mystudentsuccesslab.com for added practice, activities, assessment, and videos.

Objectives

- Identify the steps for building a résumé package
- Write a career objective or personal profile
- Distinguish between a *functional résumé* and a *chronological résumé*
- Identify personal *soft skills, job-specific skills,* and *transferable skills*
- Create a winning *résumé*
- Write a *cover letter*

How-Do-You-Rate

	Test your resume expertise	True	False
1.	Paper résumés are not necessary in today's electronic age.	☐	☐
2.	Career objectives are used on all resumes.	☐	☐
3.	Unique skills such as being bilingual or serving in the military can lead to discrimination and should not be listed on a formal résumé.	☐	☐
4.	Using a word-processing résumé template is best when creating a résumé.	☐	☐
5.	If I have a job gap on my résumé it is acceptable to make up a job to fill in the gap.	☐	☐

If you answered "true" to at least two questions, use the information and tools in this chapter to improve your chances of creating and utilizing a winning résumé.

Building Your Résumé Package

Before an employer meets you, they first view your résumé package. A résumé package includes a résumé and a cover letter. Your résumé needs accents package needs to efficiently and effectively sell your skills and communicate how your attributes are unique compared to those of all the other candidates vying for your target job. A **résumé** is a formal written profile that presents a person's knowledge, skills, and abilities to potential employers. Your résumé is an important job search tool that should be continually updated throughout your career. You may not be planning to find a new job or get promoted today, but a time will come when a current résumé is needed. Do not wait until that time to create or update your résumé. As you increase your job skills and accomplishments, add these new skills and experiences to your résumé.

When you begin to create your résumé, you will quickly discover that there are various types of résumés and résumé formats. You may also receive conflicting advice as to how the perfect résumé should look and what it should include. The appropriate type of résumé used depends upon your work experience. A well-written résumé makes it easy for potential employers to quickly and easily identify your skills and work experience.

This chapter will present the tools for creating a professional résumé and cover letter. As you go through the process of constructing your résumé package, make every word, the visual presentation, and the information sell your skills and career accomplishments. There are five steps toward building a winning résumé:

- *Step One:* Career Objective/Personal Profile
- *Step Two:* Gathering Information

- *Step Three:* Proper Layout
- *Step Four:* Skills, Accomplishments, and Experience
- *Step Five:* The Final Résumé

Step One: Career Objective/Personal Profile

The first step in developing a winning résumé is to write a career objective or personal profile. As presented in chapter 13, a career objective is a statement that presents your key skills in a brief statement for individuals with little or no work experience. A personal profile is used for individuals with more extensive career experience. Create a career objective or personal profile using the information from chapter 13. Use your career objective or personal profile as the foundation for your résumé. Make your career objective or personal profile specific to the job for which you are applying.

Exercise 14-1   Your Career Objective or Personal Profile

Refer back to chapter 13 and write a career objective or personal profile.

_____

_____

_____

_____

Step Two: Gathering Information

The second step in building a résumé is to create a draft document with key headings. This step involves collecting and merging all relevant information into one document. Begin identifying and listing the following information into an electronic document:

1. *Education.* List schools, dates, degrees, certificates, credentials, GPA, licenses, and other relevant education information, including military experience.
2. *Skills.* List all skills you possess.
3. *Employment.* Starting with the most recent job, list the employer, dates of employment (month and year), job title, and responsibilities.
4. *Languages.* List all foreign languages, fluency levels, and if you can read, speak, and/or write the foreign language.
5. *Honors and Awards.* List any honors and awards you have received at school, work, or from the community.
6. *Professional/Community Involvement.* List volunteer work and community service projects. Include any leadership role you took in these activities.

Note that when compiling information to include in your résumé, there is no personal information listed. Personal information including birth date, marital/child status, ethnicity, or religion should not be included on a résumé. It is also inappropriate to list hobbies or include photographs. There are laws that protect employees from discrimination in hiring and advancement in the workplace, and employers should not be aware of personal information unless it is relevant to the job for which you are applying. Additional information regarding this subject is presented in chapter 15. Older job seekers should not list the date of graduation on a résumé as it could be used for age discrimination.

Exercise 14-2   Gather Information

Complete the following table:

Education (list most recent first)

School Name	City, State	Dates	Degree, Certificate, Credential, Licenses

Skills

Employment (list most recent first)

Employer	Employment Dates	Job Title	Duties

Exercise 14-2 Gather Information (continued)

Languages	Fluency (Read, Write, and/or Speak)	

Honors and Awards	Dates	Place

Professional/Community Involvement

Step Three: Proper Layout

The third step in developing a successful résumé is to identify and arrange your information in the proper résumé layout. If you are at the start of your career and/or do not have extensive work experience, create a résumé using the **functional résumé layout.** This layout is used to emphasize relevant skills when you lack related work experience. A functional résumé focuses on skills and education. When writing a functional résumé, list your career objective, relevant skills, and education before any work experience. Include only your high school in the education section if you are using a functional layout and have not yet graduated from college. Most functional résumés are only one page in length. Refer to Figure 14-1 for the functional résumé layout, and see Figures 14-2 and 14-3 for examples of a functional résumé with and without career-related work experience.

Those with extensive career experience should use a **chronological résumé layout.** In the chronological layout, note that the career objective is replaced with a personal profile. General skills emphasized in a personal profile are key skill sets. These skill sets will be used as subheadings in the professional experience section on a chronological résumé. The chronological layout presents related work experience, skills, and significant accomplishments under each respective skill set subheading. When writing a personal profile, include

Functional Résumé Layout, see Figure 14-1 on page 239

Functional Résumé Example with Minimal Career Work Experience, see Figure 14-2 on page 240

Functional Résumé Example without Career Work Experience, see Figure 14-3 on page 241

Talk It Out

Which résumé layout is best for your situation? Why?

Chronological Résumé Layout, see Figure 14-4 on page 242

Chronological Résumé Example with Degree, see Figure 14-5 on pages 243–244

Chronological Résumé Example with No Degree, see Figure 14-6 on pages 245–246

key general skills and key qualities desired by your target employer. Specific skills will be detailed under each respective professional experience subheading. Share major accomplishments and responsibilities from each position. Include important activities you have accomplished in your job. If necessary, add a second page to your résumé. A chronological layout best highlights, communicates, and sells specific job skills and work accomplishments. Refer to Figure 14-4 for the chronological résumé layout, and see Figures 14-5 and 14-6 for examples of chronological résumés.

For both functional and chronological résumé layouts, present employment history and education in reverse time order (most recent job first). When listing work history, bold your job title, not the place of employment. When listing dates of employment, use only month and year. Be consistent in how dates are listed on the résumé.

When you have determined which résumé layout is best for your current situation, electronically arrange the information you have compiled into the correct résumé layout. Avoid résumé templates. Résumé templates can be difficult to update, modify, and personalize.

Step Four: Skills, Accomplishments, and Experience

Once you have electronically arranged your information into the correct layout, it is time to move to the fourth step in developing your résumé. This involves detailing the information listed in your skills, work experience, and professional accomplishments. Work experience includes learned skills, job duties, and accomplishments. Professional accomplishments communicate specific activities you achieved beyond your job duties. Whenever possible, quantify your skills, responsibilities, and professional accomplishments. Do not assume the reader will know what you have done. As you insert professional accomplishments and responsibilities into your electronic file, include both job-specific skills and transferable skills. **Job-specific skills** are those that are directly related to a specific job or industry. If you were to change careers, job-specific skills would probably not be useful. For example, if you are a medical billing clerk who knows how to use a specific software program such as Medical Manager, you will not need to use this skill if you become a preschool teacher.

Transferable skills are skills that are transferred from one job to the next. If you change careers, you will still be able to use (transfer) these skills in any job. For example, if you are a medical billing clerk, you may have learned customer service skills from consistent contact with patients and must practice being positive when dealing with customers. If you become a preschool teacher, the customer service skill of being positive is transferable to the children in your classroom. Employers need employees with job-specific skills and transferable skills, so list both types on your résumé. The term **soft skills** refers to the people skills necessary when working with others in the workplace. Employers want employees that are reliable, team players, good communicators, and able to get along well with others.

When listing work experience on your résumé, include the job title, company name, city, and state where the company is located, and the duties of the position. When listing job duties, be specific with common workplace skills, such as computer skills. The term computer skills can be too general and typically includes many different areas: networking, programming, applications, data processing, and/or repair. An employer needs to know what specific computer skills you possess. For example, inform the employer of your computer skill level (e.g., basic, intermediate, or advanced) with a specific software. When listing your skills, first list the skills relevant to your target job. If you are bilingual include this information in your résumé. Let the employer know what second language you read, write, or only speak that second language.

Résumés do not normally contain complete sentences. They contain statements that sell your skills, qualifications, and work experience. Except for the career objective on a functional résumé, the words "I" and "my" should not appear.

Exercise 14-3   Detail Your Skills

List as many job-specific and transferable skills as possible. If you do not have any job-specific skills, list the job skills you will have after finishing your schooling.

Job-Specific Skills (Related to Your Career Job)	Transferable Skills (Can Be Used in Any Job)
1.	1.
2.	2.
3.	3.
4.	4.
5.	5.

When applying for a specific position, identify the key knowledge, skills, and abilities the employer desires. General information regarding a specific position will be listed in the job announcement. If possible, secure a copy of the job description. If this is not possible, use the target job information or conduct an occupational quick search on the O*Net database. This database of occupational information was developed for the U.S. Department of Labor and provides key information by job title. Match the key knowledge, skills, and abilities required for your target job with the knowledge, skills, and abilities you possess. Then emphasize this information on your résumé.

Organize your skills and work experience by first listing the key skills required for your target job. When communicating your skills, experience, and accomplishments, write with energy. Use action verbs, also referred to as **power words.** Power words are action verbs that describe your accomplishments in a lively and specific way. For example, instead of stating "started a new accounts receivable system," use "developed a new accounts receivable system that reduced turnaround time by 20 percent." Power words are listed in Table 14-1 and Table 14-2.

Exercise 14-4   Accomplishments

Refer back to the accomplishments worksheet you completed in Exercise 13-1. Review these accomplishments and turn them into powerful action statements. Quantify whenever possible.

Choose Your Top Five Accomplishments from Exercise 13-1	Change to Powerful Action Statements
1.	
2.	
3.	
4.	
5.	

Table 14-1   Skills Power Words

Sample Power Statements for Skills

- Ideal oral and written communications skills

- Understanding of office practices and procedures; ability to operate fax machine, copy machine, and ten-key machine; ability to enter data; ability to effectively interpret policies and procedures; work well under the pressure of deadlines; establish and maintain a positive working relationship with others; ability to communicate

- Accurate typing skills at _____ wpm

- Experienced with Microsoft Office, including Word, Excel, Access, PowerPoint, and Outlook

- Excellent English grammar, spelling, and punctuation skills

- Accurately proofread and edit documents

- Strong attention to detail

- Accurately follow oral and written instructions

- Excellent attendance and punctuality record

- Maintain confidentiality

- Positive attitude, motivated, and organized

Step Five: Complete the Résumé

Prior to finalizing your résumé, ensure that you have added all information identified in steps one through four to your electronic document. As you finalize your résumé, check for information that too frequently is forgotten or not presented appropriately. This is the fifth step in finalizing the information

Table 14-2 Experience Power Words

Sample Power Statement for Work Experience

- Prepared reports and other materials requiring independent achievement

- Enjoy working in a flexible team situation

- Established and maintained positive and effective working relationships

- Planned, scheduled, and performed a variety of clerical work

- Maintained office equipment and supplies

- Proofread forms and materials for completeness and accuracy according to regulations and procedures

- Processed and prepared materials for pamphlets, bulletins, brochures, announcements, handbooks, forms, and curriculum materials

- Provided training of temporary or new employees

- Maintained department files and records

- Demonstrated ability to receive incoming calls and route them efficiently

- Processed purchase requisitions, ordered and distributed supplies, and maintained inventory control

- Responsibly planned and conducted meetings

on your résumé. The top of your résumé is called the **information heading.** An information heading contains relevant contact information including name, mailing address, city, state, ZIP code, contact phone, and e-mail address. Include your complete and formal name, including a middle initial if you have one. When listing your e-mail address, remove the hyperlink so the print color is consistent. If your current e-mail address is unprofessional, secure an address that is professional. Include only one contact phone number. Whatever number is listed should be active and have a professional voice-mail message. Check the spelling and numbers for accuracy. Spell out the names of streets. If you use abbreviations, check for appropriate format, capitalization, and punctuation.

Immediately after your information heading is the career objective or personal profile created in step one. Review this opening statement to ensure it introduces the reader to who you are and motivates him or her to learn more about your specific knowledge, skills, abilities, and key accomplishments.

In step three, you determined whether a functional or chronological résumé layout was appropriate for your situation. Review the respective layout for proper order and refer to the sample résumés. Confirm that your experience and education are listed chronologically (most recent first). Keep your résumé consistent in its setup, including all periods or no periods at the end of each line, line spacing, alignment of dates, date format, bold/italics, upper- and lowercase words, and underlines. Be consistent with word endings and the use of tense in each section (e.g., -*ing* and -*ed*). Also be consistent with the use of the postal abbreviation for your state (e.g., the state is *CA*, not *Ca.*, not *Ca,* not *C.A*). When your draft résumé is complete, spell-check and proofread the document to ensure it is free of typographical errors and inconsistencies.

As for proper résumé layout and design, underlines, bold, and italic print are acceptable for emphasis but should not be overdone. Do not use bullets throughout your résumé; use bullets only to emphasize key skills. Use easy-to-read fonts and sizes. Times New Roman or Arial are most common. Apart from your name on the information heading of your résumé, do not use more than two different font sizes, preferably 12 to 14 points. Do not use different color fonts, highlights, or graphics on your résumé; use only black ink. It is not appropriate to include personal information such as a photograph of yourself, your birth date, marital status, Social Security number, or hobbies. It is also no longer appropriate to state, "References Available Upon Request" at the close of your résumé. Professional references should be on a separate sheet and provided only when requested. Refer to figure 14-11 for proper format for a professional reference list.

Tailored Package, See
Figure 14-11 on page 254

Check to ensure your résumé is presented professionally, is free of errors, and does not contain unnecessary or inappropriate information. Print the résumé in black ink on 8½ × 11–inch, letter-sized paper. Laser print is ideal. Double-sided résumés are not appropriate. If your résumé is more than one page, place your name at the top of each page after page one. Proper résumé paper is cotton-fiber, 24-pound white (not bond or card stock) paper of good quality. Colored paper, especially if dark, is both difficult to read and does not photocopy well. Do not use fancy paper stocks or binders. Do not staple your résumé or other job search documents. Since résumés are frequently photocopied, stapled résumés and other job search documents may be torn in the process.

When you have completed your résumé and believe it is ready for distribution, have several individuals whom you trust review it for clarity, consistency, punctuation, grammar, typographical errors, and other potential mistakes. Remember that complete sentences are not necessary and, with the exception of your career objective, the words "I" or "my" should not be used. Your résumé must create a positive, professional visual image and be easy to read.

Sharing Your Résumé

As you begin to share your completed résumé with both potential employers and members of your professional network, you may have the option of presenting your résumé on résumé paper (traditional hard copy) or electronically (online) as an attachment. Résumés printed on résumé paper are designed to be used for face-to-face job searches. Regardless of which method you choose, the first step is to perfect your traditional (hard-copy) résumé, as this document contains key information you will need to share with all potential employers. When converting a traditional (hard-copy) résumé into an online version, consider content. When forwarding a résumé to an employer or posting your résumé online, such as on a job board, consider key words that reflect your target job. When employers and job boards receive résumés, the résumés are commonly dropped into a database or résumé tracking system that allow recruiters to search for potential applicants based on key words and phrases

Exercise 14-5 Check for Inconsistencies

Circle the fifteen inconsistency errors on the following résumé.

1100 EAST FAVOR AVENUE • POSTVILLE, PA 16722
PHONE (555) 698-2222 • E-MAIL AERIE@PBCC.COM

AMANDA J. ERIE

OBJECTIVE

Seeking a position as an Administrative Assistant where I can utilize my office skills

SUMMARY OF QUALIFICATIONS

- Computer software skills include Microsoft Word, Excel, Outlook, Access, and PowerPoint
- Knowledge of Multi-line telephone system, filing, data entry, formatting of documents and reports, and operation of office equipment.
- Excellent interpersonal skills and polished office etiquette.
- written and oral communication skills
- Typing skills at 50 WPM
- Bilingual in English/Spanish (speaking)

EDUCATION

Reese Community College, Postville, PA Currently pursuing AA Degree in Office Occupations.

Calvin Institute of Technology, Cambridge, OH Office Technology Certificate Spring 2010

WORK AND VOLUNTEER EXPERIENCE

01/11 – Present   *Rigal Entertainment Group*   Postville, CA
Usher – Responsible for ensuring payment of services. Answer customer inquiries. Collect and count ticket stubs.

11/07 – 02/09   Lablaws   Cambridge, OH
Cashier – Operated cash register, stocking, assisting customers

01/07 – 04/07   Jolene's Diner   Cambridge, OH
Server – Provided customer service by waiting tables, cleaned, and operated cash register

that match the position they are trying to fill. Sometimes, when posting an online résumé, you may be required to cut and paste sections from your traditionally formatted résumé. During this process, you may lose the formatting. Do not worry. Visual appeal is not an issue for this process and formatting does not matter. You are merely dropping your information into a database. Your focus should be on utilizing key words and phrases that sell your skills and quantify your accomplishments.

The second consideration when converting a traditional résumé to an online version is sending it as an attachment while preserving formatting. If you are sending your résumé electronically as an attachment, it is best to send it either as a Microsoft (MS) Word file or as a portable document file (.pdf). Doing so ensures that the résumé layout is properly maintained through the file transfer. Sending your résumé as a .pdf file also ensures that those who do not use the same word processing software as you are able to read the file.

Most colleges and career centers now have electronic job boards that allow students to upload their résumés for recruiters and employers to view. There are also many niche job boards specific to industries. Another popular means of sharing an electronic résumé is through social media sites. Just be certain that you are posting your information on valid business sites and not personal sites. As with a traditional job search, keep track of and monitor all activity with your online search.

When posting your résumé online, always date your resume and update it every two to three months. Most employers won't view online résumés that are more than six months old. Guard your personal information by posting your résumé only on reputable job search sites. Just as with a hard-copy résumé, protect your identity and do not include personal information of any kind, including photographs, marital status, birth dates, or your Social Security number.

In some instances employers, will request that an **electronic formatted résumé** be submitted. Electronic formatted résumés are résumés that are submitted in American Standard Code for Information Interchange (ASCII) format. Once the employer receives your electronic formatted résumé, the résumé is added to a specialized database/software that routinely scans résumés based on key words (qualifications/skills) for specific jobs. The résumé is used to match key words contained in your résumé with specific jobs. Therefore, on this type of résumé, list as many key words as possible related to your target job. For electronic formatted résumés, visual appeal is not an issue. Electronic formatted résumés use Times New Roman font size 10 to 14. An electronic formatted résumé should be left-justified. Avoid tabs and centering. Headings should be in all capital letters. Hard returns must be used instead of word wrap. Avoid bold, italics, underlines, graphics, percent signs, and foreign characters. Also avoid boxes, horizontal and vertical lines, solid/hollow bullets, and table and column formatting.

Content for electronic formatted résumés include having your name at the top of the page on its own line. Standard address formatting (as when addressing a letter) should be used. Use key words specific to your desired job category and/or when communicating your knowledge, skills, and abilities. Work experience dates should have beginning and ending dates on the same line. Use asterisks or dashes (no bullets or boxes of any kind) and list each telephone number on its own line (no parentheses around area codes). Date your electronic résumé. Just as with hard-copy résumés, do not include personal information of any kind, including photographs, marital status, birth dates, or your Social Security number. See Figure 14-7 for an example of an electronic formatted résumé.

Electronic Résumé Example, see Figure 14-7 on page 247

Cover Letters

A **cover letter** is often the first impression a potential employer will have of you. It serves as an introduction to your résumé. Employers use cover letters as screening tools.

When writing a cover letter, use a friendly but professional tone. Use complete sentences and proper grammar. When tailoring your cover letter, include information about the target company that communicates to the employer you have conducted research on the company. In a cover letter, communicate how your key skills, experience, and accomplishments can meet the employer's needs. This is accomplished by identifying the skills and qualifications the target employer is requesting in the job announcement and/or job description and matching these needs with your key skills and qualifications. Let the employer know what you can offer the company, not what you want from the company. In the paragraph where you are communicating your key skills and experience, refer the reader to the attached résumé. Do not duplicate what is already listed on your résumé; instead, emphasize your experience and key skills. Although it is acceptable to utilize the words "I and my" in a cover letter, be careful to not begin most of your sentences with the word "I". Instead, focus the attention toward the employer. This puts the company first and makes its needs more important. Attempt to begin a sentence with what the company will receive with your skills. For example:

Instead of writing, "*I* am proficient in Word,"

Write, "*Your* company will benefit from my proficiency in Word."

Address the cover letter to a specific person. This should be the person who will be making the hiring decision. Do not address your cover letter to a department, the company name, or "to whom it may concern." Call the company and ask for a specific name and title, identifying the appropriate spelling and gender. If you have conducted research and still cannot secure a specific name, use a subject line instead of a salutation. For example, instead of writing, "To Whom It May Concern," write, "Subject: Account Clerk Position." If you have talked to a specific person at your target company, refer to the previous communication. Include the specific position you are seeking in your cover letter and how you learned about the job opening. At the end of your cover letter, request an interview (not the job). Do not write that you look forward to the employer contacting you. Display initiative by stating that you will follow up on your request for an interview within the next week. Include an enclosure notation for your résumé and close courteously.

In chapter 9, you learned how to write a business letter. Use the proper business-letter format for your cover letter. Each word and paragraph in your cover letter must have a purpose. Your goal is to communicate how your knowledge, skills, abilities, and accomplishments fill a targeted company's needs and make the reader want to review your résumé. The cover-letter setup in Figure 14-8 and sample cover letters in Figures 14-9 and 14-10 will help you create a winning cover letter.

Cover Letter Setup, see Figure 14-8 on page 248

Cover Letter Example 1, see Figure 14-9 on page 249

Cover Letter Example 2, see Figure 14-10 on page 250

Print your cover letter on the same type of paper used for your résumé. Copy the information heading you created for your résumé and use it on your cover letter. This creates a consistent and professional visual appeal for your résumé package. Avoid making common mistakes, including typographical or grammatical errors, forgetting to include a date, or forgetting to sign the cover letter. Complete and grammatically correct sentences must be used on a cover letter. As with your résumé, have someone you trust proofread your letter before you send it to a potential employer. Any error communicates a lack of attention to detail. Even minor errors have the potential to disqualify you from securing an interview.

Tailoring Your Résumé and Cover Letter

Tailor your résumé and cover letter specifically to each job and company for which you are applying. Carefully review the target job announcement. If possible, secure a copy of the job description from the company's human resource department if it is not available or attached to the job posting. Identify key job skills that the position requires, and highlight the company needs with your skills. As you learned in step four of creating your résumé, utilize the O*Net website to identify key skills for your targeted position. If necessary, rearrange the order of the information presented on your résumé so that the key skills required for your target position are presented first. On your cover letter, emphasize your specific qualifications that match those required for the open position. Figure 14-11 provides an example of a résumé and cover letter tailored to a specific job announcement.

Tailored Package, see Figure 14-11 on page 251–254

Although mentioned earlier, it cannot be stressed enough that a daytime phone number and e-mail address need to be listed on both the cover letter and résumé. Because most invitations for job interviews occur over the phone, your phone voice-mail and/or message machine need to be professional. Do not include musical introductions or any other greeting that would not make a positive first impression to a potential employer. As mentioned in chapter 13, maintain a professional e-mail address to use in your job search.

Cory's friend Rebecca was a practical joker. Cory enjoyed calling Rebecca because her voice-mail message started with a joke or had some strange voice and/or music. However, the last time Cory called Rebecca, Cory noticed that Rebecca's message was normal. The next time Cory saw Rebecca, Cory asked Rebecca why her voice message was suddenly so serious. Rebecca explained that she had recently applied for a job and had been selected to interview. However, she was embarrassed because when the interviewer called to arrange the appointment, the interviewer left a message and also suggested that Rebecca change her voice-mail message to a more professional message.

Tips for Ex-Offenders

If you have served time in prison and are now attempting to reenter the workforce, you are to be congratulated for wanting to move forward with your life. Others have made poor choices in their past, and you have made restitution for yours. Be honest with the potential employer.

On your résumé, include all jobs you have held and skills you learned while incarcerated. List the correctional facility in place of the employer for these jobs. List all education, including degrees and courses you received while incarcerated. Include the educational institution that provided the training.

The employment application is a legal document. At the bottom of this document, applicants sign a statement that affirms that all information provided on the application is true. Therefore, you must not lie. If, after being hired, your employer discovers that you have lied on the application, you may be immediately terminated. The majority of applications ask if you have been convicted of a felony. Please note that arrests are not convictions. If you have been convicted of a felony, check "Yes." The application should also have a space to write a statement after the felony question. Do not leave this space blank. In this space, write, "Will explain in detail during interview."

Workplace Dos and Don'ts

Do keep your résumé updated with skills and accomplishments	*Don't* wait until the last minute to update your résumé
Do change your résumé format after you have gained work experience	*Don't* use outdated reference names and letters
Do use the correct format for your résumé	*Don't* send out a résumé or cover letter that has not been proofread by someone you can trust
Do check your résumé and cover letter for errors before sending them to employers	*Don't* forget to sign your cover letter

YOUR NAME (16 point, bold)
Your Address (12 or 14 point, bold)
City, State ZIP
Phone Number (Include Area Code)
E-Mail Address (Remove Hyperlink)

Horizontal line optional and thickness varies

OBJECTIVE Headings can be on the left or centered, 12- or 14-point font, and uppercase or initial cap.
Format headings the same throughout the resumé.
Keep spacing equal between each section.

QUALIFICATIONS (OR SKILLS)
- Relate to target job, all job-related skills and transferable skills
- Most relative to the job are listed first
- Bullet (small round or small square only) these items to stand out

> Emphasize skills and education. List your skills and education before any work experience.

EDUCATION
You may list before qualifications
Do not list high school if you have graduated from college
Include the dates and align to the right
List schools in chronological order, most recent attended first

WORK EXPERIENCE
Include: *Name of Company* and City, State—No Addresses
Job title bolded, if part-time, dates employed (month, year)
List the jobs in chronological order, most recent first align dates to the right
Align dates to the right
List the duties, responsibilities, and achievements
Be consistent in your setup
Use the same tense throughout (*ed* or *ing*)
Do not use complete sentences or *I, me,* or *my*

OTHER CAPABILITIES
Optional items in this section may not be directly related to the job but may interest the employer such as honors or awards.

> **Keep in mind**
> - Watch periods, punctuation
> - Watch spelling
> - Use a regular font, no color, 12-point font (except heading)
> - Use résumé paper, no dark or bright colors
> - Do not use full sentences or *I, me,* or *my*
> - References are not necessary; you will have a separate sheet with references
> - Do not use graphics

Figure 14-1

Functional Résumé Layout

Suzie S. Kringle
1234 Tolearn Avenue, Meadeville, PA 16335
555-555-5555
skringle05@careerssuccess.lns

OBJECTIVE

To obtain a position as a Junior Accountant with Owen Company where I can utilize my general accounting skills in a dynamic company.

SKILLS

- Knowledgeable and accurate in general ledger and journal posting
- Basic software knowledge of QuickBooks
- Knowledge of account receivables and account payables
- Experienced with Microsoft Office, including Word, Excel, Access, PowerPoint, and Outlook
- Ten-key at 150 cspm
- Type 50 wpm accurately
- Excellent English grammar, spelling, and punctuation skills
- Accurately follow oral and written instructions
- Strong attention to detail
- Positive attitude, motivated, and organized

EDUCATION

State University, Meadeville, PA   5/12
Bachelor of Science Degree in Business, Accounting

Meadeville City College, Meadeville PA   5/10
Associate in Arts Degree in Business, Certificate of Completion in Account Clerk Program

WORK EXPERIENCE

S and L Accounting   Edinboro, PA   1/10–present
Account Clerk
Assist the Accountant by answering telephone, bookkeeping, data entry in Excel and QuickBooks, verifying totals, making copies, faxing, and other clerical duties when needed.

Bret's Hamburger Haven   Edinboro, PA   1/07–12/09
Cashier/Food Service
Worked as a team member to assist customers with food orders, cleaned, handled cash, and trained new employees.

Figure 14-2

Functional Résumé Example
with Minimal Career Work
Experience

HEIDI H. KRINGLE

1234 Tolearn Avenue, Meadeville, PA 16335
555-555-5555   hkringle02@careersuccess.lns

OBJECTIVE

To obtain a position as an Office Assistant with Austin Office Supplies that will enable me to utilize my current skills and education.

QUALIFICATIONS

- Type 50 wpm
- Experienced with Microsoft Office, including Word, Excel, Access, PowerPoint, and Outlook
- Accurately proofread and edit documents
- Knowledge of records management
- Positive telephone skills
- Excellent oral and written communications skills
- Positive attitude, motivated, and organized
- Excellent customer services skills

EDUCATION/CERTIFICATION

2010–2012   Meadeville City College   Meadeville, PA
Associate of Art Degree, Business & Technology
Clerical Administration Certificate
GPA 3.9, Dean's list

EXPERIENCE

06/2009–present   Fine Linens by Jen   Meadeville, PA
Cashier
Responsibilities include: providing customer service, cashiering, placing merchandise on the floor, helping return go backs, processing merchandise on the floor, stocking merchandise in back/stockroom, training new hires.

02/2003–05/2009   Jerry's Burger Place   Meadeville, PA
Cashier/Counter Person
Responsibilities included: assisted guests with their orders, ensured a safe and clean work environment, and assisted other team members as needed.

Figure 14-3

Functional Résumé
Example without Career
Work Experience

YOUR NAME (16 point, bold)

Your Address (12 or 14 point, bold) ■ **City, State ZIP** ■ **Phone Number** (Include Area Code)
E-Mail Address (Remove Hyperlink)

PERSONAL PROFILE:
Include key skill sets. Headings can be on the left or centered, 12- or 14-point font, and uppercase or initial cap. Format headings the same throughout the resumé. Keep the spacing equal between each section.

PROFESSIONAL EXPERIENCE:
Group key skills, experience, and accomplishments under each major skill set heading.

First Skill Set Subheading
- Communicate experience, and key accomplishments relating to your first skill set subheading
- Using power words, quantify as much as possible
- Include duties, responsibilities, and achievements

> Emphasize key skill sets and accomplishments. List work experience before education and employment history.

Second Skill Set Subheading
- Relate statements to target job. Communicate both job-related skills or transferable skills
- Accomplishments and experience most relative to target job are listed first
- Bullet (small round or small square only) accomplishments and experience to stand out

> **Keep in mind**
> - Watch punctuation, and spelling
> - Can be one or two pages. If two pages, place name on second page
> - Use a regular font, no color, 12-point font (except heading)
> - Do not use full sentences or *I, me,* or *my*
> - Do not use graphics
> - Align bullets to the right

Third Skill Set Subheading
- Be consistent in setup
- Use same tense throughout (ed or ing)
- Do not use complete sentences or I, me, or my

WORK HISTORY:
Name of Company and City, State—No Addresses—dates employed (month, year)
Job title (bold title, NOT employer)
List jobs in chronological order with most recent date first

EDUCATION:
Do not list high school
Include the years attended, areas of study, and degrees earned
List schools in chronological order, most recent attended first

PROFESSIONAL AFFILIATIONS/CERTIFICATIONS:
List professional memberships including the name of the organization, status (member, board member, etc.) and dates of membership. Also include any certifications or community service activities that are relevant to the target job.

Figure 14-4

Chronological
Résumé Layout

PEARL B. KRINGLE, CPA

1234 Tolearn Avenue ▲ Meadeville, PA 16335 ▲ 555.555.5555
pbkringle@careerssuccess.lns

PROFILE:
Highly experienced, personable, and detail-oriented Certified Public Accountant with expertise and demonstrated leadership in the areas of accounting, computer information systems, and quantitative analysis.

PROFESSIONAL EXPERIENCE:

Accounting
- Audit cash, investments, payables, fixed assets, and prepaid expenses for small business enterprises, corporations, and not-for-profit organizations.
- Collect and analyze data to detect deficient controls, extravagance, fraud, or non-compliance with laws, regulations, and management policies.
- Prepare detailed reports on audit findings, report to management about asset utilization and audit results, and recommend changes in operations and financial activities.
- Inspect account books and accounting systems for efficiency, effectiveness, and use of accepted accounting procedures to record transactions.
- Examine and evaluate financial and information systems, recommending controls to ensure system reliability and data integrity.
- Confer with company officials about financial and regulatory matters.

Computer Information Systems
- Developed information resources, providing data security/control, strategic computing, and disaster recovery.
- Consulted with users, management, vendors, and technicians to assess computing needs and system requirements.
- Stayed abreast of advances in technology and forwarded research and recommendations to ensure company and respective clients were utilizing proper and most efficient tools and information systems.
- Met with department heads, managers, supervisors, vendors to solicit cooperation and resolve problems.
- Provided users with technical support for computer problems.

Quantitative Analysis
- Assembled computerized spreadsheets, draw charts, and graphs used to illustrate technical reports.
- Analyzed financial information to produce forecasts of business, industry, and economic conditions for use in making investment decisions.
- Maintained knowledge and stayed abreast of developments in the fields of industrial technology, business, finance, and economic theory.
- Interpreted data affecting investment programs, such as price, yield, stability, future trends in investment risks, and economic influences.

Figure 14-5

Chronological Résumé
Example with Degree

PEARL B. KRINGLE, CPA

Page Two

- Monitored fundamental economic, industrial, and corporate developments through the analysis of information obtained from financial publications and services, investment banking firms, government agencies, trade publications, company sources, and personal interviews.
- Recommended investments and investment timing to companies, investment firm staff, or the investing public.
- Determined the prices at which securities should be syndicated and offered to the public.
- Prepared plans of action for investment based on financial analyses.

WORK HISTORY:

Coopers & Lion, LLP, Alltown, PA *Auditor*	May 2010–present
Mitchell Ho, CPA, Atlanta, GA *General Accountant*	May 2007–April 2010
U.S. Department of Labor, Atlanta, GA *Program Assistant*	January 2005–February 2007
Grace's Burger Palace, Riverside, GA *Server*	August 2001–December 2004

EDUCATION AND LICENSE:

Masters of Computer Information Systems Georgia State University, Atlanta, GA	August 2012
Certified Public Accountant – State of Georgia	May 2010
Bachelor of Science in Accounting Heather Glenn College, Heather Glenn, NC	May 2007

PROFESSIONAL AFFILIATIONS:

American Institute of Certified Financial Accountants
Beta Alpha Psi Fraternity
National Association of Black Accountants

Figure 14-5

Chronological Resumé
Example with Degree page 2
(*continued*)

Steven Mark Kringle

1234 Tolearn Avenue   ■   Meadeville, PA 16335   ■   555.555.5555

smkringle@careersuccess.lns

PERSONAL PROFILE

Results and efficiency focused professional with experience in sales/vendor relations, inventory/ warehousing, and management/supervision. Proven ability in relationship management with demonstrated and consistent increase in sales over a five-year period. Inventory expertise includes streamlined operations, improved productivity, and favorable inventory ratio utilization for wholesale food supplier. Management ability to create goal-driven teams, groom leaders, and facilitate the creation of a learning organization.

PROFESSIONAL EXPERIENCE

Customer Service Orientation   ■   Innovative Risk Taker   ■   Excellent Quantitative Skills ■ Purchasing, Inventory Planning & Control   ■   Supply Chain Management   ■   Warehouse Operations   ■   Process Improvement   ■   Cost Containment   ■   Hiring, Staffing & Scheduling Safety Training   ■   Excellent Computer Knowledge

Sales/Vendor Relations

- Through the establishment of vendor relationships, schedule product installations, exchanges, buy-backs or removals of equipment or other assets including supplier networks and agent contacts in order to meet customer expectations for private soda company. Have grown sales territory from two county area to tri-state contract area over four-year period.

- Source and facilitate delivery of product (e.g., beverage equipment, parts, point of sale material, return of assets) for retail suppliers. Sales complaints are consistently .05% per year, while sales volume and customer satisfaction rates are the highest of all sales team and consistently grow.

- Research and resolve issues for customers, business partners, and Company associates in order to expedite service, installations, or orders using information systems and working with supply chain partners.

- Create and maintain partnerships with customers, clients or third party service providers (e.g., contract service/installation agents, distributors) by establishing common goals, objectives, and performance target requirements in order to improve customer service and satisfaction.

- Created troubleshooting equipment process which allows retail suppliers to receive immediate response on service issues (e.g., beverage vending, dispensing) via telephone or Internet to minimize customer down time and service cost.

Figure 14-6

Chronological Résumé
Example with No Degree

Steven Mark Kringle

Page Two

Inventory/Warehousing

- Responsible for maintaining customer contact to confirm service or orders including accuracy, service follow up, equipment service confirmation, product delivery confirmation, and routine service scheduling for local foodservice broker.

- Received, recorded, and responded to customer or consumer inquiries/feedback using specially designed database which documented best practices from nationwide foodservice association in an effort to provide improved service, order accuracy, and optimized supply chain efficiency. Information was collected, analyzed, and reported to all members of the supply chain for feedback and control purposes.

- Processed orders for goods and services with food service business partners, customers, suppliers, and company associates, either through direct telephone contact or electronic means, to increase speed and accuracy of order transactions and improve loss prevention systems.

Management/Supervision

- Developed and trained team members on inventory control, customer service, and safety for local foodservice provider. Program was so successful customers within the company supply chain requested and received training. To date, over 500 individuals have received custom training.

- Supervised cross-functional team of 100 including order technicians, outside repair personnel, transportation associates, warehouse attendants, and loss prevention specialists.

- As assistant-manager for college-town restaurant, assisted in the hiring, training, scheduling, and performance evaluation of staff for small soda company and local food service supplier.

WORK HISTORY

Christopher Cola Company, Susanville, NE **Vendor Relations Associate**	2007–2012
Joshua Food Service, Pocatoe, NE **Warehouse Manager**	2005–2007
Nick-Mike Ribs 'N Stuff, Pocatoe, NE **Assistant Restaurant Manager**	2003–2005

EDUCATION/PROFESSIONAL DEVELOPMENT

University of Nebraska, Lincoln, NE Business Management/Marketing	2009–2012

Figure 14-6

Chronological Résumé
Example with No Degree
(*continued*)

AUTUMN S. KRINGLE
1234 TOLEARN AVENUE,
MEADEVILLE, PA 16335
555-555-5555
askringle@careersuccess.Ins

OBJECTIVE

Bookkeeper

KEY WORD SUMMARY

Bookkeeping skills, financial management, accounting, receivables and payroll, organized, data entry, communication skills, problem solving, responsible, team player, computer skills.

EDUCATION

City College: City, WA
2012
Associate Degree in Accounting

COURSES OF STUDY
----

* Intro to Accounting
* Intro to Business
* MS Office
* Workplace Communication
* Office Accounting
* Business Law
* Intro to Marketing

COMPUTER SKILLS
----

* Microsoft Office: Word, Excel, Access, PowerPoint
* WordPerfect
* Internet

WORK EXPERIENCE

Yang Enterprises: Fresno, CA
2010 – Present
Bookkeeping Assistant: Responsible for assisting accounting department with payroll, budgets, planning, and forecasting, purchasing, and managing accounts.

Figure 14-7

Electronic Résumé Example

Date of Letter

Employer's Name, Title
Company Name
Address
City, State Zip

Dear Mr./Ms./Dr.:

First Paragraph. Give the reason for the letter, the position for which you are applying, and how you learned of this position. Note any previous contact you may have had with the employer.

Second Paragraph. Tell why you are interested in the position, the organization, and its products or services. Indicate any research you have done on the position and/or the employer.

Third Paragraph. Refer to the attached resumé and highlight relevant aspects of your resumé. Emphasize the skills mentioned in the advertisement or on the job description. Provide specific reasons why the organization should hire you and what you can do to contribute to the organization's success.

Last Paragraph. Indicate your desire for an interview, and offer flexibility as to the time and place. Thank the employer for his or her consideration and express anticipation in meeting him or her. Include a phone number and e-mail address for contact.

Sincerely,

(Do not forget to sign your cover letter)

Your Name
Your Address
City, State Zip

Enclosure

Figure 14-8

Cover Letter Setup

September 25, 2015

Owen Corporation
Attention Brandon Owen
435 East Chesny Street
Meadeville, PA 16335

Dear Mr. Owen:

As a recent accounting graduate of State University, Meadeville, I was delighted to learn from your web site of the available Junior Accountant position. The purpose of this letter is to express a strong interest in becoming an Owen Company Accountant at your Meadeville facility. In addition to possessing a B.S. degree in Business, Accounting, I am responsible and consider myself a leader.

Owen Company sponsors a variety of community services and employee recognition programs, which I have read a great deal about. Your company has earned my respect, as it has from much of the community for your involvement in the after-school programs in Meadeville Unified School District.

As you will see on the attached resumé, Owen Company would benefit from the skills I have learned throughout college. These include: general ledger and journal posting; Microsoft Word, Excel, and Access programs; Quickbooks; and accurate ten-key (150 cspm). In addition, I also offer a superior work ethic, strong communicative abilities, attention to detail, and a keen interest in upgrading my skills.

I am confident that my skills and abilities will make me an ideal candidate for a position in this field. I would appreciate an opportunity to meet with you to discuss how my skills can meet the needs of Owen Company. I will contact you by phone within the week to discuss the possibility of an interview.

Sincerely,

Suzie Kringle

Suzie Kringle
1234 Tolearn Avenue
Meadeville, PA 16335

Enclosure

Figure 14-9

Cover Letter Example 1

HEIDI H. KRINGLE   **1234 Tolearn Avenue, Meadeville, PA 16335**
555-555-5555   hshore02@careersuccess.lns

September 21, 2015

Mr. Jared Bill
Austin Office Supplies
1122 Friendly Road
Meadeville, PA 93725

Dear Mr. Bill:

I recently spoke with Gene Armstrong, an employee at your company, and he recommended that I send you a copy of my resume. Knowing the requirements for the position and that I am interested in working at this type of establishment, he felt that I would be an ideal candidate for your office assistant position.

My personal goal is to be a part of an organization such as yours that wants to excel in both growth and profit. I would welcome the opportunity to be employed at Austin's Office Supplies since this is the largest and best-known office supply company in the city. Your company has a reputation of excellent products and service.

Austin's Office Supplies would benefit from someone such as I who is accustomed to a fast-paced environment where deadlines are a priority and handling multiple jobs simultaneously is the norm. As you can see on the attached resumé, my previous jobs required me to be well organized, accurate, and friendly. I enjoy a challenge and work hard to attain my goals. Great customer skills are important in a business such as yours.

Nothing would please me more than to be a part of your team. I would like very much to discuss with you how I could contribute to your organization with my office skills and my dependability. I will contact you next week to arrange an interview. In the interim, I can be reached at 555-555-5555.

Sincerely,

Heidi H. Kringle

Heidi H. Kringle

Enclosure

Figure 14-10

Cover Letter Example 2

ACCOUNT CLERK – position #022394   full time, permanent posit

The current vacancy is a full-time position at Viau Technical College.

Definition: Under direction performs a wide variety of entry-level accounting/busines office work.

Compensation: Starts at $3,176 per month. Full-time permanent positions provide an attractive benefit package which include health, dental, and vision coverage for the employee and eligible dependents, as well as life insurance and disability coverage for employees.

Experience: Entry-level experience performing general accounting duties.

Education: Formal or informal education equivalent to completion of an Associate Degree in accounting.

Examples of Duties: Performs a wide variety of duties including but not limited to: basic accounting work; verifying, balancing, and posting/recording accounting informatic verifying and preparing invoices, checks, correspondence, and statistical information; proof-reading; and filing. Calculates, prepares, and reconciles various financial reports. Entering and retrieving data from computer system as needed. Assigning and/or reviewi the work of other employees and students. May perform other related duties as needed.

Required Knowledge and Abilities:
Knowledge of sequence of procedures in the accounting cycle, analysis, use, and interpretation of accounting and financial data; and modern office practices. Knowledge of and ability to employ proper English usage, spelling, grammar, and punctuation. Skil make deposits, process checks, and reconcile accounts; employ mathematical and statistic techniques sufficient to maintain district records; keyboard; utilize word processing software, email, online calendaring, and data entry/retrieval from database programs; and create and utilize spreadsheets. Ability to assign, monitor, and/or review the work of others; receive and follow instructions and appropriately interact with students, staff, faculty, and the public; and learn and apply college and district policies and procedures.

Selection Process: The selection process will include screening to ensure applicatior are complete and meet all minimum qualifications. This process will also include a written test of knowledge and abilities (35% weight), a performance test (35% weight), a an oral appraisal board interview (30% weight). Of those candidates achieving a passir score on the first test, only the 30 highest scoring candidates, plus ties, will be invited the performance exam. Of those candidates achieving a passing score on the performan exam, only the 15 highest scoring candidates, plus ties, will be invited to the oral appraisal board interview. Passing score is 75% out of 100% on each testing section.

FIRST EXAM IS TENTATIVELY SCHEDULED FOR SATURDAY, JUNE 20, 2015.

To move forward in the selection process, you must complete an online application through our web site at www.viaucommunitycollege.com. Resumes may also be submitted by mail, in person, or by emailing to job@viaucommunitycollege.com.

Filing Deadline: 4:30 p.m., Monday, June 1, 2015.

Figure 14-11

Tailored Package—Page 1
Job Announcement

Jolene M. Kringle

1234 Tolearn Avenue ■ Meadville, PA ■ 555.555.5555

jmkringle@careersuccess.lns

Objective

Highly motivated, responsible, and ethical individual seeks an entry-level accounting position with Viau Technical College in an effort to apply newly acquired general business and accounting skills. Experienced in basic accounting procedures, operational efficiencies, and logistics.

Key Skills & Qualifications

- Strong math and analytical skills
- Data entry
- Bilingual (Spanish–speak and write)
- Works well in group environments
- Excellent grammatical and English usage
- Proficient in MAS 90 and Quickbooks

- Demonstrate leadership
- Maintain records and filing
- Strong attention to detail
- Experience with balancing and posting
- Accurately proofread and edit documents
- Proficient in Word, Excel, Access, Outlook

Education

Hill Valley Technical College, Clarkville, PA   01/10–06/12
Associate of Arts Degree, Accounting

Work Experience

El Montes Restaurant, Reedville, PA   12/08–present
Bookkeeper/Server
Perform bookkeeping functions for small family business including creation and analysis of financial statements, cash/banking functions, and communication with CPA firm. Implemented electronic accounting and inventory system which saved the company an estimated $50K. Serve as Lead Server for evening staff. In addition to exemplary customer service and cashier duties, responsibilities include inventory control, and training of new staff training in both customer service and food safety/handling for busy Mexican food restaurant.

Freshwide Marketing, Lewis, PA   05–09/08, 09, 10
Quality Control Clerk (*seasonal*)
Received and counted stock items and recorded data. Monitored fruit and produce as it arrived or was shipped from cold storage for twenty independent fruit growers. Verified inventory computations by comparing them to physical counts of stock, and investi-gated discrepancies or adjusted errors. Stored items in an orderly and accessible man-ner in cold storage and warehouse.

Starlight Produce, Lewis, PA   06/06–09/08
Shipping Manifest Clerk
As a shipping clerk for regional fruit packer, prepared, monitored, and facilitated orders for shipping to over fifty clients throughout the United States. Duties included examining contents and comparing with records, such as manifests, invoices, or orders, to verify accuracy of incoming or outgoing shipment. Prepared documents, such as work orders, bills of lading, and shipping orders to route materials. Determined shipping method for materials, using knowledge of shipping procedures, routes, and rates.

Figure 14-11

Tailored Package—Page 2
Resumé (*continued*)

Jolene M. Kringle

1234 Tolearn Avenue ■ Meadeville, PA 16335 ■ 555.555.5555

jmkringle@careersuccess.lns

April 21, 2015

Monique Marshall, Director
Human Resource Department
Viau Community College
60157 S. Holbrook
Viau, PA 12150

RE: Account Clerk Position #022394

Dear Ms. Marshall:

It is with great excitement that I am submitting the following application package for consideration of your current full time Account Clerk Position posted on the Viau Community College web site. Viau Community College has a legacy of quality and excellence in education and nothing would please me more than to apply my newly acquired accounting education to your organization.

As you can see on the attached resumé, your company will benefit from my demonstrated leadership in the areas of general accounting, business, and computer applications. Excelling in the creation and quantitative analysis of basic financial statements, I am familiar with both the installation and utilization of common accounting software programs. At my current job, interaction with both the company owners and the company's contracted CPA firm is a weekly required activity which has greatly improved my communication and presentation skills. In my opinion, diversity is a valuable asset and I enjoy utilizing my fluency in speaking Spanish when interacting with customers. I consider myself an ethical and responsible individual with excellent verbal and written communication skills.

It would be a privilege to have the opportunity to discuss how my knowledge, skills, and professional experience can contribute to the continued success of the Viau Community College. I will contact you within the next week to follow-up on my application materials. In the interim, I can be reached at 555-555-5555 or via e-mail at jmkringle@careersuccess.lns.

Sincerely,

Jolene M. Kringle

Jolene M. Kringle

Enclosures

Figure 14-11

Tailored Package—Page 3
Cover Letter (*continued*)

Jolene M. Kringle

1234 Tolearn Avenue ■ Meadeville, PA 16335 ■ 555.555.5555
jmkringle@careersuccess.lns

Professional Reference List

Name	Relationship	Phone	E-mail	Mailing Address
Autumn Hart	Former Accounting Instructor, Hill Valley Technical College	555.555-1111	atmnhrt@hillvalley.scl	123 Hillvalley Clarkville, PA
Gloria Montes	Owner, El Montes Restaurant	555.555-1112	gloria@eatelmontes.fat	5432 Food Ct. Reedville, PA
Gary Solis	Floor Manager, Freshwide Marketing	555.555-1113	solisg@freshwide.fruit	2220 Tulare Lewis, PA
Patty Negoro	Office Manager, Starlight Produce	555.555-1114	pattyn@starlight.sun	444 Adoline Lewis, PA

Figure 14-11

Tailored Package—Page 4
Reference List (*continued*)

Concept Review and Application

Summary of Key Concepts

- A winning résumé makes it easy for potential employers to quickly and easily identify your skills and experience
- Update your résumé with new skills and accomplishments at least once a year
- Include both job-specific skills and transferable skills on your résumé
- Use the correct résumé layout for your career work experience
- A cover letter is most often an employer's first impression of you
- Check that your résumé and cover letter are free of typographical and grammatical errors
- Share your résumé electronically as a .pdf file to ensure the résumé layout is maintained

Key Terms

chronological résumé
functional résumé
  layout
résumé

cover letter
information heading
job-specific skills
soft skills

electronic formatted
  résumé
power words
transferable skills

If You Were the Boss

1. What would you look for first when reviewing a résumé?
2. What would your reaction be if you were reading a cover letter that had several typing and grammar errors?

Video Case Study: Résumé and Cover Letter Tips

This video presents expert advice on how to write a winning résumé and cover letter. To view these videos, visit the Student Resources: Professionalism section in www.mystudentsuccesslab.com. Then answer the following questions.

1. Share four common résumé mistakes and solutions.
2. Explain how to utilize a job announcement when preparing a résumé and cover letter.
3. Share four common cover-letter mistakes and solutions.
4. What information should be repeated in a cover letter that is already included on a résumé?

Web Links

www.onetcenter.org/
http://resume.monster.com
http://jobstar.org/tools/resume/index.htm
http://jobsearch.about.com/od/networking

Activities

Activity 14-1

Conduct an Internet search to identify five new power words to include in your résumé.

1. _____

2. _____

3. _____

4. _____

5. _____

Activity 14-2

Search for a job you would like to have when you graduate, and fill in the following information that will be used to tailor your résumé and create a cover letter.

Position for which you are applying	
How you learned about the job	
Any contact you have had with the employer or others about the job	
Why are you interested in this job?	
Why are you interested in this company?	
What products or services are provided?	
List relevant skills related to the job description	
List reasons this company should hire you	
Indicate your desire for an interview	
Indicate your flexibility for an interview (time and place)	

Activity 14-3

Using a word-processing program and the steps and/or exercises from this chapter, create a résumé for the job you found in Activity 14-2.

Activity 14-4

Using a word processing program and the information from this chapter, create a cover letter for the job you found in Activity 14-2.

Activity 14-5

Change the résumé from activity 14-3 to an electronic formatted résumé.

1. Update your résumé at least _____.

2. If you are starting a new career, create a résumé using the _____.

3. A/An _____ résumé format emphasizes your related work experience and skills.

4. _____ skills are those that are directly related to a specific job.

5. _____ skills are transferable from one job to the next.

6. Use _____ words whenever possible in your résumé; they describe your accomplishments in a lively and specific way.

7. The _____ is an introduction to your résumé.

Interview Techniques

chapter 15

All the world's a stage.

William Shakespeare (1564–1616)

Objectives

- Demonstrate strategies to implement when invited to interview
- Conduct company and job-specific research for interview preparation
- Prepare a *personal commercial* to sell skills and tie them to a target job
- Identify pre-interview preparation activities including creating an *interview portfolio* and practice interview questions
- Demonstrate how to behave during technology-based interviews
- Explain key areas of employee rights and how to respond to discriminatory questions
- Describe specific statements and behaviors to exhibit at the close of an interview and job offer
- Discuss salary negotiation strategies

How-Do-You-Rate

	Have you mastered interview techniques?	True	False
1.	Arriving more than ten minutes early to the office where your interview is to take place is considered unprofessional.	❑	❑
2.	It is best to have a draft of a post-interview thank-you note written prior to an interview.	❑	❑
3.	The same amount of pre-interview preparation should be made for an Internet and/or telephone interview as is made for a traditional face-to-face interview.	❑	❑
4.	Employers expect a job candidate to ask valid questions during interviews.	❑	❑
5.	When offered a job, it is acceptable to negotiate a salary for entry-level positions.	❑	❑

If you answered "true" to the majority of these questions, congratulations. You are already aware of successful interview techniques and are ready to successfully interview.

The Interview

You've conducted a targeted job search, and created and distributed your résumé, and now it is time to interview. A successful interview involves more than dressing sharp. It includes advance preparation; confidence; and a strategy to be used before, during, and after this important meeting. During an interview, an employer is looking to hire the best person to represent his or her company. Your goal is to communicate visually and verbally that you are the right person for the job. A job search takes work, takes time, and can sometimes be frustrating. Do not get discouraged if you do not get an interview or job offer on your first try. The purpose of this chapter is to provide you the skills and confidence to secure a good job in a reasonable time period.

The Invitation to Interview

There is a strategy to successful interviews, and it starts as soon as you receive an invitation to interview. Most interview invitations are extended by phone or electronic mail. Therefore, regularly check and respond to both phone and electronic messages. This is a good reminder to maintain a professional voice-mail message and e-mail address. When you are invited to interview, attempt to identify with whom you will be interviewing. You may be meeting with one person or a group of individuals. Your first interview may be a pre-screening interview where a human resource representative or some other representative from the company briefly meets with you to ensure you are qualified and the right fit for the job.

Ask how much time the company has scheduled for the interview. If possible, identify how many applicants are being called for interviews. Although this is a lot of information to secure, if you are friendly, respectful, and professional, most companies will share this information. Attempt to arrange your interview at a time that puts you at an advantage over the other candidates. The first and last interviews are the most memorable, so try to be the first or last interview. If you are given a choice of times to interview, schedule your interview in the morning. People are much more alert at that time, and you will have a greater advantage of making a favorable and memorable impression. If this is not possible, try to be the last person interviewed prior to the lunch break or the first person interviewed immediately after the lunch break. Be aware that sometimes you will have no say in when your interview is scheduled. Do not make demands when scheduling your interview. Politely ask the interview scheduler if it is possible for him or her to tell you who will be conducting the interview. Finally, note the name of the individual who is assisting you in arranging the interview. This will allow you to contact him or her should you need information and also allow you to personally thank him or her if you meet on the day of the interview. The goal is to secure as much information as possible prior to the interview so you are prepared.

Company-Specific Research

Prior to your interview, conduct research on the company and the specific position for which you are applying. Many candidates ignore this step, thinking it is unnecessary or takes too much time. Planning better prepares you for your interview, increases your confidence, and provides you a greater advantage over other candidates. Learn as much as you can about the company's leadership team, strategy, and any current event that may have affected the company. Review the company web and social network sites if available, or conduct a general Internet search to read blogs and other posts related to the company. Note products the company produces, identify the company's key competitors, and note any recent community activities or recognized accomplishments the company has been involved with.

In addition to the Internet, other sources for securing company information include company-produced brochures/literature, industry journals, and interviews with current employees and business leaders. Job-specific information is easily gathered by conducting a quick search on the O*Net database using the position title as your key word. As mentioned in the résumé chapter, this database of occupational information provides key information by job title.

The pre-interview research will assist you during your job interview. Identify as much as you can about the company, its administrators, and the department of your target job. Not only will you have an advantage in the interview, but you will know if this company is the right fit for you and your career goals. Use the company-specific research information to tailor your résumé, cover letter, and interview responses. This provides you an advantage over others who do not research the company.

In your interview, mention specific information about the company. This shows you have conducted research. For example, a popular interview question is, "Why do you want to work for this company?" If you have conducted research, be specific in your answer and respond with information that reflects your research. For example, say, "Your company has been green-conscious in the last two years, which is an area I, too, believe is important," instead of saying, "I have heard it is a great company."

Cory's friend Tomasz was excited about an interview he would be having in a week. When Tomasz was sharing his excitement with Cory, Cory asked him if he had conducted research on the company. Tomasz said he really didn't need to conduct research because the company was pretty well known. Cory explained that it was important to conduct research beyond general knowledge to make sure Tomasz stood out from the other candidates. Cory and Tomasz conducted an extensive Internet search on the target company, and Tomasz discovered useful information that Tomasz was able to use throughout his interview. After a successful interview, Tomasz thanked Cory and told Cory that the research prior to his interview gave him a lot of confidence that ultimately helped him secure the job.

The Personal Commercial

Prepare a **personal commercial** that sells your skills and ties these skills to the specific job for which you are interviewing. A personal commercial is a brief career biography that conveys your career choice, knowledge, skills, strengths, abilities, and experiences that make you uniquely qualified for the position for which you are applying. Include your interest in the targeted position, and use this personal commercial at the beginning or end of an interview. The purpose of the commercial is to sell your skills in a brief statement. Your goal is to sell yourself and match your skills to fit the company needs by adapting them to the requirements for each target job. Your personal commercial is essentially your "sales pitch" that communicates your key and unique knowledge, skills, and abilities that make you the right choice for your target job.

Exercise 15-1   Communicating Key Information

If you were alone in an elevator with the hiring manager of your target job, what key pieces of information would you communicate about yourself as you rode from the fifth floor to the first floor?

Do not include marital status, hobbies, or other personal information in your personal commercial. In chapter 13 you completed an accomplishments worksheet that assisted you in identifying your personal qualifications for a target job. This information was used to create a career objective for the résumé you built in chapter 14. Use this information in your personal commercial. When you write your personal commercial make it reflect your personality. Include your interest in your chosen career, activities related to the career, the skills you have acquired, and why you have enjoyed learning these skills. Your personal commercial should take no more than two minute to deliver. The following is an example of a personal commercial.

Personal Commercial Example

Since I can remember, I have been interested in math, numbers, and counting money. In junior high, I started myself on a budget and kept track of saving and spending. By high school I knew I wanted to become an accountant.

After finishing my classes at our local community college, I started working as an account clerk for a hospital. In addition to my regular duties, I was able to attend conferences and workshops where I expanded my knowledge and skills in different areas of accounting.

I am a recent college graduate from State University, where I received a bachelor's of science in accounting. With the additional education, I utilized these new skills and knowledge to work with general ledgers, accounts payable, and accounts receivable. I plan to apply my abilities and improve constantly.

With my experience as an Account Clerk, I have developed soft skills including how to deal with customers and coworkers in good and bad situations. In addition to the skills I have obtained working with MAS 90, I am proficient in MS Word and Excel. I have basic skills with Access, Outlook, and PowerPoint.

My goal is to become a CPA. Your company will benefit from my work ethic, which is to give 100 percent of my ability to all clients and provide them the confidence they need for someone handling their money. My values include integrity and innovation. I am organized, dedicated, responsible, punctual, and willing to learn. I believe I am the best candidate for this position. Since your company is committed to clients and the community, I would like to be a part of your team.

Exercise 15-2   Starting a Personal Commercial

Identify key points to include in your personal commercial.

_____

_____

_____

_____

_____

_____

Use your personal commercial during your interview when asked, "Tell me about yourself." If you are not given this instruction during the interview, include your personal commercial at the end of the interview. Practice delivering your commercial in front of a mirror.

The Interview Portfolio

An **interview portfolio** is a small folder containing relevant documents that are taken to an interview. Use a professional looking business portfolio or paper folder with pockets for your interview portfolio. Include copies of items pertinent to the position for which you are applying. Original documents (unless required) should not be given to the employer, only photocopies. Have the following items in your interview portfolio: copies of résumé, cover letter, reference list, generic application, and personal commercial. Also, include a calendar, note paper, a pen, and personal business cards. Print copies of your résumé, cover letter, and references on résumé paper. Copies of other items such as skill or education certificates and recent performance evaluations may be included if the information is relevant to the job. Keep your interview portfolio on your lap during the interview. Place your personal commercial on the top of your portfolio for easy access. Do not read the commercial. You may glance at it if you become nervous and forget what to say.

Practice Interview Questions

Another activity when preparing for an interview is to practice interview questions. Table 15-1 identifies common interview questions, the purpose of each question, and an appropriate way to answer each question. Review this list and begin creating appropriate responses to each question. Whenever you are answering interview questions, be honest and provide examples of specific skills and experiences that support your answers and meet the key requirements of the target job. The more real-life examples you provide, the more you demonstrate your experience and skill level to the employer. Anyone can say, "I can handle stress on a busy day"; however, by providing a specific example of how you handled stress on a busy day, you have demonstrated how you realistically handle stress.

Practice answering interview questions in front of a mirror, and, if possible, create a practice interview video of yourself answering common interview questions. Critically analyze your responses to see if you are appropriately answering the questions, selling your key skills, and projecting a professional image. Also check for nervous gestures. Doing this will better prepare you for an interview and help increase your self-confidence.

Talk It Out

Identify the most difficult questions to answer, and formulate appropriate responses that sell your skills.

Pre-Interview Practice

Prior to the day of your interview, visit the interview location, pre-plan your interview wardrobe, ensure your interview portfolio is up-to-date, and prepare post-interview thank-you notes.

Conduct a "practice day" prior to the day of your interview. If possible, drive or find transportation to the interview location. Ideally, do this on the same hour as your scheduled interview to identify potential transportation problems including traffic and parking. Once at the site, walk to the location where the interview will be held. This will enable you to become comfortable and familiar with your surroundings and let you know how much time you will

Table 15-1   Common Interview Questions

Question	Answer	Do Not
Tell me about yourself.	Use your personal commercial modified to the job description.	Do not divulge where you were born, hobbies, or other personal information.
What are your strengths?	Include how your strengths meet the job requirements and how they will be an asset to the company.	Do not include strengths that are not related to the job. Do not include personal information (e.g., "I'm a good mother").
Tell me about a time you failed.	Use an example that is not too damaging. Turn it into a positive by including the lesson learned from your mistake.	Do not exclude the lesson learned from the failure. Do not place blame for why the failure occurred.
Tell me about a time you were successful.	Use an example that relates to the job for which you are applying.	Do not take full credit if the success was a team effort.
How do you handle conflict?	Use an example that is not too damaging. Include how the conflict was positively resolved. Apply the lesson from chapter 12.	Do not provide specifics on how the conflict occurred, and do not use a negative example or place blame on others.
Would you rather work individually or in a team? Why?	State that you prefer one or the other and why, but relate your answer to the job requirements.	Do not state that you will not work one way or the other.
Why do you want this job?	Convey career goals and how the job supports your current skills. Include company information learned through research.	Do not state money or benefits in your response.
How do you deal with stress?	Share positive stress reducers addressed in chapter 3.	Do not state that stress does not affect you. Do not use negative examples.
What is your greatest weakness?	Use a weakness that will not damage your chance of getting the job. Explain how you are minimizing your weakness or are turning it into a strength (e.g., "I'm a perfectionist, but I don't allow it to interfere with getting my job done on time").	Do not state, "I don't have any."
Where do you want to be in five years?	Share the career goals you created in chapter 1.	Do not say you want the interviewer's job.
Tell me about a time you displayed leadership.	Use a specific example, and try to relate the example to the needed job skills.	Do not appear arrogant.

need to arrive at the interview on time. Do not go into the specific office, just the general area. Make note of the nearest public restroom so you can use it the day of the interview to freshen up prior to your meeting.

Ensure that your interview attire is clean and professional prior to the day of the interview. Refer to chapter 6 to review professional dress in greater detail. Dress at a level above the position for which you are interviewing. For example, if you are interviewing for an entry-level position, dress like you are interviewing for a supervisor position. Check that your clothes are spotless and fit appropriately and your shoes are clean. Women, if relevant, it is a good idea to have an extra pair of nylons available in case of snags or tears. Ensure that your hair and fingernails are professional and appropriate for an interview. If necessary, get a haircut prior to your interview. Use little or no perfume/aftershave and keep jewelry to a minimum. Cleanliness is important.

Prior to the interview, customize your interview portfolio for the target job. Place your portfolio in a place where you will not forget it when you leave your home.

Purchase a package of simple but professional thank-you notes. The evening before your interview, write a draft thank-you note on a blank piece of paper. Keep your thank-you note brief, only three to four sentences. In the note, thank the interviewer for his or her time. State that you enjoyed learning more about the position, are very interested in the job, and look forward to hearing from the interviewer soon. This draft note will be used as a foundation for notes you will be writing immediately after your interview. Place the draft note, the package of thank-you notes, and a black pen alongside your interview portfolio to take with you.

Exercise 15-3 Thank-You Note

Write a draft thank-you note.

The Day of the Interview

Be well rested and have food in your stomach prior to leaving your home for the interview. Look in the mirror to check your appearance and clothing. Your clothes should fit properly and project a professional image. If you smoke, refrain from smoking prior to the interview. The smell may be a distraction to the interviewer.

Plan to arrive at your destination fifteen minutes early. This provides time to deal with unforeseen traffic and/or parking issues. If there is a public restroom available, go to the restroom and freshen up. Check your hair, clothing, and makeup, if applicable. Turn off your phone, and if you are chewing gum, throw it away. Enter the specific meeting location five minutes prior to your scheduled interview. This is where your interview unofficially begins. First impressions matter, and any interaction with representatives of the organization must be professional.

Immediately upon entering the interview location, introduce yourself to the receptionist. Offer a smile and a handshake, and then clearly and slowly state your name. For example, "Hi, I'm Cory Kringle, and I am here for a 9:00 a.m. interview with Ms. Dancey for the accounting clerk position." If you recognize the receptionist as the same individual who arranged your interview appointment, make an additional statement thanking the individual for his or her assistance. For example, "Mrs. Wong, were you the one that I spoke with on the phone? Thank you for your help in arranging my interview." Be sincere in your conversation, and convey to the receptionist that you appreciate his or her efforts. The receptionist will most likely ask you to have a seat and wait to be called into the interview. Take a seat and relax. While you are waiting, use **positive self-talk.** Positive self-talk is a mental form of positive self-reinforcement. It helps remind you that you are qualified and deserve both the interview and the job. Mentally tell yourself that you are prepared, qualified, and ready for a successful interview. Review your personal commercial, your qualifications, and the key skills you want to convey in the interview.

Cory's friend Shelby had been asked to interview with one of her target companies. Shelby really wanted the job but was afraid she was not going to do well during her interview. Cory worked with Shelby the evening before the interview by role-playing interview questions and reviewing Shelby's company research. The next day, when Shelby arrived for the interview, she arrived early, thanked the receptionist, and took a seat. As Shelby waited to be called in to the interview, she began getting extremely nervous. Remembering Cory's tips, Shelby briefly closed her eyes and used positive self-talk to improve her attitude, increase her confidence, and calm her nerves. After doing this, she felt more confident when called into the office to begin the interview.

The Interview

During an interview, communicate confidence. Your primary message during the interview will be how your knowledge, skills, and abilities will be assets to the company. When you are called to interview, stand up and approach the individual who called your name. If it is not the receptionist who called you, extend a smile and a handshake, then clearly and slowly state your name. For example, "Hi, I'm Cory Kringle. It's nice to meet you." Listen carefully to the interviewer's name so you will remember it and use it during the interview. He or she will escort you to an office or conference room where the interview will take place. If you enter a room and there is someone in the room that you have not met, smile, extend a handshake, and introduce yourself. Once in the room, do not be seated until you are invited to do so. When seated, if possible, write down the names of the individuals you have just met. Inject the interviewer's name(s) during the interview. Although you may be offered something to drink, it is best to decline the offer so there is nothing to distract you from the interview. If you are sitting in a chair that swivels, put your feet flat on the floor to remind yourself not to swivel. If you forgot to turn off your phone and it rings during the interview, do not answer the phone. Immediately, apologize to the employer and turn it off.

The interview may be conducted different ways. It may involve only one person, it may involve several individuals, it may involve testing, or it may be a combination of interviewing and testing. Testing activities must be job-related, such as typing tests for office work, lifting for a warehouse position, or demonstrating other skills that are included in the job requirements and/or job duties. If the interview is taking place in an office, look around the room to get a sense of the person who is conducting the interview, assuming it is his or her office. This provides useful information for conversation, should it be necessary. Depending on the time available and the skills of the interviewer(s), you may first be asked general questions, such as, "Did you have trouble finding our office?" The interviewer is trying to get you to relax. During the interview, pay attention to body language—both yours and that of the individual conducting the interview. Sit up straight, sit back in your chair, and try to relax. Be calm but alert. Keep your hands folded on your lap or ready to take notes, depending on the situation. If you are seated near a desk or table, do not lean on the furniture. Make eye contact, but do not stare at the interviewer.

If you are given the opportunity to provide an opening statement, share your personal commercial. If you are not able to open with your personal commercial, include it in an appropriate response or use it at the end of the interview. When asked a question, listen carefully. Take a few seconds to think and digest what information the interviewer truly wants to know about your skill sets. Formulate an answer. Interview answers should relate back to the job qualifications and/or job duties. Your goal is to convey to the interviewer how your skills will assist the company in achieving success. Keep your answers brief but complete. Sell your skills and expertise by including a specific but short example. Whenever possible, inject information you learned about the company during your research.

Phone- and other Technology-Based Interviews

In some situations, your first interview may take place over the phone. Phone interviews may occur without prearrangement, while others are scheduled. During your job search, consistently answer your phone(s) in a professional manner and keep your interview portfolio in an accessible place. If a company calls and asks if it is a good time to speak with you and it is not, politely respond that it is not a good time and ask if you can reschedule the call. Try to be as accommodating as possible to the interviewer.

Those being interviewed by phone should follow these tips:

- *Be professional and be prepared.* Conduct the interview in a quiet room. Remove all distractions, including music, pets, television, and other individuals from your quiet area. Company research, personal examples, and the use of your personal commercial are just as important to inject into the phone conversation as during a face-to-face interview. Just as in a face-to-face interview, take notes and ask questions.

- *Be concise with your communication.* Those conducting the interview are not able to see you; therefore, they are forming an impression of you by what you say and how it is stated. Speak clearly and slowly, and do not interrupt. Smile while you speak, and speak with enthusiasm. Use proper grammar and beware of "ums" and other nervous verbal phrases. If you stand while conducting your phone interview, you will keep alert, focused, and more aware of your responses.
- *Be polite.* Utilize what you learned in both the etiquette and communication chapters. Exercise good manners. Do not eat or chew gum during your interview. It is not appropriate to use a speaker phone when being interviewed, nor is it polite to take another call, or tend to personal matters. Your attention should be completely focused on the interview. When the conversation is over, ask for the job, and thank the interviewer for his or her time.

Due to a tight economy, it is becoming increasingly common for interviews to take place through video chat venues such as Skype, WebEx, and Google Talk. An individual participating in a video chat interview needs a computer, a web cam, and a reliable Internet connection. When taking part in a video chat interview, the participant will receive a designated time and specific instructions on where and how to establish the connection. In addition to following the phone interview tips, the interviewer needs to prepare and treat the video chat interview as if it were a face-to-face interview. Therefore,

- *Plan ahead.* Research the venue you will be using to address any unforeseen issues. Identify where you will conduct the interview and what technology is required. If possible, arrange a pre-interview trial to ensure all equipment works properly and you know how to use it (including your volume and microphone).
- *Dress professionally.* You will be in plain view of the interviewer, so visual impressions matter.
- *Maintain a professional environment.* Conduct your interview in a quiet and appropriate location. A bedroom, public place, or outside location is not appropriate.
- *Speak to the camera.* Focus on the web cam as if it were the interviewer's face. Feel free to ask questions, take notes, and use hand gestures. While it may be more difficult to communicate, make every effort to not only project your personality, but, more importantly, sell your knowledge, skills, abilities, and unique qualifications. As with a traditional face-to-face interview, your job is to connect with the interviewer.

Additional information regarding technology-based meetings was presented in chapter 10.

Interview Methods and Types of Interview Questions

There are several common types of interviews. These include one-on-one interviews, group interviews, and panel interviews. **One-on-one interviews** involve a one-on-one meeting between the applicant and a company representative. The company representative is typically either someone from the human resource department or the immediate supervisor of the department with the open position.

Group interviews involve several applicants interviewing with each other while being observed by company representatives. The purpose of a group interview is to gauge how an individual behaves in a competitive and stressful environment. In a group interview situation, practice positive human relation and communication skills toward other applicants. Listening and communicating that you are the best candidate is critical to a successful group interview. If another applicant is first asked a question and you are immediately asked the same question, do not repeat what the other applicant said. If you agree with the first applicant's response, state, "I agree with Ms. Bell's response and would like to add that it's also important to...," and then elaborate or expand on the first applicant's response. If you do not agree with the first applicant's response, state, "I believe...," and then confidently provide your response. Do not demean other applicants. Be professional, do not interrupt, and behave like a leader. Be assertive, not aggressive.

Panel interviews involve the applicant meeting with several company employees at the same time. During a panel interview, make initial eye contact with the person asking the question. While answering the question, make eye contact with the other members of the interview panel. Whenever possible, call individuals by name.

The three general types of interview questions are structured, unstructured, and behavioral. **Structured interview questions** address job-related issues where each applicant is asked the same question(s). An example of a structured question is, "How long have you worked in the retail industry?" The purpose of a structured interview question is to secure information related to a specific job. An **unstructured interview question** is a probing, open-ended question. The purpose of an unstructured interview question is to identify if the candidate can appropriately sell his or her skills. An example of an unstructured interview question is, "Tell me about yourself." When you are asked to talk about yourself, state your personal commercial. This is where you begin using the interview portfolio. Whenever possible, pull job samples from your interview portfolio if you are referring to a specific skill. Relate answers back to the job for which you are applying. **Behavioral interview questions** are questions that ask candidates to share a past experience related to a workplace situation. An example of a behavioral question is: "Describe a time you motivated others." Prior to answering the question, take a moment to formulate your answer. Use an example that puts you in a positive light and utilizes key skills that are necessary for your target job.

Discrimination and Employee Rights

Title VII of the Civil Rights Act was created to protect the rights of employees. It prohibits employment discrimination based on race, color, religion, sex, or national origin. Other federal laws prohibit pay inequity and discrimination against individuals forty years or older, individuals with disabilities, and individuals who are pregnant. This does not mean that an employer must hire you if you are a minority, pregnant, forty or older, or have a disability. Employers have a legal obligation to provide every qualified candidate equal opportunity to interview. Their job is to hire the most qualified candidate. Unfortunately, some employers ask interview questions that can be discriminatory. Discriminatory questions are illegal. Table 15-2 was taken from the

Table 15-2	Illegal Interview Questions	
Acceptable	**Subject**	**Unacceptable**
Name	**Name**	Maiden name
Place of residence	**Residence**	Questions regarding owning or renting
Statements that employment is subject to verification if applicant meets legal age requirement	**Age**	Age Birth date Date of attendance/completion of school Questions that tend to identify applicants over forty
Statements/inquiries regarding verification of legal right to work in the United States	**Birthplace, citizenship**	Birthplace of applicant or applicant's parents, spouse, or other relatives Requirements that applicant produce naturalization or alien card prior to employment
Languages applicant reads, speaks, or writes if use of language other than English is relevant to the job for which applicant is applying	**National origin**	Questions as to nationality, lineage, ancestry, national origin, descent or parentage of applicant, applicant's spouse, parent, or relative
Statement by employer of regular days, hours, or shifts to be worked	**Religion**	Questions regarding applicant's religion Religious days observed
Name and address of parent or guardian if applicant is a minor. Statement of company policy regarding work assignment of employees who are related	**Sex, marital status, family**	Questions to indicate applicant's sex, marital status, number/ages of children or dependents Questions regarding pregnancy, child birth, or birth control Name/address of relative, spouse, or children of adult applicant
Job-related questions about convictions, except those convictions that have been sealed, expunged, or statutorily eradicated	**Arrest, criminal record**	General questions regarding arrest record

California Department of Fair Employment and Housing to provide examples of acceptable and unacceptable employment inquiries.

If an interviewer asks you a question that is illegal or could be discriminatory, do not directly answer the question; instead, address the issue. For example, if the interviewer states, "You look Hispanic—are you?" Your response should not be "Yes" or "No." Politely smile and say, "People wonder about my ethnicity. What can I tell you about my qualifications for this job?" Also, do not

Talk It Out

Role-play an interview. During the interview, ask one legal question and one illegal question. Practice answering the illegal question with confidence but in a non-offensive manner.

accuse the interviewer of asking an illegal question or say, "I will not answer that question because it is illegal." Most employers do not realize they are asking illegal questions. However, some employers purposely ask inappropriate questions. In this case, you need to decide if you want to work for an employer who intentionally asks illegal questions. If employers are behaving inappropriately during an interview, one would wonder how they will treat the applicant after he or she is hired.

Know and protect your rights. It is inappropriate to disclose personal information about yourself during an interview. Avoid making any comment referring to your marital status, children, religion, age, or any other private issue protected by law.

Tough Questions

Life is unpredictable and sometimes results in situations that can be embarrassing or difficult to explain during a job interview. These situations may include a negative work experience with a previous employer, time gaps in a résumé, or a prior felony conviction. The following information provides the proper response to interview questions related to these difficult situations.

Some job seekers have had negative work-related experiences that they do not want to disclose during an interview. Disclosing such information could be potentially devastating to a job interview if it is not handled properly. Some of these experiences include being fired, having a poor performance evaluation, or knowing that a former manager or teacher will not provide a positive reference if called. Perhaps you behaved in a negative manner prior to leaving your old job.

If you did have a difficult circumstance and are not asked about the situation, you have no need to disclose the unpleasant event. The only exception to this rule is if your current or former boss has the potential to provide a negative reference. If this is the situation, tell the interviewer that you know you will not receive a positive reference from him or her and request that the interviewer contact another manager or coworker who will provide a fair assessment of your performance.

Being honest and factual is the best answer to any difficult question. If you were fired, performed poorly, or left in a negative manner, state the facts, but do not go into great detail. Tell the interviewer that you have matured and realize that you did not handle the situation appropriately. Add what lesson you have learned. Do not speak poorly of your current or previous employer, boss, or coworker. It is also important to not place blame by stating who was right or wrong in your negative workplace situation.

It is common for an individual to have time gaps in a résumé as a result of staying at home to raise a young child, care for an elderly relative, or continue his or her education. Those who have gaps in their résumé may need to be prepared to explain what they did during the time gap. Identify a key skill you sharpened during your time gap and relate this experience to a key skill necessary for your target job and industry. For example, if you stayed at home to care for an elderly relative and are asked about the time gap, explain the situation without providing specific details, and then share how the experience improved your time management and organizational skills in addition to improving your awareness of diverse populations including the elderly and disabled.

If you have a felony record, you may be asked about your conviction. As with other difficult interview questions, be honest and factual in your response. Explain the situation, and tell the interviewer that you are making every attempt to start anew and are committed to doing your very best. Sell your strengths, and remember to communicate how your skills will help the company achieve its goals. Your self-confidence and honesty will be revealed through your body language and eye contact. Be sincere. Depending on the type and severity of your offense, it may take more attempts to secure a job than during a typical job search. You may also need to start at a lower level and/or lower pay than desired. The goal is to begin to reestablish credibility. Do not give up. Each experience, be it positive or negative, is a learning experience.

Closing the Interview

After the interviewer has completed his or her questioning, you may be asked if you have any questions. Having a question or closing statement prepared for use at the close of your interview demonstrates to your prospective employer that you have conducted research on the company. A good question refers to a current event that has occurred within the company. For example, "Ms. Dancey, I read about how your company employees donated time to clean up the ABC school yard. Is this an annual event?" A statement such as this provides you one last opportunity to personalize the interview and demonstrate that you researched the company. This is also a good time to share any relevant information you have in your portfolio.

Do not ask questions that imply you did not research the company or that you care only about your needs. Inappropriate questions include questions regarding salary, benefits, or vacations. These questions imply that you care more about what the company can do for you than what you can do for the company. However, it is appropriate to ask what the next steps will be in the interview process, including when a hiring decision will be made.

Questions You *May* Ask the Interviewer

1. Does your company have any plans for expansion?
2. What type of formal training does your company offer?
3. What is the greatest challenge your industry is currently facing?
4. What is the next step in the interview process?
5. What are the required work days and hours of the position?
6. When will you be making a hiring decision?

Questions You *Should Not* Ask During an Interview

1. How much does this job pay?
2. How many sick days do I get?
3. What benefits will I get?
4. What does your company do?
5. How long does it take for someone to get fired for poor performance?

After the interviewer answers your general questions, make a closing interview statement. Restate your personal commercial and ask for the job. An example of a good closing statement is to restate your personal commercial and add: "Once again, thank you for your time, Ms. Dancey. As I stated at the beginning of our meeting, I feel I am qualified for this job based upon my experience, knowledge, and demonstrated leadership. I would like this job and believe I will be an asset to XYZ Company." The purpose of the job interview is to sell you and your skills. A sale is useless if you do not close the sale.

After you make your closing statement, the interviewer will signal that the interview is over. He or she will do this either through conversation or through body language, such as standing up and walking toward the door. Prior to leaving the interview, hand the interviewer your personal business card and ask the interviewer for a business card. You will use this business card for the interview follow-up. As you are handed the card, shake the interviewer's hand using a firm shake and eye contact, and thank him or her for his or her time and state that you look forward to hearing from him or her. Remember to continue communicating confidence, friendliness, and professionalism to every company employee you encounter on your way out of the building.

When you leave the building, retrieve your draft thank-you note. Modify your draft thank-you note to include information that was shared during your interview. Handwrite a personalized thank-you note to each individual who interviewed you. Use your finest handwriting and double-check your spelling and grammar. Refer to the business card(s) you collected for correct name spelling. After you have written your note, hand deliver it to the reception area and ask the receptionist to deliver the notes. Your goal is to make a positive last impression and stand out from the other candidates.

After the Interview

After delivering your thank-you notes, congratulate yourself. If you did your best, you should have no regrets. Prior to leaving the company property, make notes regarding specific information you learned about your prospective job and questions you were asked during the interview. Through the excitement of an interview, you may forget parts of your meeting if you do not immediately write notes. Write down what you did right and areas in which you would like to improve. This is a good time for you to evaluate your impressions of the company and determine if it is a company where you will want to work. This information will be helpful in the future.

Salary Negotiation

Soon after your initial interview, you should hear back from the company. At that point, you may be called in for a second interview or may receive a job offer. A job offer may be contingent upon reference and background checks. This will be a good time to contact the individuals on your reference list to provide them an update on your job search and ensure your references are prepared to respond appropriately to the individual conducting your reference check.

If you are a final candidate for the job, the interviewer may ask you about your salary requirements. In order to negotiate an acceptable salary, first conduct research and compare your research to the salary range that was included in the job announcement. Check job postings and conduct online research to determine local and regional salaries. When conducting your salary research, attempt to match the job description as closely as possible to that of the job for which you are applying. Depending on your experience, start a few thousand dollars higher than your desired starting salary and do not forget to consider your experience and/or lack of experience. Some companies do not offer many benefits but offer higher salaries. Other companies offer lower salaries but better benefits. Weigh these factors when determining your desired salary. Prior to stating your salary requirement, sell your skills. For example, "Ms. Dancey, as I mentioned in my initial interview, I have over five years' experience working in a professional accounting office and an accounting degree; therefore, I feel I should earn between $55,000 and $65,000." If you are offered a salary that is not acceptable, use silence and wait for the interviewer to respond. This minute of silence may encourage the employer to offer a higher salary.

Cory's friend Kenny was invited to a second interview. Prior to the interview, Cory and Kenny prepared for potential questions and situations Kenny might encounter during the interview. In their practice, Cory asked Kenny about his starting salary. Kenny said he did not care; he would just be happy to get a job. Cory reminded Kenny that he needed to sell his skills and go into the interview with a desired target salary. Cory and Kenny then conducted an Internet search of both local and statewide jobs that were similar to the one Kenny wants. Kenny was surprised that starting salaries were much higher than he expected. Fortunately, the next day, when the interviewer asked Kenny about his desired starting salary, Kenny was prepared to answer.

Pre-Employment Tests, Screenings and Medical Exams

Pre-employment tests are assessments that are given to potential employees as a means of determining if the applicant possesses the desired knowledge, skills, or abilities required for the job. Pre-employment tests can be giving during the application process, during the interview process, or prior to receiving a job offer. Some employers require applicants to take online pre-employment tests. Some tests may require lifting, others are skills-based, while others measure listening or logic. Legally, pre-employment tests must be job-related. Depending on the type of test, you may be given the results immediately. In other cases, you may need to wait for the results. If you pass the employment test(s), you will be invited to proceed with the interview process. It is common for employers to have applicants who did not pass a pre-employment test to wait a predetermined period prior to reapplying.

Employers may also conduct pre-employment screenings and medical exams. The most common pre-employment screenings include criminal checks, education verification, driver's license history, security checks, employment checks, credit checks, and reference checks. The number and type of pre-employment screenings performed will be based upon how relevant the check is to the job you will be performing. Legally, employers can require medical exams only after a job offer is made. The exam must be required for all applicants for the same job, and the exam must be job-related. Employers are not allowed to ask disability questions related to pre-employment screenings and medical exams. Common medical exams include vision and strength testing. Employers may also require pre-employment drug tests.

An employer legally cannot conduct these checks without your permission. Most employers will secure your permission in writing when you complete an employment application or when you are a finalist for the position.

When You Are Not Offered the Job

As stated at the beginning of the chapter, a job search is similar to a full-time job. It takes time and can sometimes be discouraging. If you are not called in for an interview or fail to receive a job offer, do not be discouraged.

When you are not invited to interview, evaluate your résumé and cover letter. Check for typographical or grammatical errors. Make sure you have listed important skills that reflect the needs of your target job. Have someone who knows you and your skills—and whom you trust—review your cover letter and résumé. Many times, a fresh perspective will catch obvious errors or opportunities for improvement.

If you are invited to interview but do not receive a job offer, do not be discouraged. Remember to make every experience a learning experience. Sit down and carefully review each step in the interview process and grade yourself. Consider your pre-interview preparation, your interview-day appearance, your interview answers, your ability to interject company research into each interview answer, and your overall attitude. Any area that did not receive an "A" grade is an area poised for improvement.

There are several steps you can take to increase the probability for success in your next interview. Consider your overall appearance. Reviewing the information in chapter 4, make sure you convey professionalism. Ensure that your clothes are clean and fit properly. Have a hairstyle that is flattering and well kempt. Check that your fingernails and jewelry are appropriate and do not distract from your personality and job skills.

Mentally review job interview questions that were asked and the responses you provided. Every answer should communicate how your skills will assist the target company in achieving success. Review the amount of company research you conducted. Did you feel amply prepared, or did you simply research the bare minimum? If you felt you did conduct the appropriate amount of research, evaluate whether you fully communicated your research to the interviewer.

Assess your body language and attitude. Stand in front of a mirror and practice your answers to difficult and/or illegal questions. If possible, have a friend videotape you and provide an honest evaluation of your appearance, attitude, and body language. Check for nervous gestures, and keep practicing until you are able to control these nervous habits.

Finally, be honest about your overall performance. Did you ask for the job? Did you immediately send a thank-you note to your interviewer(s)? Sell your skills through your mannerisms, answers, and attitude. Your goal is to stand out above the other candidates.

Workplace Dos and Don'ts

Do tailor your résumé and personal commercial to the needs of your targeted employer	*Don't* have unprofessional introductions on your voice-mail message
Do try to schedule your interview at a time that puts you at an advantage over the other candidates and secure information that better prepares you for the interview	*Don't* make demands with the individual scheduling the interview
Do learn as much as you can about the company, its strategy, and its competition	*Don't* forget to include your research information in your interview answers
Do practice interview questions and formulate answers that highlight your skills and experience	*Don't* show up to an interview unprepared
Do remember that your interview begins the minute you step onto company property	*Don't* let your nerves get the better of you in a job interview
Do know how to handle inappropriate questions that may be discriminatory	*Don't* answer an illegal question. Instead address the issue

Concept Review and Application

Summary of Key Concepts

- Create and modify your personal commercial and adapt it to the requirements of your target job
- Review common interview questions and formulate answers as part of your interview preparation

- Conduct a pre-interview practice to ensure you are prepared the day of the interview
- During your interview, communicate how your knowledge, skills, and abilities will be assets to the company
- Understand the laws that protect employees from discrimination in the interviewing and hiring process
- Be prepared to confidently handle gaps in employment and other difficult interview questions
- Know how to sell yourself and professionally ask for the job at the close of an interview

Key Terms

behavioral interview question

personal commercial

unstructured interview question

group interview

one-on-one interview

positive self-talk

interview portfolio

panel interview

structured interview question

If You Were the Boss

1. What kind of information should you share with your current staff members as they prepare to interview a new employee?
2. How would you handle a prospective employee who disclosed inappropriate information during the job interview?

Video Case Study: Good, Bad, and Ugly

This video addresses improper and proper behavior in a job interview. To view these videos, visit the Student Resources: Professionalism section in www.mystudentsuccesslab.com. Then answer the following questions.

1. Of the three candidates, who was dressed appropriately for the interview and who was not?
2. Name four interview recommendations for Shawn.
3. What interview advice would you give to Kevin?
4. How did Francesca specifically use her interview portfolio and personal commercial during her interview?

Video Case Study: Interview Walk-Through

This video presents expert advice on how to prepare and what to expect the day of an interview. To view these videos, visit the Student Resources: Professionalism section in www.mystudentsuccesslab.com. Then answer the following questions.

1. Name three activities to perform prior to entering the specific interview location.
2. How specifically should you greet the receptionist?
3. What three activities does the expert recommend you do and what are two activities to avoid while waiting in the reception area?

Video Case Study: Preparing for a Phone Interview

This video presents a phone interview between a job applicant and a potential employer. To view these videos, visit the Student Resources: Professionalism section in www.mystudentsuccesslab.com. Then answer the following questions.

1. What improvements could be made to Kevin's voice mail message?
2. Did Kevin answer his phone appropriately and what kind of impression did he make on Karen Gonzales when he answered the phone?
3. Did Kevin handle the background noise appropriately? Why or why not?
4. How could Kevin have been better prepared for this phone interview?
5. If you were Karen would you call Kevin in for a second interview? Why or why not?

Video Case Study: Pre-Interview Activities

This video presents expert advice regarding activities to conduct before the day of an interview. To view these videos, visit the Student Resources: Professionalism section in www.mystudentsuccesslab.com. Then answer the following questions.

1. What scheduling strategy should you utilize when invited to an interview?
2. Name four specific items to be included in an interview portfolio and explain the purpose of each.
3. Name four specific activities that need to take place in preparing your interview outfit.
4. Why is it important to visit the interview site prior to the day of an interview?

Video Case Study: Tough Interview Questions

This video presents expert advice on how to respond to tough interview questions. To view these videos, visit the Student Resources: Professionalism section in www.mystudentsuccesslab.com. Then answer the following questions.

1. How does the expert recommend you prepare for a tough interview question?
2. What specific advice does the expert share on how to respond to a tough interview question?
3. Provide specific information the expert shared on how to deal with illegal interview questions.

Web Links

http://www.onetcenter.org/
http://jobstar.org/electra/question/sal-req.cfm
http://www.collegegrad.com/intv
http://www.careercc.com/interv3.shtml
http://interview.monster.com
http://www.rileyguide.com/interview.html

Activities

Activity 15-1

Identify a local company for which you would like to interview. Using the following table, conduct a thorough targeted job search on this company. Answer as many of the questions as possible.

1. Company name	
2. Company address	
3. Job title	
4. To whom should the cover letter be addressed?	
5. What are the job requirements?	
6. Is this a full-time or part-time job?	
7. What are the hours/days of work?	
8. What are the working conditions?	
9. Is there room for advancement?	
10. What kind of training is offered?	
11. What other positions at this company match my qualifications?	
12. What are the average starting salaries (benefits)?	
13. Is traveling or relocation required?	
14. Where is the business located (home office, other offices)?	
15. What are the products or services that the employer provides or manufactures?	
16. What is the mission statement?	
17. What kind of reputation does this organization have?	
18. What is the size of the employer's organization relative to the industry?	
19. What is the growth history of the organization for the past five, ten, or fifteen years?	
20. How long has the employer been in business?	
21. Who is the employer's competition?	

Activity 15-2

Write a statement to use during an invitation to an interview that will help you secure all relevant interview information.

_____

_____

Activity 15-3

Using information obtained in your target company research (Activity 15-1), write three common interview questions and answers. Integrate relevant company information in your answers.

Question	Answer
1.	
2.	
3.	

Activity 15-4

Conduct a salary search for a target job. Identify the salary range. Using your research data, write out a statement you could use to negotiate a higher salary.

Lowest Salary	Highest Salary
$	$

Salary Negotiation Statement

_____

_____

1. The purpose of a/an _____ is to identify _____ and identify companies for which you would like to work.

2. In addition to finding out with whom you will be interviewing, identify how much _____ _____ the company has scheduled and _____ are being called in to _____.

3. Prior to your interview, _____.

4. If possible, prior to the interview day, _____.

5. When asked a difficult question, be _____ and _____.

Career Changes

chapter 16

Real success is finding your lifework in the work that you love.

David McCullough (b. 1933)

MyStudentSuccessLab   Visit www.mystudentsuccesslab.com for added practice, activities, assessment, and videos.

Objectives

- Explain the importance of *training* and *development*
- Define the importance of continual *formal learning* and *informal learning*
- Know the various ways employment status can change
- Define the various types of workplace terminations
- Demonstrate how to write a *letter of resignation*
- Know the appropriate behavior to exhibit when leaving a position
- Understand the opportunities of becoming an *entrepreneur*

How-Do-You-Rate

	Do you understand job transition?	True	False
1.	It is normal to change jobs within the same company.	❏	❏
2.	Being fired is not the same as being laid off.	❏	❏
3.	It is appropriate to look for a new job while still employed.	❏	❏
4.	With the exception of being fired, when leaving a job, an employee should always write a thank-you note to his or her former boss.	❏	❏
5.	Many people start their own business if they are unable to find a job.	❏	❏

If you answered "true" to the majority of these questions, well done. You are aware of important concepts related to career and life changes.

Career Changes

Where do you want to be in five years? While this is a common interview question, it is also part of goal setting. Based upon the career and life plan you created in chapter 1, career changes should be welcome, because they mean you are accomplishing and updating your goals. Career changes are normal and common occurrences. While most of these changes can be controlled, some career changes are unexpected. Make a commitment to become a lifelong learner so you have current knowledge and skills to deal with unexpected change. This chapter explores the various career changes that may occur and teaches you how to welcome change as an opportunity for both personal and career growth.

Training and Development

Many companies offer current and new employees **training** to learn new skills. The teaching of new skills may be used to promote employees and/or increase their responsibilities. With the increase of technology usage, employee training is important for many companies. Training is usually provided and/or paid for by the company.

In addition to learning new skills through training, make every effort to attend **development** sessions designed to enhance existing skills or increase your skills. Development sessions make employees more diverse in knowledge, skills, and abilities, which provides an advantage when promotional or other opportunities arise in the workplace. Even if you do not think a development session is in your area of expertise, continue expanding your knowledge and skills in as many areas as possible. This is especially helpful if you are considering a promotion into a management position.

As an employee who is considering a management position, learn not only the skills needed for your job, but also other skills. Be aware of the key duties within other departments. The development of these skills will increase your knowledge and understanding of the company's mission and goals. When you can see beyond your job, you become more aware of what you are contributing to the company and how you are helping make it more successful.

The marketing department for Cory's company invited all employees to meet in the conference room during lunch hour to learn more about how to conduct a media interview. Cory did not know a lot about marketing and did not think media interviews were a part of Cory's job. However, Cory attended because it would be not only a good skill to learn, but also a good way to meet people in other departments.

Continual Learning

In addition to training and development programs offered by a company, there are other ways to improve and increase your skills and knowledge. **Continual learning** is the ongoing process of increasing knowledge in the area of your career. This can be accomplished by formal and/or informal learning.

Formal learning involves returning to college to increase knowledge, improve skills, or receive an additional or advanced degree. This can be done while you continue working. Consider taking one or two night classes a semester while you work. Be cautious about taking too many classes while working full-time, because that might stress you to a point that you will perform poorly at both work and school. Many colleges offer online classes, which have become increasingly popular for working adults. These classes allow more freedom and flexibility by allowing students to complete coursework on the Internet.

In addition to college, seminars and conferences are available. Some of these seminars and conferences offer college credit. Many seminars and conferences are offered by vendors or industry experts. Although you may have to pay for a conference, your company may be willing to reimburse you or share the cost with you. Conferences may last one day or may take place over a period of several days. Seminars and conferences are also excellent methods of expanding your professional network.

Informal learning is increasing knowledge by reading career-related magazines, newsletters, and electronic articles associated with your job. Another means of informal learning is using the Internet to research career-related information. Informal learning is an ongoing process and can occur during informational interviews, in conversations with professionals in your career area, and by attending association meetings. Make every opportunity a learning opportunity.

Talk It Out

Based on your target career, name two professional conferences or associations you would like to join/attend.

Exercise 16-1   Additional Career Interests

What additional classes might be helpful to you when you start working in your new job? Name at least three classes.

1. _____

2. _____

3. _____

Changes in Employment Status

Throughout this text, we have stressed the importance of goal setting. As you begin meeting your stated career goals, establish new ones. If you are following your life plan, you will have the desire to change jobs as you advance in your area of expertise. If and when this job change occurs depends upon many factors. Some reasons for changing jobs include a(n):

- Acquired experience for an advanced position
- Opportunity for higher salary
- Desire for improved work hours
- Need for increased responsibility, status, and/or power
- Perceived decrease in stress
- Desire for different work environment and/or colleagues

It is normal for employees to move within and outside of their company. A poor economy forces some employees to change positions and, in some cases, careers. Changes in employment status include promotions, voluntary terminations, involuntary terminations, lateral transfers, and retirement. The following section presents and discusses these changes in employment status and provides tips on how to handle each situation in a proactive and professional manner.

New Job Searches

Depending on their work situation, some employees determine that they must find a new job immediately, while other employees are constantly exploring opportunities. No matter your situation, identify when to share your desire for a new job and when to keep your job search private. If you have recently received a college certification or degree that qualifies you for a higher position, approach your supervisor or human resource department to inform the appropriate individuals of your increased qualifications and desire for additional responsibilities and/or promotion. It is also appropriate to share your need to change jobs if a situation is requiring you to move out of the area. In this instance, your employer may have contacts to assist you in securing a new job in another city. If you have had good performance evaluations and are leaving voluntarily, ask your immediate supervisor, another superior, or coworkers if they are willing to serve as references for future employers. If they agree to serve as references, secure letters of recommendation written on company letterhead. It is helpful to write and provide a draft letter for your reference that highlights your accomplishments and favorable work attitude. Finally, if you have mastered your job duties, have had good performance evaluations, and are beginning to feel bored, respectfully share your desire for increased responsibilities with your boss.

Apart from the previously mentioned circumstances, do not share your desire to change jobs with anyone at work. This includes close coworkers. Oftentimes, sharing secrets at work can be used against you. Therefore, keep your job search private. Conduct your job search outside of work hours and schedule job interviews before or after work.

Exercise 16-2   Employer Recommendations

List at least four key points to include in a draft letter of recommendation from your employer. Provide an example for each key point.

Key Point (Quality)	Example
1.	
2.	
3.	
4.	

Grace and style are two key words to remember if coworkers learn you are looking for a new position. When confronted about your job search, be brief and positive. State that you desire a move, be it the need for additional responsibility or the need for more money, but keep your explanation simple. You do not have to share details as to why you want to move on. It is also not necessary to share details about potential employers or the status of your job search.

Promotions

A **promotion** is when someone moves to a position higher in the organization with increased pay and responsibility. The first step in securing a future promotion within your company is to begin behaving and dressing for advancement. Secure a copy of the job description and/or research key skills necessary for your desired position. Begin acquiring work experience in the target area by volunteering for assignments that provide the needed experience. Develop new skills through appropriate classes, job training, and other educational experiences to increase your qualifications. Watch and learn from those who are already in the position you desire. Implement this plan and you will gain the necessary qualifications and have the experience when an advanced position becomes available.

If you receive a promotion, congratulate yourself. Your hard work has been noticed by others within your company, and they want to reward your excellent behavior. A promotion also means that you are advancing toward your career goals. When you are promoted, thank your former boss either verbally or with a simple handwritten thank-you note. Communicate to your former boss how he or she has helped you acquire new skills. Be sincere. Even if your former boss was less than perfect, his or her behavior taught you how to lead and manage. Keep your note positive and professional. With your promotion, you most likely will see an increase in pay, a new title, and new responsibilities. If your promotion occurred within the same company, do not gloat; there were probably others within the company who also applied for the job. Behave in a positive, pleasant, and professional manner that reinforces that your company made the right choice in selecting you for the position.

In your new job, do not try to reinvent the wheel. Become familiar with the history of your department or area. Be sensitive to the needs and adjustments of your new employees. Review files and begin networking with people who can assist you in achieving department goals. When you are new to a position, you do not know everything. Ask for and accept help from others.

With a history of favorable performance evaluations, Cory wants a promotion. Cory decided to take responsibility and began evaluating potential positions for which Cory might qualify. While conducting research, Cory created a list of additional knowledge, skills, and abilities needed for the promotion. Cory began taking classes, attending training seminars, and watching leaders within the company to prepare for a future promotion.

Voluntary Terminations

Leaving a job on your own is called a **voluntary termination.** Voluntary terminations frequently occur when an employee has taken a job with a new employer or when retiring. While at times the workplace can be so unbearable that you want to quit without having another job, it is best to not quit your job unless you have another job waiting. No matter what the situation, when voluntarily leaving a job, be professional and do not burn bridges.

When taking a voluntary termination, resign with a formal letter of resignation. A **letter of resignation** is a written notice of your voluntary termination. Unless you are working with a contract that specifies an end date of your employment, you are technically not required to provide advance notice of your voluntary termination. It is, however, considered unprofessional to resign from work and make your last day the same day you resign. Typically, two weeks' notice is acceptable. State your last date of employment in your letter of resignation. Include a positive statement about the employer and remember to sign and date your letter. Figure 16-1 is a sample letter of resignation.

In your final days of employment, do not speak or behave negatively. Leave in a manner that would make the company want to rehire you tomorrow. Coworkers may want to share gossip or speak poorly of others, but you must remain professional. It is also inappropriate to damage or take property that belongs to the company. Do not behave unethically. Take only personal belongings, and leave your workspace clean and organized for whoever assumes your position. Preserve the confidentiality of your coworkers, department, and customers.

February 1, 2015

Susie Supervisor
ABC Company
123 Avenue 456
Anycity, USA 98765

Re: Notice of Resignation

Dear Ms. Supervisor:

While I have enjoyed working for ABC Company, I have been offered and have accepted a new position with another firm. Therefore, my last day of employment will be February 23, 2012.

In the past two years, I have had the pleasure of learning new skills and of working with extremely talented individuals. I thank you for the opportunities you have provided me and wish everyone at ABC Company continued success.

Sincerely,

Jennie New-Job

Jennie New-Job
123 North Avenue
Anycity, USA 98765

Figure 16-1

Cory had a coworker who had been looking for a job over the past few months. Cory knew this because the coworker not only told everyone, but used the company equipment to update and mail her résumé. Cory often heard the coworker talking to potential employers on the telephone. On the day Cory's coworker finally landed a new job, the coworker proudly announced to everyone in the office that she was "leaving the prison" and that afternoon would be her last day at work. The coworker went on to bad-mouth the company, her boss, and several colleagues. As she was cleaning out her desk, Cory noticed that the coworker started packing items that did not belong to her. When Cory shared this observation, the coworker said she deserved the items and that the company would never miss them. A few weeks later, Cory's former coworker came by the office to say hello. Cory asked her how her new job was going. "Well…" said the coworker, "the job fell through." The coworker explained that she was stopping by the office to see if she could have her old position back. Unfortunately, the former coworker left in such a negative manner that the company would not rehire her.

On the last day of employment with your company, you may meet with a representative from the human resource department or with your immediate supervisor to receive your final paycheck. This paycheck should include all unpaid wages and accrued vacation. This is also when you will formally return all company property, including your keys and name badge. You may receive an

exit interview. An exit interview is when an employer meets with an employee who is voluntarily leaving a company to identify opportunities for improving the work environment. During this interview, a company representative will ask questions regarding the job you are leaving, the boss, and the work environment. The company's goal is to secure any information that provides constructive input on how to improve the company. Share opportunities for improvement, but do not turn your comments into personal attacks. While it is sometimes tempting to provide negative information in the interview, remain positive and professional.

Involuntary Terminations

Talk It Out

If you were to be laid off, what are the first three things you would do, and why?

Involuntary terminations are when you lose your job against your will. Types of involuntary terminations include **firing,** which happens when you are terminated because of a performance issue; a **layoff,** which is a result of the company's financial inability to keep your position; or a restructuring, which is when the company has eliminated your position due to a change in strategy.

If you are fired, you have lost your job as a result of a performance issue. Unless you have done something outrageous (such as blatant theft or harassment), you should have received a poor performance warning prior to being fired. Typically, this progressive discipline includes a verbal and/or written warning prior to termination. If you are totally unaware of why you are being fired, ask for documentation to support the company's decision. Firing based on outrageous behavior will be supported by a policy, while any performance issue should be supported with prior written documentation. When you are informed of your firing, you should immediately receive your final paycheck. You will also be asked to return all company property on the spot (including keys and name badge). Do not damage company property. Doing so is not only immature, but punishable by law. While you may be angry or caught off guard, do not make threats against the company or its employees. Remain calm and professional. If you think you are being wrongfully terminated, your legal recourse is to seek assistance from your state's labor commission or a private attorney.

Many people consider a layoff a form of firing. This is not true. Firing is a result of poor performance. A layoff is a result of a company's change of strategy or its inability to financially support a position. While some companies lay off employees based upon performance, most do it on seniority. Frequently, when the company's financial situation improves, employees may be recalled. A **work recall** is when employees are called back to work after being laid off. If you have been laid off, remain positive and ask your employer for a letter of reference and job-search assistance. This job-search assistance may include support with updating a résumé, counseling, job training, and job leads. Some companies require employees to take unpaid work days, called **furloughs.** Employees are required to take these unpaid work days. Work furloughs are not a result of poor performance. They are a result of employers trying to save financial resources. If your company implements a work furlough program, make the best of the situation. Be happy you still have a job, and find ways to assist the company in improving

Talk It Out

What is the best way to use your time during a furlough day?

its financial situation. Knowing your current employer is experiencing economic challenges provides you an opportunity to update your résumé and create a plan should your employer need to take additional steps toward saving resources.

In today's competitive environment, it is common for companies to restructure. **Restructuring** involves a company changing its strategy and reorganizing resources. This commonly results in eliminating unnecessary positions. If your position is eliminated, remain positive and inquire about new positions. In a restructuring situation, it is often common for new positions to be created. Once again, do not bad-mouth anyone or openly express your anger or dissatisfaction over the situation. If you have recently acquired new skills, now is the time to communicate and demonstrate them. Keep a record of your workplace accomplishments, and keep your ears open for new positions for which to apply.

Other Moves Within the Organization

In addition to promotions and terminations, there are several other methods of moving within and outside the company. These include lateral moves, demotions, and retirement. A **lateral move** is when you are transferred to another area of the organization with the same level of responsibility. Lateral moves involve only a change in department or work area. A change in pay is not involved in a lateral move. If you are moved to a different position and experience a pay increase, it is considered a promotion. If you are moved to a different position and experience a pay decrease, you have been demoted. While **demotions** are rare, they can occur if one's performance is not acceptable but the employee chooses to not leave the company. Of all the changes an employee can make, a demotion is by far the most difficult. You experience not only a decrease in pay, but also a decrease in job title and status. If you are demoted, remain professional and be respectful of your new boss.

The final change in employment status is called **retirement.** Retirement is when you are voluntarily leaving your employment and will no longer be working. Although this text addresses those entering the workforce, it is never too early to start planning for your retirement, both mentally and financially. This can be done by establishing career goals and deadlines, in addition to contributing to a retirement fund.

Entrepreneurship

Some individuals do not want to work for others and have a desire to be their own boss. A final and common form of career transition is that of becoming an entrepreneur. An **entrepreneur** is someone who assumes the risk of succeeding or failing in business through owning and operating a business. While owning and operating your own business may sound glamorous, doing so involves work. Individuals become entrepreneurs for several reasons. The most common reason is when someone has identified a business opportunity he or she wants to exploit. People also become entrepreneurs because they would rather work for themselves, want more control of their work environment, want more income, or have lost their jobs and have been unable to find another.

Individuals with full-time jobs sometimes supplement their income by running a business on the side. It is unethical to run a side business that competes with or utilizes your employer's resources or confidential information. If your current employer allows employees to run side businesses, do not allow your side business to interfere with your full-time employment. Keep the two ventures separate.

Entrepreneurship is a rewarding career option for many and plays a valuable role in the U.S. economy. There are various methods of becoming an entrepreneur. You can start your own business, purchase an existing business, or operate a franchise. From a home-based business to running a chain of retail sites, every entrepreneur started with a dream. To be a successful entrepreneur, you need to have a passion for your business. You also need to know how to plan, manage finances, and make yourself creatively and professionally stand out from a crowd. These are all skills you have started to develop by reading this text.

If you are interested in becoming an entrepreneur, there are many resources available to you. Start by exploring the Small Business Administration website at www.sba.gov. Here you will find online, local, and national resources to get you started on the road to entrepreneurial success.

Career Success

As you have learned, there are several methods of advancing your career both within and outside of an organization. Although it is not good to change jobs too frequently, those with healthy careers move and rarely stay in one position their entire career. Personal issues frequently influence the choices we make in our careers. Health matters, changes in marital status, children, and elder care are just a few of these issues. There is a French proverb that states that some work to live, while others live to work. While there are trade-offs, your personal life must be a priority. Any change in your career will not only affect you, but those to whom you are close. Therefore, make them a consideration in your career decisions.

Career success is all about personal choice and maintaining an attitude of success. Regardless of when you plan to advance your career, keep your résumé updated, make a commitment to continuous learning, and display leadership. Doing so keeps you motivated to take on additional responsibilities and increases your knowledge, skills, and abilities. This will prepare you if some unforeseen opportunity comes your way. Keep focused on your life plan and consistently display professionalism. By consistently displaying professionalism, you will possess skills that position you for a lifetime of workplace success.

Talk It Out

What kind of business would you like to own? What steps would you need to take to make this occur?

Workplace Dos and Don'ts

Do continually update your skills and knowledge through training and development	*Don't* assume additional skills and knowledge are not necessary for advancement
Do keep an open mind for job advancement opportunities	*Don't* openly share your dissatisfaction for your current job
Do write a formal resignation letter when leaving a company and a thank-you note to a boss or mentor when receiving a promotion	*Don't* leave your job abruptly without providing adequate notice to your current employer
Do behave professionally when leaving a position	*Don't* take or ruin company property when leaving a position
Do provide valuable feedback and opportunities for improvement during an exit interview	*Don't* turn an exit interview into a personal attack on your former boss or coworkers

Concept Review and Application

Summary of Key Concepts

- Continue learning new skills to help reach your career potential
- Formal learning is another way to increase skills and knowledge
- Changes in employment status include promotions, voluntary terminations, involuntary terminations, lateral moves, and retirement
- Be cautious about sharing your desire for a new job
- There are two types of terminations: voluntary and involuntary
- When leaving voluntarily, submit a letter of resignation
- When leaving in an involuntary manner, do not burn bridges or behave in an unprofessional or unethical manner
- There is a difference between being fired and being laid off
- It is never too early to begin planning for your retirement
- Becoming an entrepreneur is an additional form of career transition

Key Terms

continual learning

entrepreneur

formal learning

involuntary
  termination

restructuring

voluntary termination

demotion

exit interview

furlough

lateral move

letter of resignation

retirement

work recall

development

firing

informal learning

layoff

promotion

training

If You Were the Boss

1. Why would it be important to encourage training and development sessions within your department?
2. You hear through the grapevine that one of your best employees is looking for another job. What should you do?
3. Management has told you that you must lay off four of your employees. How do you determine whom to lay off and how best to tell them? How do you defend your decision?

Web Links

http://marciaconner.com/intros/informal.html

http://careerplanning.about.com/od/quittingyourjob

http://www.insiderreports.com/bizltrs/resign1.htm

Activity 16-1

Based on your career plan in chapter 1, identify additional training, development, and continual learning you will need for professional success.

Training	Development	Continual Learning

Activity 16-2

Identify your ideal job. What continual learning will you need to secure this job?

Job Move	Continual Learning

Activity 16-3

Name at least five ways you can begin to develop additional skills for a future promotion.

1. _____

2. _____

3. _____

4. _____

5. _____

Activity 16-4

Throughout this text, you have learned good human relations for the workplace. Name at least three things you can do to decrease your chances of being laid off if that becomes necessary within your company.

1. _____

2. _____

3. _____

Activity 16-5

Write a draft letter of reference for yourself.

_____

_____

_____

_____

_____

_____

_____

1. To make you more diverse in your skills, attend _____ and
   _____.

2. The process of increasing knowledge in your career area is referred to as _____
   and _____.

3. Changes in employment status include promotions, _____ terminations,
   involuntary _____, lateral moves, and _____.

4. If you have had positive performance evaluations and are leaving voluntarily, secure a
   _____.

5. A/An _____ is a written notice of your voluntary termination.

6. Your _____ should include all unpaid wages and _____.

7. Employees who are _____ are terminated due to a/an
   _____ issue.

8. Employees who are _____ are terminated due to the company's
   _____.

9. A/An _____ is when you are transferred to another area of the organization.
   A change in pay is not involved.

10. A/An _____ is someone who assumes the risk of _____ or
    _____ through owning and operating a _____.

abusive boss: a boss who is constantly belittling or intimidating his or her employees

accommodating conflict management style: a conflict management style that allows the other party to have his or her own way without knowing there was a conflict

accountability: accepting the responsibility to perform and reporting back to whoever gave the power

active listening: when a receiver provides a sender full attention without distraction

adjourning stage: when team members bring closure to a project

aggressive behavior: the behavior of an individual who stands up for his or her rights in a manner that violates others' rights in an offensive manner

appearance: how you look

assertive behavior: the behavior of an individual who stands up for his or her rights without violating the rights of others

assets: items that you own that are worth money

attitude: a strong belief toward people, things, and situations

autocratic leaders: leaders who make decisions on their own without input from others

automatic deduction plan: when funds are automatically deducted from an employee's paycheck and placed into a bank account

avoiding conflict management style: a passive conflict management style used when one does not want to deal with the conflict so the offense is ignored

behavioral interview question: interview question that asks candidates to share a past experience related to a specific workplace situation

board of directors: a group of individuals responsible for developing the company's overall strategy and major policies

brainstorming: a problem-solving method that involves identifying alternatives that allow members to freely add ideas while other members withhold comments on the alternatives

budget: a detailed financial plan used to allocate money for a specific time period

business letter: a formal written form of communication used when a message is being sent to an individual outside of an organization

business memo: written communication sent within an organization (also called *interoffice memorandum*)

capital budget: a financial plan used for long-term investments including land and large pieces of equipment

career objective: an introductory written statement used on a résumé for individuals with little or no work experience

casual workdays: workdays when companies relax the dress code policy

chain of command: identifies who reports to whom within the company

character: the unique qualities of an individual, which usually reflect personal morals and values

charismatic power: a type of personal power that makes people attracted to you

chronological résumé layout: a résumé layout used by those with extensive career experience that emphasizes related work experience, skills, and significant accomplishments

coercive power: power that uses threats and punishment

collaborating conflict management style: a conflict management style in which both parties work together to arrive at a solution without having to give up something of value

communication: the process of a sender transmitting a message to an individual (receiver) with the purpose of creating mutual understanding

company resources: financial (fiscal), human (employees), and capital (long-term investments) resources that the company can utilize to achieve its goals

competent: having the ability to answer questions when a customer asks

compromising conflict management style: a conflict management style that is used when both parties give up something of importance to arrive at a mutually agreeable solution to the conflict

confidential: matters that should be kept private

conflict: a disagreement or tension between two or more parties (individuals or groups)

conflict of interest: when someone influences a decision that directly or indirectly benefits him or her

connection power: based on using someone else's legitimate power

continual learning: the ongoing process of increasing knowledge in the area of your career

corporate culture (organizational culture): values, expectations, and behavior of people at work; the company's personality being reflected through employees' behavior

cost of living: average cost of basic necessities such as housing, food, and clothing for a specific geographic area

courtesy: exercising manners, respect, and consideration toward others

cover letter: a letter that introduces your résumé

creativity: the ability to produce something new and unique

credit report: a detailed credit history on an individual

culture: different behavior patterns of various groups

customer service: the treatment an employee provides the customer

debt: money owed

decoding: when a receiver interprets a message

delegate: when a manager or leader assigns part or all of a project to someone else

democratic leaders: leaders who make decisions based upon input from others

demotion: when an employee is moved to a lower position with less responsibility and a decrease in pay

dental benefits: insurance coverage for teeth

department: sub-area of a division that carries out specific functions respective of its division

dependable: being reliable and taking responsibility to assist a customer

development: sessions to enhance or increase existing skills

direct benefits: monetary employee benefits

directional statements: a company's mission, vision, and values statements; these statements are the foundation of a strategic plan explaining why a company exists and how it will operate

diversity statements: corporate statements that remind employees that diversity in the workplace is an asset and not a form of prejudice and stereotyping

diversity training: company training designed to teach employees how to eliminate workplace discrimination and harassment

division: how companies arrange major business functions

documentation: a formal record of events or activities

dress code: an organization's policy regarding appropriate workplace attire

e-dentity: another name for an electronic image

electronic formatted résumés: résumés that are submitted in American Standard Code for Information Interchange (ASCII) format

electronic image: the image formed when someone is communicating and/or researching you through electronic means such as personal web pages and search engines

electronic job search portfolio: a computerized folder that contains electronic copies of all documents kept in hard-copy job search portfolio

employee assistance program (EAP): an employee benefit that typically provides free and confidential psychological, financial, and legal advice

employee handbook: a formal document provided by the company that outlines an employee's agreement with the employer regarding work conditions, policies, and benefits

employee loyalty: an employee's obligation to consistently support a company and its mission

employee morale: the attitude employees have toward the company

employee orientation: a time when a company provides new employees important information including the company's purpose, structure, major policies, procedures, benefits, and other matters

employment-at-will: a legal term for noncontract employees that states that an employee can quit any time he or she wishes

empowerment: pushing power and decision making to the individuals who are closest to the customer in an effort to increase quality, customer satisfaction, and, ultimately, profits

encoding: identifying how a message will be sent (verbally, written, or nonverbally)

entrepreneur: someone who assumes the risk of succeeding or failing in business through owning and operating the business

ethics: a moral standard of right and wrong

ethics statement: a formal corporate policy that addresses the issue of ethical behavior and punishment should someone behave inappropriately

ethnocentric: when an individual believes his or her culture is superior to others

etiquette: a standard of social behavior

executive presence: having the attitude of an executive

executives (senior managers): typically have title of vice president; individuals who work with the president of a company in identifying and implementing the company strategy

exit interview: when an employer meets with an employee who is voluntarily leaving a company to identify opportunities to improve the work environment

expense: money going out

expert power: power that is earned by one's knowledge, experience, or expertise

external customers: customers outside of the company including vendors and the individuals or businesses that purchase a company's product

extrinsic rewards: rewards that come from external sources including such things as money and praise

Fair Isaac Corporation (FICO) score: the most common credit rating

feedback: when a receiver responds to a sender's message based upon the receiver's interpretation of the original message

finance and accounting department: a department that is responsible for the securing, distribution, and growth of the company's financial assets

firing: when an employee is terminated because of a performance issue

fixed expenses: expenses that do not change from month to month

flexible expenses: expenses that change from month to month

forcing conflict management style: a conflict management style that deals with the issues directly

formal communication: workplace communication that occurs through lines of authority

formal learning: returning to college to increase knowledge or improve skills or receive an additional or advanced degree

formal teams: developed within the formal organizational structure and may include functional teams or cross-functional teams

forming stage: when team members first get to know each other and form initial opinions about other members

full-time employee: an employment status for employees who work forty or more hours per week

functional résumé layout: a résumé layout that emphasizes relevant skills when related work experience is lacking

furloughs: when employees are required to take unpaid work days

glass ceiling: invisible barrier that frequently makes executive positions off-limits to females and minorities, thus prohibiting them from advancing up the corporate ladder through promotions

glass wall: invisible barrier that frequently makes certain work areas such as a golf course off-limits to females and minorities, thus prohibiting them from advancing up the corporate ladder through promotions

goal: a target

good: a tangible item produced by a company

good boss: a boss who is respectful and fair

gossip: personal information about another individual that is hurtful and inappropriate

grapevine: an informal communication network where employees talk about workplace issues of importance

grievance: a problem or conflict that occurs in a union setting

grievance procedure: formal steps taken in resolving a conflict between the union and an employer

gross income: the amount of money in a paycheck before paying taxes or other deductions

group interview: an interview that involves several applicants interviewing with each other while being observed by company representatives

harassment: offensive, humiliating, or intimidating behavior

hostile behavior harassment: any behavior of a sexual nature by another employee that someone finds offensive, including verbal slurs, physical contact, offensive photos, jokes, or any other offensive behavior of a sexual nature

human relations: interactions occurring with and through people

human resource department (HR): a department responsible for hiring, training, compensation, benefits, performance evaluations, complaints, promotions, and changes in work status

implied confidentiality: an obligation to not share information with individuals with whom the business is of no concern

income: money coming in

indirect benefits: nonmonetary employee benefits such as health care and paid vacations

informal communication: workplace communication that occurs among individuals without regard to the formal lines of authority

informal learning: increasing knowledge by reading career-related magazines, newsletters, and other articles associated with a job

informal team: group of individuals who get together outside of the formal organizational structure to accomplish a goal

information heading: a résumé heading that contains relevant contact information including name, mailing address, city, state, ZIP code, contact phone, and e-mail address

information power: power based upon an individual's ability to obtain and share information

information systems (IS) department: a business function that deals with the electronic management of computer-based information within the organization

informational interview: when a job seeker meets with a business professional to learn about a specific career, company, or industry

innovation: the process of turning a creative idea into reality

interest: the cost of borrowing money

internal customers: fellow employees and departments that exist within a company

interview portfolio: a folder to be taken on an interview that contains photocopies of documents and items relevant to a position

intrinsic rewards: internal rewards that include such things as self-satisfaction and pride of accomplishment

introductory employee: newly hired full-time employee who has not yet successfully passed his or her introductory period

involuntary termination: when an employee loses his or her job against his or her will

job burnout: a form of extreme stress where you lack motivation and no longer have the desire to work

job description: a document that outlines specific job duties and responsibilities for a specific position

job search portfolio: a collection of paperwork needed for job searches and interview

job-specific skills: skills that are directly related to a specific job or industry

labeling: when one describes an individual or group of individuals based upon past actions

laissez-faire leaders: leaders who allow team members to make their own decisions without input from the leader (also known as *free reign leaders*)

lateral move: when an employee is transferred to another area (department) of an organization with the same level of responsibility

layoff: when a company releases employees as a result of a company's inability to keep the position

leadership: a process of one person guiding one or more individuals toward a specific goal

learning style: the method of how you best take in information and/or learn new ideas

legal counsel: a function within a business that handles all legal matters relating to the company

legitimate power: the power that is given to an employee from the company

letter of recommendation: a written testimony from another person that states that a job candidate is credible

letter of resignation: a written notice of your voluntary termination

letterhead: paper that has the company logo, mailing address, and telephone numbers imprinted on quality paper

levels of ethical decisions: the first level is the law; the second level is fairness; the third level is one's conscience

liability: an obligation to pay what you owe

life plan: a written document that identifies goals in all areas of your life

listening: the act of hearing attentively

loan: a large debt that is paid in smaller amounts over a period of time and has interest added to the payment

locus of control: identifies who you believe controls your future

long-term goal: a target that takes longer than one year to accomplish

marketing: responsible for creating, pricing, selling, distributing, and promoting the company's product

McClelland's Theory of Needs: holds that people are primarily motivated by one of three factors: achievement, power, or affiliation

mediator: a neutral third party whose objective is to assist two conflicting parties in coming to a mutually agreeable solution

medical benefits: insurance coverage for physician and hospital visits

meeting agenda: an outline of all topics and activities that are to be addressed during a meeting

meeting chair: the individual who is in charge of a meeting and has prepared the agenda

mentor: someone who can help an employee learn more about his or her present position, provide support, and help develop the employee's career

middle manager: typically has the title of *director* or *manager;* these individuals work on tactical issues

mirror words: words that describe the foundation of how you view yourself, how you view others, and how you will most likely perform in the workplace

mission statement: a company's statement of purpose

money wasters: small expenditures that consume a larger portion of one's income than expected

morals: a personal standard of right and wrong

motivation: an internal drive that causes people to behave a certain way to meet a need

negative stress: an unproductive stress that affects your mental and/or physical health including becoming emotional or illogical or losing your temper

negotiation: working with another party to create a situation (resolution) that is fair to all involved parties

net income: the amount of money you have after all taxes and deductions are paid

net worth: the amount of money that is yours after paying off debt

network list: an easily accessible list of all professional network contacts' names, industries, addresses, and phone numbers

networking: meeting and developing relationships with individuals outside one's immediate work area; the act of creating professional relationships

noise: anything that interrupts or interferes with the communication process

non-listening: when a receiver does not make any effort to hear or understand the sender's message

nonverbal communication: what is communicated through body language

norming stage: when team members accept other members for who they are

objectives: short-term goals that are measurable and have specific time lines that occur within one year

one-on-one interview: an interview that involves a one-on-one meeting between the applicant and a company representative

open-door policy: a management philosophy, the purpose of which is to communicate to employees that management and the human resource department are always available to listen should the employees have a concern or complaint

operational budget: a financial plan used for short-term items including payroll and the day-to-day costs associated with running a business

operational issue: organizational issues that typically occur on a daily basis and/or no longer than one year

operations: a business function that deals with the production and distribution of a company's product

operations manager: first-line manager who is typically called a *supervisor* or *assistant manager*

organizational chart: a graphic visual display of how a company organizes its resources; identifies key functions within the company and shows the formal lines of authority for employees

organizational structure: the way a company is organized

panel interview: an interview that involves the applicant meeting with several company employees at the same time

part-time employee: an employment status for employees who work fewer than forty hours a week

passive behavior: the behavior exhibited when an individual does not stand up for his or her rights by consistently allowing others to have their way

passive listening: the receiver is selectively hearing parts of a message

perception: one's understanding or interpretation of reality

performance evaluation: a formal appraisal that measures an employee's work performance

performing stage: when team members begin working on their task

personal commercial: a brief career biography that conveys one's career choice, knowledge, skills, strengths, abilities, and experiences

personal financial management: the process of controlling personal income and expenses

personal profile: an introductory written statement used on a résumé for individuals with professional experience related to their target career

personality: a stable set of traits that assist in explaining and predicting an individual's behavior

physiological needs: an individual's need for basic wages to obtain food, shelter, and other basic needs

politics: obtaining and utilizing power

positive self-talk: a mental form of positive self-reinforcement that helps remind you that you are qualified and deserve both the interview and the job

positive stress: productive stress that provides strength to accomplish a task

power: one's ability to influence another's behavior

power words: action verbs that describe your accomplishments in a lively and specific way

prejudice: a favorable or unfavorable judgment or opinion toward an individual or group based on one's perception (or understanding) of a group, individual, or situation

president or chief executive officer (CEO): the individual responsible for operating the company; this individual takes his or her direction from the board of directors

priorities: determine what needs to be done and in what order

procrastination: putting off tasks until a later time

product: what is produced by a company

productivity: to perform a function that adds value to a company

professionalism: workplace behaviors that result in positive business relationships

profit: revenue (money coming in from sales) minus expenses (the costs involved in running the business)

projection: the way you feel about yourself is reflected in how you treat others

promotion: moving to a position higher in the organization with increased pay and responsibility

proxemics: the study of distance (space) between individuals

quality: a predetermined standard that defines how a product is to be produced

quid pro quo harassment: a form of sexual harassing behavior that is construed as reciprocity or payback for a sexual favor

race: a group of individuals with certain physical traits

reciprocity: creating debts and obligations for doing something

respect: holding someone in high regard

responsibility: accepting the power that is being given and the obligation to perform

responsive: being aware of a customer's needs, often before the customer

restructuring: when a company eliminates a position due to a change in corporate strategy

résumé: a formal written profile that presents a person's knowledge, skills, and abilities to potential employers

retirement: when an employee voluntarily leaves the company and will no longer work

retirement plan: a savings plan for retirement purposes

reward power: the ability to influence someone with something of value

right to revise: a statement contained in many employee handbooks that provides an employer the opportunity to change or revise existing policies

Robert's Rules of Order: a guide to running meetings, oftentimes referred to as *parliamentary procedure*

safety needs: an individual's need for a safe working environment and job security

self-actualization: when an employee has successfully had his or her needs met and desires to assist others in meeting their needs

self-concept: how you view yourself

self-discovery: the process of identifying key interests and skills built upon career goals

self-efficacy: your belief in your ability to perform a task

self-esteem needs: an individual's need for public titles, degrees, and awards

self-image: your belief of how others view you

sender: an individual wanting to convey a message

senior managers or executives: individuals who work with the president in identifying and implementing the company strategy

service: an intangible product produced by a company

sexual harassment: unwanted advances of a sexual nature

shop steward: a coworker who assists others with union-related issues and procedures

short-term goals: goals that can be reached within a year's time (also called *objectives*)

slang: an informal language used among a particular group

SMART goal: a goal that is specific, measurable, achievable, relevant, and time-based

social needs: an individual's need for investment in workplace relationships

soft skills: people skills that are necessary when working with others in the workplace

stereotyping: making a generalized image of a particular group or situation

storming stage: when team members have conflict with each other

strategic issues: major company goals that typically range from three to five years or more

strategic plan: a formal document that is developed by senior management; the strategic plan identifies how the company secures, organizes, utilizes, and monitors its resources

strategy: a company's road map for success that outlines major goals and objectives

stress: a body's reaction to tense situations

structured interview question: a type of interview question that addresses job-related issues where each applicant is asked the same question

supervisor: first-level manager who concerns him- or herself with operational issues

synergy: two or more individuals working together and producing more than the sum of their individual efforts

tactical issues: business issues that identify how to link the corporate strategy into the reality of day-to-day operations; the time line for tactical issues is one to three years

targeted job search: job search process of discovering positions for which you are qualified in addition to identifying specific companies for which you would like to work

team: a group of people linked to a common purpose

teleconference: an interactive communication that connects participants through the telephone without the opportunity of visually seeing all participants

temporary employee: an employee who is hired only for a specified period of time, typically to assist with busy work periods or to temporarily replace an employee on leave

time management: how you manage your time

trade-off: giving up one thing to do something else

training: the process of learning new job skills for the purpose of an employee promotion and/or increased responsibility

transferable skills: skills that can be transferred from one job to another

union: a third-party organization that protects the rights of employees and represents employee interests to an employer

union contract: the formal document that addresses specific employment issues including the handling of grievances, holidays, vacations, and other issues

unstructured interview question: a probing, open-ended interview question intended to identify if the candidate can appropriately sell his or her skills

value: getting a good deal for the price paid for a product

values: things that are important to an individual

values statement: part of a company strategic plan that defines what is important to (or what the priorities are for) the company

verbal communication: the process of using words to send a message

video conference: a form of interactive communication using two-way video and audio technology

virtual teams: teams that function through electronic communications because they are geographically dispersed

vision benefits: insurance coverage for vision (eye) care

vision statement: part of a company's strategic plan that describes the company's viable view of the future

voluntary termination: leaving a job on your own

Vroom's Expectancy Theory: holds that individuals will behave in a certain manner based upon the expected outcome

work recall: when employees are called back to work after a layoff

work wardrobe: clothes that are primarily worn only to work and work-related functions

workplace bullies: employees who are intentionally rude and unprofessional to coworkers

workplace discrimination: acting negatively toward someone based on race, age, gender, religion, disability, or other areas

workplace diversity: differences among coworkers including culture, race, age, gender, economic status, and religion

written communication: a form of business communication that is printed, handwritten, or sent electronically

Suggested Readings

Chapter 1

Rotter, J. B. "Generalized Expectancies for Internal versus External Control of Reinforcement." *Psychological Monographs*, Vol. 80, No. 1 (1966): 1–28.

Taylor, M. "Does Locus of Control Predict Young Adult Conflict Strategies with Superiors? An Examination of Control Orientation and the Organizational Communication Conflict Instrument." *North American Journal of Psychology*, Vol. 12, No. 3 (2010): 445–458.

Anderson, C. R. and Schneider, C. E. "Locus of Control, Leader Behavior and Leader Performance among Management Students." *Academy of Management Journal*, Vol. 21, No. 4 (1978): 690–698, doi:10.2307/255709

Bandura, A. "Self-efficacy". In V. S. Ramachaudran (Ed.), *Encyclopedia of Human Behavior*, Vol. 4 (New York: Academic Press 1994), pp. 71–81.

Bandura, A. "Human Agency in Social Cognitive Theory." *American Psychologist*, Vol. 44, No. 9 (1989): 1175–1184.

"Work-Family Conflicts Affect Employees at All Income Levels," *HR Focus* 87 (April 2010): 9.

Golden, E. Organizational Renewal Associates. 1971. Golden LLC, May 2011, www.goldenllc.com

Isabel Briggs, M. Introduction to Type: A Guide to Understanding Your Results on the Myers-Briggs Type Indicator (Mountain View, CA: CPP, Inc., 1998).

O'Reilly, C. A., III, Chatman, J., and Caldwell, D. F. "People and Organizational Culture: A Profile Comparison Approach to Assessing Person-Organization Fit." *The Academy of Management Journal*, Vol. 34, No. 3 (September 1991): 487–516.

Hoel, H., Glasco, L., Hetland, J., Cooper, C. L., and Einarsen, S. "Leadership Styles as Predictors of Self-reported and Observed Workplace Bullying." *British Journal of Management*, Vol. 21, No. 2 (2010): 453–468.

Newhouse, N. "Implications of Attitude and Behavior Research for Environmental Conservation." *Journal of Environmental Education*, Vol. 22, No. 1 (Fall 1990): 26–32.

Doran, G. T. "There's a S.M.A.R.T. Way to Write Management's Goals and Objectives." *Management Review*, Vol. 70, No. 11 (AMA FORUM, 1981): 35–36.

Platt, G. "SMART Objectives: What They Mean and How to Set Them." *Training Journal* (August 2002): 23.

Chapter 2

Fair Isaac Corporation, Minneapolis, MN, www.myfico.com

Federal Reserve Bank, Washington, DC, www.federalreserve.gov

Annual Credit Report Request Service, Atlanta, GA, www.annualreditreport.com

Kim, J., Sorhaindo, B., and Garman, E. T. "Relationship between Financial Stress and Workplace Absenteeism of Credit Counseling Clients." *Journal of Family and Economic Issues*, Vol. 27, No. 3 (2006): 458–478, doi:10.1007/s10834-006-9024-9

Peete, S. S. "Employers Are Stung with a Hefty Price When Employees Suffer an Identity Theft." *Supervision*, Vol. 69, No. 7 (July 2008): 10–12.

The Motley Fool, Alexandria, VA, www.fool.com (how to invest, personal finance)

The Lampo Group, Inc., Brentwood, TN, www.daveramsey.com

Garman, E. T., Kim, J., Kratzer, C. Y., Brunson, B. H., and Joo, S. "Workplace Financial Education Improves Personal Financial Wellness." *Financial Counseling and Planning*, Vol. 10, No. 1 (1999): 79–88.

Joo, S. and Garman, E. T. "Personal Financial Wellness May Be the Missing Factor in Understanding and Reducing Worker Absenteeism." *Personal Finances and Worker Productivity*, Vol. 2, No. 2 (1998): 172–182.

Kim, J. "Impact of a Workplace Financial Education Program on Financial Attitude, Financial Behavior, Financial Well-Being, and Financial Knowledge." Proceedings from the Association for Financial Counseling and Planning Education, 2004, 1–8.

Quinn, J. M. "Mainstreaming Financial Education As an Employee Benefit." *Journal of Financial Planning*, Vol. 13, No. 5 (2000): 70–79, www.Personalfinancefoundation.org

Bernheim, B. D. and Garrett, D. M. "The Effects of Financial Education in the Workplace: Evidence from a Survey of Households." *Journal of Public Economics*, Vol. 87, No. 7–8 (2003): 1487–1519.

Armour, S. "Workers' Financial Stress May Hurt Productivity," *USA Today* (September 7, 2007).

Chapter 3

Jobson, K. "Beware: Your Job May Be Killing You," *U.S. News & World Report* 147 (February 2010): 50.

"Leading Productivity Killers in Today's Market: Overwork, Stress," *HR Focus* 85 (April 2008): 8.

Macan, T., Gibson, J. M., and Cunningham, J. "Will You Remember to Read This Article Later When You Have Time? The Relationship between Prospective Memory and Time Management." *Personality and Individual Differences*, Vol. 48, No. 6 (2010): 725–730, doi:10.1016/j.physletb.2003.10.071

Rosekind, M. R., Gregory, K. B., et. al. "The Cost of Poor Sleep: Workplace Productivity Loss and Associated Costs." *Journal of Occupational & Environmental Medicine*, Vol. 52, No. 1 (2010): 91–98, doi: 10.1097/JOM.0b013e3181c78c30

Babcock, P. "Getting the Weight Off," *HR Magazine* 53 (January 2008): 60–66.

Leeds, R. One Year to an Organized Work Life. (Cambridge, MA: Da Capo Press, 2008).

DeVries, G. "Innovations in Workplace Wellness: Six New Tools to Enhance Programs and Maximize Employee Health and Productivity." *Compensation Benefits Review*, Vol. 42, No. 1 (January/February 2010): 46–51.

Richardson, N. "10 Ways the CEO Can Reduce Office Stress." *Inc.* (April 30, 2010).

Ford, M. T., Heinen, B. A., and Langkamer, K. L. "Work and Family Satisfaction and Conflict: A Meta-analysis of Cross-domain Relations." *Journal of Applied Psychology*, Vol. 92, No. 1 (January 2007): 57–80.

"The 2008 Wasting Time at Work Survey Reveals a Record Number of People Waste Time at Work." *Salary.com, Inc.* (2008).

Chandola, T. "Stress at Work," British Academy Policy Centre. October 2010.

Centers for Disease Control and Prevention/National Institute for Occupational Safety and Health, www.cdc.gov/niosh/

Chapter 4

The Emily Post Institute, Burlington, VT, www.emilypost.com

Wayne, T. "Why Etiquette Schools Are Thriving," *Bloomberg Business Week* (October 14, 2010).

Fisher, A. "Is Cubical Etiquette an Oxymoron?" *CNNMoney* (October 22, 2010).

McAfee, A. "Mistakes Millennials Make at Work," *Harvard Business Review* (August 30, 2010).

"Discovering Hats, a New Generation Brims with Anxiety Over Etiquette," *Wall Street Journal* (August 11, 2010).

Schrage, M. "Why Your Looks Will Matter More," *Harvard Business Review* (April 22, 2010).

Tillotson, K. "Manners Mean More in Tough Job Market," *Minneapolis Star Tribune* (March 22, 2010).

Chapter 5

Taylor, B. "Money and the Meaning of Life," *Harvard Business Review* (May 17, 2011).

Etzioni, A. Comparative Analysis of Complex Organizations (New York: Free Press, 1961), pp. 4–6.

French, John R. P. and Raven, B. "The Bases of Social Power." In D. Cartwright (Ed.), *Studies in Social Power* (Ann Arbor, MI: University of Michigan Press, 1959), pp. 150–167.

Kotter, J. P. "Power, Dependence and Effective Management," *Harvard Business Review* (July–August 1977): 131–136.

Vigoda, E. "Stress-related Aftermaths to Workplace Politics: The Relationships among Politics, Job Distress, and Aggressive Behavior in Organizations." *Journal of Organizational Behavior*, Vol. 23 (2002): 1–21.

Peale, N. V. and Blanchard, K. The Power of Ethical Management. (New York: William Morrow, 1988).

Weissenberger, B. "How to Win at Office Politics," *BusinessWeek* (February 23, 2010).

Business Ethics, New York, www.businessethics.com

Wells, S. J. "Counting on Workers with Disabilities," *HR Magazine* (April 2008): 45–49.

Chapter 6

"How 'Recession-Proof' Will Millennial Workers Be?" *HR Focus* 86 (March 2009): 6–7.

Leyes, M. "Talking' 'Bout My Generation," *Advisor Today* 105 (April 2010): 34–38.

Deming, W. E. Quality, Productivity and Competitive Position (Cambridge, MA: MIT Press, 1982).

Connors, R. and Smith, T. How Did That Happen?: Holding People Accountable for Results the Positive, Principled Way (New York: Penguin Group, Inc., 2009).

Wakeman, C. Y. "Why Empowerment without Accountability Is Chaos at Work," *Fast Company* (April 7, 2009).

Pugh, K. and Dixon, N., "Don't Just Capture Knowledge—Put It to Work," *Harvard Business Review* (May 2008).

Welch, J. and Welch, S. "Emotional Management," *BusinessWeek* (July 28, 2008).

Staub, R. "Accountability and Its Role in the Workplace," *The Business Journal.* Greensborough, NC, January 13, 2005, www.bizjournals.com/triad/stories/2005/01/17/smallb3.html

Chapter 7

Schultz, H. Onward: How Starbucks Fought for its Life without Losing its Soul (New York: Rodale, Inc., 2011).

Fenn, D. "10 Ways to Get More Sales from Existing Customers," *Inc.* (August 31, 2010), www.inc.com/guides/2010/08/get-more-sales-from-existing-customers.html.

Smith, C. "About Customer Service in a Bad Economy," *The Houston Chronicle* (May 27, 2011), www.smallbusiness.chron.com/customer-service-bad-economy-740.html

Mathews, S. "Why Basic Business Principles Still Matter," September 15, 2010, www.samanthamathews.com/general/why-basic-business-principles-still-matter/

Pleshette, L. A. "Understanding Basic Business Principles," *PowerHomeBiz.com.* Retrieved May 2011, www.powerhomebiz.com/vol50/charan.htm

Sawhney, M., Woldcott, R. C., and Arroniz, I., "The 12 Different Ways for Companies to Innovate." *MIT Sloan Management Review*, Vol. 47, No. 3 (Spring 2006): 75–81.

Von Hippel, E. The Sources of Innovation (Oxford, UK: Oxford University Press, 1994); and Leonard, D. Wellsprings of Knowledge: Building and Sustaining the Sources of Innovation (Cambridge, MA: Harvard Business School Press, 1998).

Chapter 8

United States Department of Labor, www.dol.gov

Society for Human Resource Management (SHRM), www.shrm.org

Business Research Lab, Houston, TX, www.busreslab.com

National Labor Relations Board, www.nlrb.gov

Wells, S. J. "Layoff Aftermath," *HR Magazine* (November 2008): 37–41.

Lichtenstein, S. D. and Darrow, J. J. "At-Will Employment: A Right to Blog or a Right to Terminate." *Journal of Internet Law*, Vol. 11 (March 2008): 1–20.

"Employees Care a Lot More About Performance Reviews Than You May Think," *HR Focus* 86 (July 2009): 9.

Stanley, T. L. "Union Stewards and Labor Relations," *Supervision* 71 (February 2010): 3–6.

Wells, S. J. "Getting Paid for Staying Well," *HR Magazine* 55 (February 2010): 59–62.

Robb, D. "Get the Benefits Message Out," *HR Magazine* 54 (October 2009): 69–71.

Fogarty, S. "EAPs New Role: A Core Strategic Element," *Employee Benefit Advisor* 8 (April 2010): 40–46.

Carvin, B. N. "The Great Mentor Match," *T&D* 63 (January 2009): 46–50.

"Share Baby Boomers' Knowledge With Intergenerational Mentoring," *HR Focus* 87 (February 2010): 7–13.

Chapter 9

Gallo C. "Why Leadership Means Listening," *Businessweek* (January 31, 2007), http://www.businessweek.com/smallbiz/content/jan2007/sb20070131_192848.htm

Dan, R. J. (2010). In the Company of Others: An Introduction to Communication (New York: Oxford University Press), pp. 157–166.

Susan, Y. "The New Trend in Communication: Silent Listening," *Salesopedia*. Retrieved May 31, 2011, www.salesopedia.com/index.php/component/content/1863?task=view&Itemid=10479

Paul, P. "Proxemics in Clinical and Administrative Settings." *Journal of Healthcare Management*, Vol. 50, No. 3 (May–June 2005): 151–154.

Carter, L. Ideas for adding soft skills education to service learning and capstone courses for computer science students. ACM Technical Symposium on Computer Science Education Proceedings. Dallas, TX. March 9–12, 2011, pp. 517–522.

Chapter 10

Ott, A. "How Social Media Has Changed the Workplace," *Fast Company* (November 11, 2010).

Friedl, J. and Tkalac Verčič, A. "Media Preferences of Digital Natives' Internal Communication: A Pilot Study." *Public Relations Review*, Vol. 37, No. 1 (March 2011): 84–86.

Bernstein, C. A., M.D. "Communication: It's Not What It Used to Be Psychiatric News." *American Psychiatric Association*, Vol. 46, No. 6 (March 18, 2011): 3.

Zielinski, D. "New Regulations Make Social Usage Policies More Imperative," *SHRM Online Technology Discipline*, June 8, 2010.

Rafferty, H. R. "Social Media Etiquette: Communicate Behavioral Expectations," *SHRM Online Technology Discipline*, March 24, 2010.

Social Media Acceptable-Use Policy, *HR Magazine* (December 2009).

Study Links Technology to Poor Workplace Manners, *SHRM Online Technology Discipline* (February 2009).

Chapter 11

Nelson, R. "The Business Case for Leadership and Engagement During Challenging Times," *Employee Benefit Advisor* 7 (May 2009): 56.

White, R. and Lippitt, R. Autocracy and Democracy: An Experiential Inquiry (New York: Harper & Brothers, 1960).

Fanelli, A. and Misangyi, V. "Bringing Out Charisma: CEO Charisma and External Stakeholders." *Academy of Management Review*, Vol. 31, No. 4 (2006): 1049–1061.

Bennis W. and Townsend, R. Reinventing Leadership (New York: William Morrow, 1995).

DeChurch, L. A., Hiller, N. J., Murase, T., Doty, D., and Salas, E. "Leadership Across Levels: Levels of Leaders and Their Levels of Impact." *The Leadership Quarterly*, Vol. 21, No. 6 (December 2010): 1069–1085.

Belbin, R. M. Management Teams: Why They Succeed or Fail (Oxford, UK: Elsevier Ltd., 1981).

Virtual team, http://www.exforsys.com/career-center/virtual-team/virtual-team-success-factors.html

Maslow, A. H. "A Theory of Human Motivation." *Psychological Review*, Vol. 50, No. 4 (July 1943): 370–396.

McClelland, D. The Achieving Society (New York: Van Nostrand Reinhold, 1961).

Bennis, W. and Nanus, B. Leaders (New York: Harper & Row, 1985).

Kotter, J. P. "What Leaders Really Do," *Harvard Business Review* 68 (May–June 1990): 103–111.

Reynolds, G. Presentation Zen: Simple Ideas on Presentation Design and Delivery (Berkeley, CA: New Riders Press, 2008).

Berkun, S. Confessions of a Public Speaker (Sebastopol, CA: O'Reilly Media, Inc., 2009).

Chapter 12

"Economic Crisis Raises Potential for Workplace Violence," *Teller Vision* (January 2009): 1–2.

"Understanding and Preventing Violence in the Workplace," *Safety Compliance Letter* (March 1, 2009): 7–16.

"What to Do When Domestic Violence Comes to Work," *HR Focus* 87 (January 2010): 10–11.

Thomas, K. W. "Conflict and Conflict Management." In M. D. Dunnette (Ed.), *Handbook of Industrial and Organizational Psychology* (Chicago, IL: Rand McNally, 1976), pp. 889–935.

Neil Browne, M. and Keeley, S. M. Asking the Right Questions: A Guide to Critical Thinking, 8th ed. (Saddleback, NJ: Pearson Education, 2010).

De Dreu, C. K. W. "Conflict at Work: Basic Principles and Applied Issues." In S. Zedeck (Ed.), *APA Handbook of Industrial and Organizational Psychology, Vol. 3: Maintaining, Expanding, and Contracting the Organization, APA Handbooks in Psychology* (Washington, DC: American Psychological Association, 2011), pp. 461–493.

Speakman, J. and Ryals, L. "A Re-evaluation of Conflict Theory for the Management of Multiple, Simultaneous Conflict Episodes." *International Journal of Conflict Management*, Vol. 21, No. 2 (2010): 186–201.

Afzalur R. M. Managing Conflict in Organizations (New Brunswick, NJ: Transaction Publishers, 2011).

Lovelle B. L. and Lee, R. T. "Impact of Workplace Bullying on Emotional and Physical Well-Being: A Longitudinal Collective Case Study." *Journal of Aggression, Maltreatment & Trauma*, Vol. 20, No. 3 (2011): 344–357.

Chapter 13

Beagrie, S. "How to Jump-Start Your Job Search," *Personnel Today* (January 8, 2008): 5.

"Nearly Half of Empoyers Use Social Media to Research Candidates," *HR Focus* 86 (December 2009): 8.

Benezine, K. "Applying for Jobs," *Caterer & Hotelkeeper* (2009 Careers Guide): 4–5.

"Feds Turning Up Heat on HR Background Checks," HR Specialists: *Employment Law* 40 (May 2010): 1–2.

Chapter 14

Schuller, N. M., Ickes, L., and Schullery, S. E. "Employer Preferences for Resumes and Cover Letters," *Business Communication Quarterly* 72 (June 2009): 163–176.

"2010 Resume: What's In, What's Out," *Administrative Professional Today* 36 (March 2010): 1–2.

Schaffer, G. "Six Ways to Ruin Your Resume," *Computerworld* 43 (April 13, 2009): 26–28.

Chapter 15

"How to Stand Out from the Crowd and Kick-Start Your Own Recovery," *U.S. News & World Report* 147 (May 2010): 14–16.

National Association of Colleges and Employers, Bethlehem, PA, www.Jobweb.com

Skorkin, A. The Main Reason Why You Suck at Interviews: Lack of Preparation. *Lifehacker.com*, http://lifehacker.com/5710712/ the-main-reason-why-you-suck-at-interviews-lack-of-preparation December 10, 2010.

Garrison, S., Gutter, M., and Spence, L. Managing in Tough Times: Building Your Assets by Volunteering. Department of Family, Youth and Community Sciences, Florida Cooperative Extension Service, Institute of Food and Agricultural Sciences, University of Florida. October 2009, http://edis.ifas.ufl.edu/fy1107#FOOTNOTE_1

Chapter 16

Shanoff, B. "Departing with Dignity," *Waste Age* 38 (September 2007): 26–28.

McKenzie, M. "Exit Interviews," *Smart Business Atlanta* 7 (March 2010): 24.

Shea, T. E. "Getting the Last Word," *HR Magazine* 55 (January 2010): 24–25.

"The Changing Organizational Chart: Up Isn't the Only Way to Success," *Health Care Collector* 21 (January 2008): 8.

Elmer, V. "The Invisible Promotion," *Fortune* (February 7, 2011): 31–32.

Gurchiek, K. "Motivating Innovation," *HR Magazine* (September 2009): 31–35.

Credits

Index